D1559624

The Origins of
the Crimean Alliance

The Origins of
the Crimean Alliance

Ann Pottinger Saab

University Press of Virginia
Charlottesville

THE UNIVERSITY PRESS OF VIRGINIA
Copyright © 1977 by the Rector and Visitors
of the University of Virginia

First published 1977

Library of Congress Cataloging in Publication Data

Saab, Ann Pottinger, 1934–
The origins of the Crimean alliance.

Bibliography: p.
Includes index.
1. Crimean War, 1853–1856—Causes. I. Title.
DK215.S23   947'.07   76-30526
ISBN 0-8139-0699-7

Printed in the United States of America

For
Elie, Georges, and David
latter-day heroes
and victims
of the Crimean War

Contents

Preface

I was first drawn to the subject of Crimean War origins under the guidance of Edward V. Gulick of Wellesley College. But my work at that time (an undergraduate paper) did not encourage me to continue with the problem as a graduate student. Brison D. Gooch summarized the thinking of the mid-fifties on Crimean War origins with the remark, "there are no important questions of specific matters of fact yet to be answered."[1] It was not until some seven or eight years later, when an instructor at Middlebury College, that I began to see where one might look for some new facts. At that time, discussions with H. McKim Steele, an enthusiastic African historian, convinced me that much insight into traditionally insoluble problems of European history can be gained from non-Western sources. Advised and encouraged by Stanford J. Shaw, I resolved to try to explore the Near Eastern background of the war through work in the then newly opened Dişişleri Bakanliği Hazine-i Evrak in Istanbul.

I shared with many others—working primarily in Russian, Austrian, and Balkan history—my hunch that the origins of the war could not be finally understood without more attention to the policy of the East European and Near Eastern powers. Many stimulating suggestions as to the causes of the war have been offered in the last decade, but the goal of a definitive interpretation of the war has perhaps receded. For the field of Ottoman diplomacy, the state of the archives—incompletely classified when I used them—precluded the possibility of a complete narrative at this time. The rich materials in Turkey open up enticing perspectives for future revisions when the time and immense scholarly capabilities necessary can be brought to bear. The enormous difficulty of the Ottoman Turkish language is a barrier to the aspiring European historian. I cannot pretend to have made more than the most limited attempt to work in this field. Even so, it is hard to strike a balance between oversimplification of Ottoman history and overabsorption in it. I have tried to focus on the process by which the British government, initially reluctant to become involved in the Eastern crisis, became the Ottoman Empire's military ally. I have emphasized those developments at Constantinople that enmeshed the British in a war they wanted to win but did not wish to fight. I hope, despite the many

shortcomings of this study, to be able to bring some new considerations to bear on the broader question of Crimean War origins and to
stimulate others, better qualified than I, to continue this approach to
the Eastern Question.

The rendering of names and terms in foreign languages presents
many problems. In general, English-language equivalents have been
preferred where they exist and can easily be found by the reader in
standard reference works such as Webster's *New International Dic-
tionary* and the *Times Atlas of the World.* Failing this, the spelling used
is the spelling current in modern Turkish. Russian words have been
transliterated according to the U. S. Board on Geographic Names system. Translations, except where otherwise indicated, are my own.

The list of those who have helped me in a task whose dimensions
far exceeded my expectations is too long for full enumeration. The aid
and encouragement of Stanford J. Shaw and Ezel Kural Shaw have
been indispensable. Roderic Davison gave me much good advice during my work in the archives in Istanbul. Necat Göyunc, of the Istanbul
University faculty, helped me to learn to decipher Ottoman documents.
The staffs of the Dişişleri Bakanliği Hazine-i Evrak and Başvekâlet
Arşivi in Istanbul, the Haus- Hof- and Staatsarchiv in Vienna, the
archives of the Ministère des Affaires Etrangères in Paris, and the
Public Record Office in London have been unfailingly courteous and
helpful. The Interlibrary Loan Service and Reference Department of
the Walter Clinton Jackson Library of the University of North Caro-
lina at Greensboro have wrestled undauntedly with unusual requests.
Particular thanks are due to Emmy Mills. The Social Science Research
Council supported a year's research in Istanbul, Paris, and London,
while the University of North Carolina at Greensboro generously financed many purchases through its Research Fund and provided a
semester's leave in the spring of 1970. My colleague, David Mac-
Kenzie, read a portion of the manuscript; so did James B. Peabody and
Walter Muir Whitehill. Their friendly encouragement had really crucial
importance. My graduate assistants, Kathleen Swiger and Sue Ann
Pennington, performed innumerable editorial chores. Muriel Dreyer,
Bobbie Tillery, Betty Hatton, and Sue Pennington coped admirably
with the problems of typing the manuscript. Georges Saab, although
not thought of when this project was originally undertaken, was old
enough before its completion to render enthusiastic service checking
references in the National Union Catalogue. Finally, my husband, by
his ability to cope with everything from illegible Ottoman Turkish
handwriting to the logistics of domestic crises proved himself to be a
man for all seasons.

Greensboro, North Carolina
November 1976

The Origins of
the Crimean Alliance

Chapter I

Introduction

DESPITE much fine scholarship, the origins of the Crimean War remain something of a mystery, particularly when seen from the British point of view. Disillusion with the war became acute long before the peace treaty was signed in 1856, and in the ensuing decades, discussions of Britain's role either deprecated British participation entirely or supported it on the somewhat specious grounds that it was unthinkable that so many Englishmen had died in vain. This contemporary revulsion has flavored a tradition of otherwise impressive study of the subject. Disraeli termed the struggle "a just but unnecessary war." Sir Robert Morier's opinion that the Crimean War was "the only perfectly useless modern war that has been waged" was repeated by J. A. R. Marriott in the book that for decades served as the standard text covering Eastern Mediterranean politics. And M. S. Anderson, in his recent general treatment of the Eastern Question, confirms this view: he tells us, "more than any great war of modern times, it took place by accident."[1]

It is now more than a hundred years since the war was fought; and since Brison D. Gooch wrote his important article on the centenary of the peace, a wealth of significant books and articles have appeared, which enable us to consider the war and its origins with greater sophistication. Particularly helpful have been the detailed investigations of the foreign policies and the domestic situations of the various powers involved. J. B. Conacher's examination of the intricacies of Parliamentary maneuver and Paul W. Schroeder's work with private papers reveal much of the interplay of personality and domestic politics that was operative in Britain. Schroeder's and Unckel's and Baumgart's work in the Austrian archival collections illuminate the subtleties of Austrian policy and offer a firmer grasp of the entire Central European condition, which was unstable in the aftermath of the 1848 revolutions. John S. Curtiss has published articles on Russian diplomacy and is at work on a book on that subject, based on extensive research in Russia. Although they do not deal explicitly with foreign policy, recent studies of Ottoman history such as Bernard Lewis's *The Emergence of Modern Turkey* and Roderic H. Davison's *Reform in the Ottoman Empire* provide insights into the state of the Ottoman Empire, and the diplomatic imperatives emerging therefrom, that need to be integrated into the general picture of mid-century international relations and to be extended by further research in the Ottoman collections, especially as more documents are classified and made available to scholars. Despite Brison Gooch's fine book on the conduct of the war,[2] the French role remains perhaps the most obscure—a fact related to the highly personal nature of Napoleon III's diplomacy, and to the consequent lack of records, especially for the earlier, more autocratic part of the reign. Finally, a number of specialized monographs present the experiences of some of the governments less directly involved in the Crimean experience.[3]

Despite all this important work, many aspects of Crimean War diplomacy remain murky. For a definitive view, we must await full publication of the information available from Russian archives, more complete classification of Ottoman materials, and fuller exploration of what can be recaptured of Napoleon III's cloudy, ambitious, yet surprisingly practical visions. However, it is possible to delineate some new themes that emerge from all this monographic work. In this chapter, an effort will be made to assess the contribution of Britain, France, Russia, Austria, and the Ottoman Empire to the creation of a warlike situation by the spring of 1853. This examination will serve as an introduction to a closer analysis of one of the themes that emerge as significant in "causing" the war: the relationship between Great Britain and the Ottoman Empire, built on an explosive combination of material interests and psychological illusions.

Central to British involvement with the Ottoman Empire after 1848 was the fact that the British had come to exercise a preponderant degree of control in Constantinople in the 1840s. The origins of this relationship go back to the first major threat to the existence of the Ottoman Empire itself in the 1830s. Although there had been crises of a greater or lesser magnitude in the provinces for many years before that time, Mohammed Ali of Egypt was the first figure to appear who was capable, and seemingly desirous, of deposing the Sultan and of providing a full-scale alternative to Ottoman rule. The French were quick to support Mohammed Ali, at least at the level of cultural and educational exchange. The Russians—who might have been expected, on the basis of earlier policy towards the Ottoman Empire, to applaud Mohammed Ali's challenge to the Porte, in the hope of winning outright gains for themselves—had swung around to a policy of upholding the Empire in 1828, with the intention of using their influence at Constantinople to affect developments behind the scenes throughout the eastern Mediterranean.[4] Tsar Nicholas I accordingly came to Sultan Mahmud's rescue, and the bargain was signalized by the treaty of Unkiar Skelessi, signed in July 1833. Although much attention was later focused on the treaty provisions (which were ambiguous and probably inoperable in their widest connotation) concerning passage of the Straits, the heart of the agreement lay in the stipulations for consultation between the Turkish and Russian governments, in case of emergency, to determine possible Russian assistance to Turkey. This was a direct effort on the Russians' part to lay the groundwork for a Russian protectorate over the Ottoman Empire.[5]

The British government, during the first months of the crisis, took a surprisingly cavalier attitude towards the whole question. The heated internal debate over the Reform Bill made it difficult for the ministry to broach controversial questions of foreign policy. The cabinet was uneasy about the new French government's intentions, particularly with regard to Belgium and the Low Countries, and did not want to be distracted. The fleet, which had declined markedly in the years of peace since 1815, was already sufficiently involved in operations off Portugal and the Netherlands. Anxious about all these problems, Lord Palmerston, then foreign secretary for the first time, evidently failed to read up on the question. However, when he did give his attention to the Eastern Question, he decided that his earlier nonchalance had been a "tremendous blunder,"[6] and his reversal inaugurated several decades of British support for the status quo in the eastern Mediterranean.

Actuated by this new concern, Palmerston took the lead in upholding the Ottoman Empire during the second Mohammed Ali crisis of 1839–40 and emerged as the principal architect of the Straits Convention of 1841, which, with its reaffirmation of closure of the Straits to warships in time of peace and its implied international guarantee of the Ottoman Empire, was to remain the basis for the five European great powers' relations with the Near East for at least the next decade and a half. Concurrently, the Porte and the British government had moved closer together. A British fleet was stationed at Malta beginning in 1834, and for a few years in the mid-thirties, the British ambassador at Constantinople had the power to summon it without further authorization from London.[7] The important commercial Convention of Balta Liman was signed in 1838; by it, the British won extensive tariff concessions that started the process of opening the Ottoman Empire to commercial exploitation and helped to give the British a significant stake in its survival. A loan was to have been raised in Great Britain, but fell through after the British government declined to guarantee it.[8] Finally Reshid Pasha, a promising young Ottoman statesman, was sent to London and other European capitals to win support. The mission was probably most important as a learning experience for Reshid; he apparently saw Palmerston only three times during the first six months of his visit, failed in his attempts to secure a British alliance broad enough to be acceptable in Constantinople,[9] and did not do much better when he tried to interest the foreign secretary in the cause of Turkish reform. Though the conversations were inconclusive, it is evident that—at least at this stage of his career—Palmerston only favored military reforms, which were directly related to the Ottoman Empire's survival capacity; political or constitutional change he regarded as controversial and hence too risky.[10]

Despite Palmerston's reluctance, the British government did become a principal foreign sponsor of the Ottoman reform movement, the Tanzimat, in the 1840s. After the high diplomatic concern of the 1830s, the Near East receded from general international importance in the 1840s. The Treaty of London (1840) and the Straits Convention (1841) had provided the basis for reasonable compromise. Nicholas I retreated from the active policy of the preceding fifteen years and decided to await the Empire's fall, meanwhile safeguarding his interests with international agreements such as the 1844 exchange of notes between Nesselrode, as Russian chancellor, and Lord Aberdeen, foreign secretary in Britain. In France, the Guizot government was absorbed by developments in western Europe, particularly Spain, and also faced growing internal disaffection. In Vienna, Metternich's position was similar. As a result, the British faced few challenges in the Near East; British representatives fell into the trap of expanding their activities without counting a cost that was largely deferred.[11]

The situation was compounded when Stratford Canning returned to Constantinople as ambassador in 1842 (a post he was to occupy almost continuously until 1858). His Near East experience, which already spanned more than thirty years, had made him a powerful, if eccentric, friend and advocate of the Porte and an almost embarassingly dedicated mentor. He lent his prestige to the efforts of Turkish reformers such as Reshid Pasha to implement a program of reforms that derived from the Hatt-i Sherif of Gulhane of 1839. Although this early period of the Tanzimat has been given short shrift by some students of Ottoman reform,[12] there is no doubt that important beginnings were made in secular and Europeanized education; in the creation of a rudimentary public opinion through publication of books, pamphlets, and the first nonofficial gazette, the *Ceride-i Havadis;* in a secularized legal system based on new law codes and mixed courts in certain areas; and in the attempts to abolish tax farming, a primary source of official corruption.

As part of the involvement with reform, the British associated themselves with two movements in Ottoman politics that were highly controversial and contained the seeds of future instability. In this sense, despite the self-proclaimed purity of their motives, the British must appear as among the instigators of the crisis that was to engulf the Empire between 1848 and 1856. One of these movements was centralization. The Tanzimat reformers kept a tight rein on provincial governors, and as posts fell vacant, they preferred candidates from the capital to members of local elites. At the same time, an effort was made to recapture for the Ottoman administration some of the civil functions that had traditionally been exercised by the religious authorities of the different sects, according to the millet system instituted at the time of the Ottoman conquest, and even earlier in some parts of the Empire.*

*According to the millet system, conquered Christians and Jews were not forced to convert but were given special status under their religious leaders. Since religion and nationality were essentially synonymous in the Near East, the resultant groupings, or millets, had both political and spiritual functions. The Greek Orthodox millet, as the most fully evolved, will serve as an example. After the Council of Chalcedon in 451, the Orthodox Church was ruled by the four Patriarchs of Constantinople, Antioch, Alexandria, and Jerusalem. Even the Russian Church, until the time of Peter the Great, was theoretically subordinate to their authority. The Patriarch of Constantinople was supposedly the first among equals; but his strategic location in the Ottoman capital made him the real head of the church. He was the spiritual director and clerical administrator over some twelve million believers. His most important jurisdiction was the Balkans, with certain exceptions, notably Moldavia, Walachia, Serbia, and Montenegro. The Patriarch also had a variety of civil tasks, such as collection of taxes, including the *kharaj* (a kind of poll tax), from all Orthodox subjects and jurisdiction over all civil cases that involved Greek Orthodox. (Criminal cases and cases that involved a Christian and a Moslem were tried in the Moslem courts on the basis of Islamic law.)

In exercising these extensive powers, the Patriarch and the hierarchy of Church officials acted in close association with the Moslem establishment. The Patriarch's lay associate, the logothete, was his liaison with the divan. At the provincial level, the metropolitans (and certain other highly selected Greek notables) advised the valis, or provincial governors. But the most impressive exercise of control came at the local level of the communes, or *nahiyes.* In the Balkans, each village usually consisted of members of a single religious group. Yearly, on St. George's Day, the men of the Orthodox villages gathered before the Church or under an old tree and elected their officials, of whom the most important was the *kocabaşı.* Under the *kocabaşı's* leadership, these officials were responsible for all the major functions of local government, including collection of taxes, hearing of civil cases in the first instance, maintenance of schools, repair of churches, and payment of the local priest. (A good contemporary description of the

This policy of centralization was a rational response to the problems of governing a multinational empire in an age of nationalism; it bears comparison with the policy of neoabsolutism in the similarly constituted Hapsburg Empire. But it was ambitious to the point of being unrealistic; as Stanford Shaw puts it, the Ottoman reformers were trying to establish a degree of control, particularly in the Balkans, that the Porte had never been able to exercise, even at the height of its power in the sixteenth century.[13] In the process, they inevitably alienated many local leaders, some of whom had national or religious ties that could serve as the basis for appeals abroad.

The other movement the British espoused was the movement towards Christian-Moslem equality. The impulse behind this support was shared almost universally by Europeans. Although British apologists often claimed that Ottoman misgovernment weighed equally on the poor, whatever their religion, it was clear to most observers, including the British, that the millet system, which in fact had made the Ottoman Empire a showcase for toleration in earlier centuries, had by the nineteenth century become the means of making the non-Moslems into second-class citizens. As Christians, European rulers favored improvement of their coreligionists' lot. The question was how to obtain this eminently desirable goal. Although the options were never mutually exclusive, two broad strategies emerged by the mid-nineteenth century. One possibility involved strengthening the millet system and bettering the position of each sect as a corporate group, probably with the help of intervention from fellow believers abroad. This program was favored by the Russians, who shared the religion of the Ottoman Empire's largest non-Moslem group, the Greek Orthodox. Another approach

---

Greek Orthodox millet may be found in F. Eichmann, *Die Reformen des osmanischen Reiches*, pp. 13–46.)

The Armenian Catholics, the Armenian Orthodox, and the Jews followed this pattern in its general outlines. The Roman Catholics and the tiny Protestant minority were never an integral part of the Empire in the way described above. The Latins only received a Patriarch in 1847, when the Latin Patriarch of Jerusalem was appointed in response to pressure from the Pope and the Catholic powers of Europe. Although there were sizable Roman Catholic groups in certain regions of the Empire, such as Bosnia, their interests had traditionally been protected by foreign governments; and in fact a relatively high proportion of the Roman Catholics residing in the Empire were foreign nationals, whether diplomatic personnel, merchants, or missionaries (ibid., pp. 99–114). These observations apply with still more force to the struggling Protestant sect, which received millet status only in 1850 (ibid., pp. 411–12), after strong representations from Stratford Canning.

was to secularize the Empire; to minimize the importance of religious ties except as a purely personal attribute; and to replace the corporate structure of the Ottoman state with an individual, strictly political, bond between Sultan and subject. This concept, known as *Osmanlılık,* obviously dovetailed with the Tanzimat reformers' ideas of administrative centralization; and although they were far from consistent, it was the policy they generally preferred and the policy that became identified with the Constitution of 1876, which climaxed the Tanzimat era. Though the British too were inconsistent (Stratford Canning worked hard for the establishment of a Protestant millet in 1850), British predilections obviously followed this line also. In the first place, the British had no significant group of coreligionists in the Ottoman Empire. If the game were to be played that way, they were clearly at a tremendous disadvantage. Equally important, the whole concept of the millet was suspicious to the British. The British had historically mistrusted groups like the Roman Catholics, who seemed to owe an allegiance to an authority outside the state. To the extent that this intolerance had abated in the nineteenth century, with moves such as the passage of Catholic emancipation, the new breadth of view was motivated by the perception that, for Englishmen, religion was no longer a prime determinant of political conduct. The least suggestion of ultramontanism revived latent fears, as witness the anti-Popery agitation centering around the Ecclesiastical Titles Bill of 1851. With this deep post-Reformation distrust of autonomous religious corporations—nourished by Irish Catholic immigration, peaking in the 1840s,[14]—the British were predisposed to find the millet system antiquated and (in a pejorative sense) "oriental." It remained to be seen whether it was feasible to diminish the power of the millets in Ottoman society. Attempts to do so not only alienated the officials whose power depended on the millet system, but also, to the extent that such attempts were fueled by the desire to improve the Christians' lot vis-à-vis the Moslems, they inevitably ignited a Moslem backlash and contributed to social disturbances.

Starting in 1848, the weaknesses of British policy began to emerge. The strains built into Ottoman society, exacerbated in many instances by the Tanzimat reforms, merged with the contagion of revolution in Europe to produce uprisings in various parts of the Empire. These revolts naturally attracted the attention of European governments, and the Near East again became a center of international rivalry. The Porte, counting on the informal protectorate of preceding years, logically turned to the British for assistance, and the British were forced to reassess a diplomacy whose implications were more than they had bargained for.

As early as March 1848, as revolutions were breaking out across Europe, Reshid Pasha, then grand vizier, tried to win an explicit promise of support from the British. Talking to Lord Cowley, who was about to return to London after a stint as ambassador, Reshid enlarged upon his fears of Russian aggression and tried to find out whether Britain would aid the Turks. Cowley was appropriately noncommittal, but he managed to find out that the Porte would be willing to sign an alliance giving the British navy access to the Dardanelles. When revolutions broke out in Moldavia and Walachia in June, the Ottoman ministers again approached the British. Stratford Canning was flattered "that in the present unsettled state of Europe the Sultan looks to England as his sheet anchor," but neither he nor the foreign secretary, Lord Palmerston, judged it wise to give a specifically encouraging reply.[15] Even when the Russians occupied both principalities, London refused to act; although Stratford warmly seconded an Ottoman request for a demonstration by the fleet at Malta, Palmerston remained uninterested.[16]

The results were not long in doubt: a defeat for Ottoman diplomacy. Since the Treaty of Adrianople in 1829, Moldavia and Walachia—though technically subject to the Sultan—had in fact existed under a Russian protectorate. The Porte hoped to use the revolutions, which were directed primarily against Russia, to loosen this foreign control. There is some evidence that Stratford sympathized with this goal.[17] However, failing material aid from Britain even at this last crucial moment,[18] the Ottoman ministers were obliged in May 1849 to sign an agreement that put an end to representative government in the Principalities and strengthened Russian control, as exercised through the hospodars, as the price of ending the Russian military occupation.[19]

Meanwhile, the Russian presence in Moldavia and Walachia provided the springboard for Russian intervention against the revolution in Hungary in the spring of 1849. Once again, Palmerston was on the side of the status quo: though he probably sympathized with some of the revolutionary leaders such as Kossuth,[20] he was convinced that maintenance of the Hapsburg Empire was the prerequisite for stability in eastern Europe; and he accordingly refused all overtures from Hungarian propagandists. Ultimately, however, the progress of Russian arms did awaken some alarm; at the end of August, Palmerston remarked to the French ambassador, Drouyn de Lhuys: "The moderation of the Czar . . . reassures me poorly. From moderation to moderation he might finish, if one let him have his way, by invading the entire world."[21] Palmerston soon found a way to serve notice on the Russians that Britain was watching: when the Russian and Austrian governments demanded extradition of some thirty-six hundred Hungarians and eight hundred Poles who had fled to the Ottoman Empire in the aftermath of the revolution, Palmerston backed up the Porte in the refusal to repatriate the refugees. Palmerston had concluded that Vienna and Saint Petersburg were bluffing in their extreme demands on the Porte; the solution was to put up a bigger bluff. As he expressed it to Lord John Russell, "With a little manly firmness we shall get successfully through this matter." Accordingly, he authorized a joint Franco-British naval demonstration in the eastern Mediterranean, urged in the strongest terms by Stratford.[22]

This response was definitely more encouraging to the Porte than the British attitude during the revolutions in Moldavia and Walachia. But it came virtually at the eleventh hour; in advising the dispatch of the fleet, Stratford warned: "I cannot conclude without repeating my conviction that if the Porte be left in this strait to it's [*sic*] own resources, there will be a complete, and perhaps an unavoidable breakdown of all that it has been hitherto the object of British policy to maintain."[23] And the support was hedged with important qualifications. Though the British fleet did eventually enter the Dardanelles, it was never clear whether this was a calculated move in aid of the Ottoman Empire or a nonpolitical attempt to escape bad weather.[24] In any event, Palmerston formally apologized to the Russian government for the breach of the Straits Convention, a step that further diminished the supportive character of the demonstration.[25] And Reshid Pasha's efforts, starting in November 1849, to interest the British in a permanent defensive alliance bogged down in British demands for reform and Ottoman wariness of alienating other powers.[26]

Yet Stratford had concluded: "The great eastern question is virtually at stake." In retrospect, his statement does not seem exaggerated. Although the British served their own interests by remaining levelheaded during the year of revolutions, a crisis of credibility was building at Constantinople. During 1851 and 1852, matters worsened as the British stayed aloof from the Holy Places Question, which they considered "an unseemly dispute."[27] It was inevitable that during 1853, as new conflicts struck to the root of the reforms that the British had encouraged, pressure would mount for Britain to act or to abdicate.

In fact, right after the 1848 revolutions, Napoleon III was more concerned about the shifting balance in the Near East than were the British. Everything in Napoleon's background set him against the

Vienna Settlement of 1815 and the Triple Alliance of Russia, Austria,
and Prussia that had maintained it. Now it seemed as though Russian
influence was expanding all across the Balkans, while the Hapsburgs,
who had seemed severely threatened in 1848, had been restored to their
old position in eastern Europe by Russian intervention. Such thinking
lay behind Napoleon's espousal of the rights of Roman Catholic pilgrims at the Holy Places in Palestine. This was an issue that aroused
considerable grass-roots support among clerical circles in France;
pressure had been growing for some years, particularly among officials
connected with the Latin, or Roman Catholic, church in the East.[28]
Many authorities have pointed to the President's need to conciliate the
party of the dévots, with whom he was not generally popular, especially
in view of his imperial ambitions.[29] But evidence in French documents
suggests that another important motive for Napoleon III was the desire
to challenge the Russians, who sponsored the rights of Greek Orthodox
pilgrims (most of whom were of Russian nationality) to the Holy Places.
Although French involvement in the preservation of the Holy Places
and in the pilgrimages to Palestine had been high in the eighteenth
century, the laicism of the governments after 1789 had meant lessened
concern, and in the early part of the nineteenth century, French influence had definitely declined, while there was a remarkable upsurge
of the Greek Orthodox Church, encouraged and partially financed by
the Russian government. Now Napoleon resolved to change this; as his
foreign minister de la Hitte wrote to Aupick, the ambassador at
Constantinople, in a passage later crossed out: "Finally, there is another consideration of great weight in our eyes because it is connected
with still higher interests yet, that is ... the utility that there is for the
Porte itself that our influence in the Orient be adequate to counter-
balance the always growing [influence] of Russia." The Holy Places
issue was particularly useful because it tended to divide Russia from
Austria, a Catholic state. Indeed, as plans were made for broaching
the Holy Places Question, the Quai d'Orsay was at some pains to involve the Austrian government on the French side. The démarche
could usefully serve to weaken the Holy Alliance, as well as affronting
Russia. Finally, it seemed likely that Napoleon's purposes could be
accomplished without serious danger of war. Aupick, consulted, judged
that Russia would operate behind the front of the Greek Orthodox
Church in the Ottoman Empire; he did not think that the Russian
government would enter into the affair directly. And the instructions
that Aupick received emphasized that France would never go beyond
diplomatic methods; Aupick was cautioned against any steps that
might make it embarassing to stop short of a recourse to force.[30]

Based on these factors alone, it might appear that Napoleon III's contribution to the creation of a warlike situation in the Near East was minimal. He was merely using diplomatic weapons to exploit the changing situation in the interest of raising French prestige and of harming Russia and the Holy Alliance, surely normal activity for a Bonaparte ruler. Unfortunately, the arguments used in support of the French case were not well chosen in view of the special nature of Ottoman society, and they made it almost inevitable that the Russians would produce counterdemands unacceptable to the Porte and to other powers that had signed treaties with the Porte. After some deliberation, on Aupick's advice, it was decided to present an inclusive demand based on the rights granted in the Capitulations of 1740. When the Porte demurred, Aupick presented the French case: the Capitulations had been a bilateral agreement; France had never sanctioned any changes; therefore, any departures from the letter of the treaty were illegal. When the Porte continued to search for a compromise, Aupick was instructed, on January 28, 1851, to inquire, "purely and simply, if the Porte considers itself as still bound by the Capitulations of 1740."[31]

However attractive this approach might be from a legal standpoint, it left a good deal to be desired from the angle of practical politics. To begin with, 1740 had represented the high point of French clerical influence in the Near East. It was not likely that the French could retrieve this status after more than a hundred years. Indeed, within a few months the Quai d'Orsay was forced to accept a procedural compromise. Aupick was recalled, and a plan suggested by Lavalette, the new minister to Constantinople, was adopted in June 1851. France would demand formal recognition of the validity of the Capitulations of 1740 but would make it clear that this did not imply a return to the status quo of 1740. After this face-saving ceremony had been executed, French and Ottoman representatives would proceed to a scrutiny of all relevant documents.[32]

Meanwhile, French action had set a damaging precedent. Until the 1840s, the Roman Catholic, or Latin, Church in the Ottoman Empire had not been headed by a patriarch—as were other, more extensively developed, millets, such as the Greek Orthodox. The Latins were comparatively few in number, and many adherents were foreign nationals. As a result, instead of entrusting their interests to a patriarch, their cause was usually presented by the mission of a foreign state. Eventually, the French took over that role, and thereafter, any disputes touching the rights of Ottoman subjects of the Catholic religion were routinely regulated by negotiation between the Porte and the French minister. In contrast, the Greek Orthodox millet had always been headed by a patriarch who had full power to speak for his coreligionists. Historically speaking, the Russian Orthodox Church stood on an equal footing with the Greek Orthodox Church in the Ottoman Empire. Technically the Patriarch in Constantinople was superior to the Church authorities in Russia. So, when Greek Orthodox rights were in question, although the Russian government might make strong diplomatic representations, any agreements were formulated as unilateral decrees from the Sultan to his subjects of the Greek Orthodox millet in response to petitions from the Patriarch of Constantinople and the millet.[33] Now the French argued that such decrees were internal arrangements which could not supersede or modify the stipulations of international treaties. The argument, generally accepted in relation to European states, was specious when applied to the Ottoman Empire. Furthermore, it invited response. If the French could win special privileges for the Latins on the grounds of international treaty rights, someone in Russia was bound to think of forcing a convention on the Porte which would envision settlement of disputes concerning the Greek Orthodox through Russo-Turkish agreements. When this demand, which had already been presented privately, was made publicly by Menshikov, the tsar's emissary, in 1853,[34] it was greeted with universal hostility; the fat was in the fire.

In 1851 and 1852, however, it seemed as though the Holy Places Question would get safely lost in a procedural morass. Conflicting claims were examined first by an international commission, then—after the Russians protested in a special mission—by a commission composed of ulema, or Moslem legal scholars and members of the Ottoman bureaucracy. The findings of that group were issued in a note sent to the French on February 8, 1852. When this document proved unsatisfactory to the Russians, the Porte simply issued a firman, which reasserted many of the Orthodox rights. All went well until early May, when the French found out the text of the firman and realized that the two documents were contradictory. A series of strong-arm measures redressed the balance during the summer of 1852. The *Charlemagne,* one of the newest French steamers, was sent up to Constantinople on a dubious pretext; captain and crew hospitably invited Turkish officials aboard for extended tours. The message was not lost. Meanwhile, a quarrel over the return of some French deserters, held by the Ottoman authorities in Tripoli in Africa, was made the occasion for a naval demonstration.[35]

As of the end of 1852, the French seemed to have won the confrontation over the Holy Places. The Porte determined to iron out the disagreements between the note and the firman by a special mission to Palestine under Afif Bey. Impressed by French bellicosity, the Porte gave Afif Bey instructions that favored the Latins. A key point was that Afif Bey was to continue the refusal to read the Greek firman publicly; without this ceremony, it would remain technically invalid.[36]

At the end of 1852, French success impelled Nicholas I and his chancellor, Count Nesselrode, to reevaluate the situation in the Near East in some detail. Apparently Nicholas believed that the Balkans represented the one unresolved trouble spot of his reign. It was tempting to try to do something about it,[37] especially when an unusual opportunity seemed to be provided by the rise of Russian power during the 1848 revolutions. It is still not entirely clear what new organization of the Balkan area Nicholas preferred. Certainly his chancellor wished for maintenance of the Ottoman Empire; but Nesselrode believed that Russia must demand solemn pledges against further disturbance of the rights of Orthodox pilgrims to the Holy Places or of the privileges of the Orthodox millet in general. To accomplish this aim, a special mission to Constantinople would be appropriate. A Russian emissary could work out, on the spot, a signed agreement concerning the rights of the different sects at the Holy Places and could win the Porte's assent to a *sened,* or convention with the force of a treaty; such an agreement would guarantee the position of the Orthodox millet and would recognize the tsar's role as its protector, thus putting the Greeks on an equal legal footing with the Latins. Nicholas espoused the idea of a mission, but apparently did not believe that the Porte would peaceably accept Russian conditions. He judged that the mission would arouse Ottoman resistance, which would lead to war and perhaps to the total collapse of Ottoman power. How to replace it? Nicholas was sure that he did not approve unilateral Russian gains, a dissolution into independent states, or the establishment of some new entity—such as a nineteenth-century version of the Byzantine Empire. The solution he preferred, assuming such extreme circumstances, was partition between Russia, Austria, Britain, and France.[38]

Nesselrode and Nicholas differed not only in their assessment of the probable future of the Balkan area; they also disagreed as to the strategy for attaining it. Nesselrode was firmly committed to peace. Although his survey of Russia's relations with foreign powers at the end of 1852 found no major sources of anxiety, he believed nonetheless that other powers would quickly unite against Russia if they suspected designs on Turkey; the result would be a general European war, which should be avoided at all costs.[39] Nicholas's later actions suggest that he, too, did not wish to unleash a major war; but he convinced himself that it would be feasible to carry out at least a partial reorganization of the Balkans through a quick Russo-Turkish war, which would be over before other powers—with the possible exception of France—could intervene. Such a war should be waged with maximum surprise effect, through a sudden march into the Principalities or an unexpected descent on Constantinople.[40] In a note of January 7, 1853, he considered in some detail the problem of military operations against Turkey. He returned to the idea of a successful attack on Constantinople as the strategy that might best accomplish the Russian goal: to win the war before the French could send aid. Nicholas outlined plans for a naval expedition to the Bosporus, consisting of sixteen thousand men with guns and horses, and a detachment of Cossacks. Such a force could be assembled at Odessa and Sevastopol and held in readiness. Nicholas did show some awareness of the difficulties of his plan: he considered, for example, the possibility that Constantinople might resist, or that the Turks might retire—in which case, they might be in a position to pin the Russians down until the French could arrive. These objections did not seem to deter Nicholas, however; rather, they seemed additional arguments for speed.[41]

Nicholas's scheme continued under discussion during the early weeks of 1853,[42] but his advisers were not happy with it. Paskevich, Nicholas's powerful field marshal, developed an alternate plan, the occupation of Moldavia and Walachia. This limited measure should suffice to make the Turks agree to the Russian proposals; and Paskevich guessed that if the Russian government made it clear that the occupation was "temporary," there would be minimal danger of European intervention.[43] But unfortunately for Nicholas, data from the foreign ministry made it easy for him to discount the likelihood of such intervention, even if his most drastic proposal were implemented. France might intervene if she could count on Britain's help; but the emergence of a Bonapartist regime in France seemed to preclude this possibility. Aberdeen told Brunnov, the Russian ambassador, that he did not expect to be able to work with Louis Napoleon.[44] And it seemed improbable that Napoleon would risk an attack on Russia alone. Nesselrode's view of Napoleon III may have influenced Nicholas here. Commenting on Louis Napoleon's humiliation in the Recognition Crisis of 1852—when Nicholas had refused to salute him with the customary polite term of "brother" upon his assumption of the imperial title—Nesselrode painted the new French ruler as an essentially mediocre man, who had achieved an inflated reputation by a series of successful bluffs. In denying Napoleon the footing of "brother," Nicholas had called his bluff and exposed the hollowness of his pretensions. It is noteworthy that Nesselrode failed to realize that the tsar's stand was ridiculed in the West, where Napoleon was generally considered to have had the best of the encounter.[45] Nicholas, being equally insensitive, however, might well conclude that—despite Napoleon's strong language in the Holy Places dispute—he would not be quick to send military aid to the Porte.

As for Britain, Nicholas's pleasant conversations with Aberdeen at the time of the 1844 Agreement, and the return of the latter as prime minister in 1852, undoubtedly disposed Nicholas to believe that British susceptibilities could be soothed. Confirmation of this estimate seemed to be offered by his conversations with Seymour, the British ambassador, during January and February of 1853. Nicholas had been advised against this démarche by Nesselrode, who argued that frank conversations with the ambassador, especially if they included revelation of any kind of partition plan, were premature, and were bound to do more harm than good in London. It is possible that Nicholas might have heeded this excellent advice had it not been for the news of Aberdeen's succession to power.[46] The opportunity to contact the statesman with whom he had, so he thought, successfully negotiated the 1844 Agreement was too much for Nicholas's vanity. Accordingly, at a diplomatic reception on January 9, 1853, Nicholas singled Seymour out for protestations of friendship. Seymour brought the discussion around to the Ottoman Empire; Nicholas, as reported by Seymour, declared: "We have a sick man on our hands, a man gravely ill, it will be a great misfortune if one of these days he slips through our hands, especially before the necessary arrangements are made." Though Seymour's reply was not enthusiastic (he proposed "a physician not a surgeon"),[47] Nicholas continued the exchange in another meeting on January 14. The conversations went on through February and into March before they tapered off into irrelevancies.[48]

In the course of the talks, most specifically on February 20, Nicholas outlined plans for partition of the Ottoman Empire. Nicholas disclaimed the desire to annex Constantinople, but he admitted to Seymour that Russia might occupy the city for a short time. Nicholas did mention to Seymour plans for some kind of control of the Straits and of strategic coastal regions, perhaps jointly with Austria. The Principalities, Serbia, and Bulgaria were to exchange Turkish rule for independence under Russian supervision. The status of Greece would not be changed. Crete and Egypt would go to Britain. This last provision was obviously designed to attract Seymour.[49]

Much controversy has surrounded the British reaction to these over-tures. Seymour, though careful to preserve his public suavity, was privately shocked. He paraphrased Nicholas's policy bitingly:

I, Nicholas, by the grace of God and so forth, not willing to incur the risk of war, and desirous not to compromise my character for magnanimity, will never seize upon Turkey; but I will destroy her independence. I will reduce her to vassalage and make her existence a burden to her and that by a process which is perfectly familiar to us, as it is the same which was employed with so much success against Poland. The danger is that England and France will foregather for the purpose of preventing this consummation. I will therefore show a decided preference for one of these powers and will do my best to disunite them.[50]

It is noteworthy, however, that Seymour did not believe that Nicholas contemplated an actual armed attack on Turkish territory in the near future. In January and February, the reaction in the British Cabinet to Nicholas's overtures seems to have been unalarmed. Even when Nicholas revealed the partition plan, there was a tendency not to take it seriously, for Nicholas had already demonstrated a penchant for this kind of scheme. The 1844 conversations were evidence of his fondness for personal diplomacy and seemed to show that this thoroughly un-British habit was relatively innocuous.[51] And this was not the first time since 1844 that Nicholas had talked of the "sick man"; in a crisis be-tween the Porte and Abbas Hilmi Pasha of Egypt in 1852, Nicholas had spoken to Seymour in terms that closely foreshadowed his over-ture of January 1853,[52] but nothing drastic had developed. The protes-tations of friendship were gratifying; so were Nesselrode's categoric assurances, through Brunnov, of Russian determination to maintain the Ottoman state as the "least bad" solution for the eastern Medi-terranean. Accordingly, the initial British response to Nicholas's soundings was somewhat encouraging; Lord John Russell even indi-cated that he thought there might be some substance to the Russian claims concerning the existing treaty status of the Greek Orthodox millet. It is doubtful that Nicholas expected anything more at this stage; Foreign Secretary Lord Clarendon's confidence in the tsar's in-tentions, repeatedly expressed during the spring in private letters to Stratford,[53] afforded a short honeymoon that reassured Nicholas.[54]

The British had misled the tsar; but they did not do it intentionally. Later in 1853, Brunnov has been blamed (with some justice), for telling the tsar what he wanted to hear, and for overemphasizing the views of the pro-Russian Aberdeen at the expense of a more balanced reportage of the attitudes of the ministry and the country at large.[55] But at this stage, the fault seems to lie with genuine British indecision and with Britain's lack of interest in the Holy Places Question. Nicholas's miscalculation concerning Austrian policy was more complicated and, in the long run, was more serious. On the one hand, after the Hungarian campaign the tsar had many sources of information about the stresses within the Austrian Empire that ultimately persuaded the Hapsburg government to stay at peace. On the other hand, Austrian readiness to exploit every opportunity to dampen revolutionary agitation in the Balkans—anytime it seemed possible to do so without starting a war—made Austrian policy look bellicose from the outside; Nicholas (and, incidentally, the Porte) had considerable reason to believe that Austria might join in an adventurous campaign to partition the Balkans.

Early in 1853, the Austrian government contributed dramatically to heightening tension in the Near East by sending a special mission under Count Leiningen to Constantinople, to press for solution of a series of grievances. In particular, the mission brought up the issue of the status of Christians in Bosnia, which had worsened in recent years—in part as a result of the introduction of the Tanzimat reforms. This issue was taken up by the Russians, and in the Menshikov mission (which the Russians originally hoped to coordinate with Leiningen's efforts), it was joined to the more limited question of the rights of the Greek Orthodox at the Holy Places. Although it was the Menshikov mission that created the immediate crisis that ended in the outbreak of war, the Austrian mission must be held responsible for exacerbating tensions; for helping to exhaust the patience of important Ottoman ministers; and for broaching some of the broad questions of principle, which were the most difficult to resolve.

Basically, the Leiningen mission dealt with the question of who was to control the western Balkans, especially Bosnia, Hercegovina, and Montenegro. Bosnia and Hercegovina had been semi-independent under local pashas in the early nineteenth century; but this period ended in 1840, with the death of Čengić Aǧa, a Bogomil (or Moslem Slav), who was a good example of the traditional ruling elite exploited by the Turks.[56] The Porte now appointed a Turkish governor from Istanbul, Tahir Pasha, to establish closer links with the capital and to improve the lot of the Christians, in accordance with the ideas of the Tanzimat. Tahir's reforms alienated the Moslem beys and led to a revolt.[57] The religious situation was compounded by the economic policy that had followed the conclusion of the Balta Liman treaty with Great Britain in 1838; that policy created preferential tariffs for for-

eigners in comparison with Ottoman subjects, who were liable to internal duties. The Bosnians, for example, found that goods sent from the
province to other parts of the Ottoman Empire were consistently under-
sold by Austrian exports, brought in at a lower duty. The Bosnian
solution was extensive smuggling over the Austrian border and reex-
portation to Ottoman territories; but this was illegal, and also created a
further problem: the strengthening of their ties with the South Slavs on
the other side of the Drava River.[58] Then came the appeal in 1848 of
Jelačić, the Ban, or governor, of Croatia, to the South Slavs of the
Ottoman Empire to join him in a general Slav revolt, directed specifically against Hungarian oppression. Though the problems of the Moslem beys were rather different from those of the Croatians, there was
considerable popular enthusiasm for South Slav unity, and the beys
accordingly joined a revolt led by a relative of Jelačić, Ali Kiedić. Tahir
Pasha failed to repress the uprising and urged the Porte to make concessions. A Slav assembly was called at Travnik, but its deliberations
soon foundered on the issue of Christian-Moslem equality. The troubles continued long after quiet had been restored in the Hapsburg
Empire across the Drava. Finally, in 1850, the Porte removed Tahir
and replaced him with Omer Pasha, a top military leader.[59]

Omer, ironically, was a Croatian by birth,[60] who had fled to the
Ottoman Empire after a scandal touching his family seemed to block
his military career. He had attracted the attention of the Sultan,
Abdul-Mejid, and had been used in a number of pacification missions.
Early in the Crimean War, he would be appointed Serdarı Ekrem
(commander in chief) of the Ottoman forces. Despite his Croatian
origins, Omer was not known for favoritism to the subject peoples.[61]
In this instance, he put down the rebellion with considerable harshness
and proceeded to administer Bosnia on the basis of a strict interpretation of the Tanzimat. Equality was rigidly enforced, and smuggling
across the Austrian border was ended.[62] Naturally, these results were
not obtained without bloodshed; and although the Porte's intention
was to help the Christians, in many cases Christians were the victims.
Literally thousands fled into Hapsburg territory, especially after Omer
tried to enforce a general disarmament. The problem of feeding and
caring for these refugees assumed serious proportions, particularly in
the economic slump caused by Omer's prohibition of smuggling. In
light of the already explosive situation in Croatia and on the military
border, the situation began to look extremely volatile. The Austrians
watched developments with anxiety. Early in 1852, the Vienna government severely curtailed Jelačić's powers as Ban of Croatia, and vir-

tually all his authority was given to General Mamula.[63] The hard line pushed by the Austrian army seemed to be gaining new adherents. The Austrian government called for the dismissal of Omer Pasha and the dismantling of the entire effort to enforce the Tanzimat, on the grounds that, whatever the Porte's ultimate intentions, the immediate results were unbearably disruptive and defeated the alleged purpose of the reform. The Porte admitted that the campaign to raise the position of the Christians would lead to disturbances sparked by the grievances of dispossessed Moslem elites; they pointed out that these growing pains were to be expected, not only in Bosnia, but also in other parts of the empire such as Kurdistan and Lebanon, where the populations were similarly mixed. In a clever attempt to outflank the Austrians' own arguments, however, the Porte reasoned that these disturbances were simply new examples of the general revolutionary movement, and should not receive the support of foreign powers any more than the Hungarian revolution against Austria in 1848 had been supported by the Ottomans.[64]

Meanwhile, the crisis in Bosnia had merged with another, originally unrelated, crisis in Montenegro. Montenegro had for many years enjoyed a peculiar status. Owing in part to its mountainous terrain and relative poverty, Montenegro had never been fully subdued by the Ottomans. Legally, the area enjoyed a state of virtually complete autonomy under the regime of the vladika, or prince-bishop. But the vladika's position was a good example of the complications that could arise when a more secular outlook had diminished the traditional Middle Eastern identification of nationality with religion. In his civil functions as quasi-independent governor of Montenegro, the vladika was theoretically subject to the Porte. But from a religious point of view, he was subject to, and was invested by, the synod at Saint Petersburg.[65] In 1851, the vladika, Peter II, died, and the position passed to one of his nephews, Prince Danilo. Danilo proceeded to secularize the office, with the approval of Saint Petersburg and Vienna. As a gesture of independence from the Porte, he did not request confirmation from Constantinople.[66]

It was perfectly evident that Danilo was really trying to increase the independence of Montenegro from the Porte through close ties with Russia and secondarily with Austria. His move came at a time when the Tanzimat reformers were trying to increase central control of the patchwork of Balkan provinces, and it coincided with the presence of an Ottoman army in Bosnia and in neighboring Hercegovina. A clash was highly likely and was certainly not unwelcome to Danilo, for he cherished hopes of annexing territories that would make his tiny mountain principality more nearly viable economically.[67] Should Omer succeed in the pacification of Bosnia-Hercegovina, this possibility might recede indefinitely.

At this juncture, a small band of some thirty Montenegrins attacked the Ottoman border fortress of Zabliak and mastered it. Danilo disavowed them, but the incident had provided Omer with an excuse to fight. He quickly overpowered the fortress (partly because Danilo had ordered the Montenegrins not to resist), took numerous prisoners, "and sent two hundred loads" of ears back to the capital. The incident was the signal for a full-scale Ottoman invasion of Montenegro.[68]

The Austrians now took up the cudgels for Danilo. The Porte argued, with considerable passion, that, though unrest in Montenegro was endemic, Danilo's challenge to Ottoman rule was new and could not be passed over. In effect, Danilo was trying to make himself a national ruler, independent of the Porte's control.[69] In opposition to this, the Austrians said that the Porte was deliberately taking advantage of the latest round of troubles in Montenegro to change the status quo and to establish a degree of control there that had no historical basis and had never been accepted by either the Montenegrins, the Austrians, or the Russians. As the pressure on Prince Danilo mounted, many figures in the Austrian government, particularly those in the military, began to urge the advisability of definitely establishing a protectorate over Montenegro; proposals circulated to offer Danilo a pension of as much as twenty thousand gulden if he would orient himself towards Vienna instead of Saint Petersburg.[70] And the Austrians took diplomatic action at the Porte. For some time, they had been pressing their right to close to Ottoman shipping the harbors of the tiny Ottoman enclaves of Klek and Suttorino, on the coast of Austrian Dalmatia. Since the ports provided the only possibility of supplying by sea Ottoman armies in the western Balkans, the point had considerable military importance. Now the Austrians mounted a major attempt to prevent the Ottoman invasion of Montenegro. The Sultan agreed to send orders to Omer Pasha forbidding the violation of Montenegrin territory under any circumstances, but Ottoman sincerity was doubtful. Ozerov, the Russian chargé d'affaires, reported a conversation with the Serasker Pasha (minister of war), Mehmet Rüştü that opened some disquieting perspectives. Mehmet Rüştü confirmed the sending of instructions to Omer to stay out of Montenegro, but suggested they might reach headquarters too late to be acted upon. Indeed, Mehmet Rüştü said he hoped Omer would not be stopped, since he would like nothing better than to see the Ottoman commander come to grief in the almost impassable mountain valleys. Though, in repeating this tidbit, Klezl, the Austrian chargé, emphasized Mehmet Rüştü's personal enmity to Omer, there is considerable plausibility to the speculation—which he also retailed—that the Porte hoped to subdue Montenegro, while holding off foreign criticism, by relying on the difficulty of communications to present everyone with a fait accompli.[71] In fact, at least one competent observer in Belgrade calculated that, unless the Porte were successful in Montenegro, Serbia would rise, and the whole Ottoman position in the western Balkans would collapse.[72]

Against this ominous background, the Austrians decided to send a mission to Constantinople under Count Leiningen. Leiningen was charged with presenting a note to Fuad Efendi, the Ottoman foreign minister, that would summarize Austrian demands. Ottoman military actions in Montenegro and Ottoman proceedings against Christians were to be the subject of explanations to Vienna. Certain revolutionaries currently serving with Omer Pasha were to be transferred away from the frontier provinces. The Austrian claim to control of maritime access to the enclaves was repeated. Finally, certain specific claims regarding individual Austrian subjects were urged.[73] These demands were supported by a buildup of troops in Croatia and Dalmatia and by reinforcement of Austrian naval units in the Adriatic. The generals proposed a full-scale Austrian protectorate over Montenegro, with provision of money, weapons, ammunition, and Austrian officers. Though Buol, the Austrian foreign minister, believed that the sending of weapons and officers might lead to international complications, proposals for munitions and money, within the very tight limits of the Austrian budget, were generally favored. Orders were given to the troops in both Croatia and Dalmatia to stand ready to attack should Omer cross the Austrian border or change the existing situation in Klek and Suttorino, while General Grünne, the head of the Military Central Chancellery, made it clear to the Porte that the Austrian moves were intended to have offensive implications, in that they were designed to increase Austrian influence in the western Balkans—specifically in relation to the Christian Slavs.[74]

The Porte at first continued immovable: Fuad Efendi's initial remarks seemed to the Austrians "more than ever elusive and unsatisfactory." However, when Leiningen sent what he considered a final note, Ottoman resistance abruptly collapsed. It seems evident that Russian cooperation with the Austrians—which was evidenced by Ozerov's informal support of the mission,[75] by a big Russian military buildup on the Ottoman border, and perhaps even by advance news of the Russian Menshikov mission—must have impressed the Porte.[76] It was obvi-

ously advisable to separate the two great powers by taking the opportunity to conciliate Austria.[77]

Although the Austrian government later went to some trouble to
publicize the results of the mission as a significant success, there were
clear losses. The Porte did indeed agree to the restoration of the status
quo in Montenegro, but this fell far short of the ambitions nourished
by Austrian military figures of gaining a decisive influence over Montenegro and the western Balkans. On the questions of the enclaves and
of the status of foreign revolutionaries in the Ottoman Empire, the
Porte, in practice, continued to stall. On the purely negative side, the
cost of the mobilization in Croatia and Dalmatia had run high, at a
time when the Austrian budget could ill afford extra strain, and Austrian handling of the crisis had contributed significantly to tension in
the Near East. Most unfortunate of all, Buol and his colleagues had
managed to project a bullying, opportunistic image that was diametrically counter to their intentions; the resulting confusion about Austria's
real aims was one of the factors that helped to bring on the war.[78]
Nicholas I, already inclined to take Austrian cooperation for granted,
was encouraged to believe that the Austrians were seriously interested
in extending their power in the western Balkans, even if war resulted,
and he concluded that some kind of deal could be struck with them in
which they would trade either benevolent neutrality or active support
for a division of the putative spoils. The Porte reacted to the episode
with deepened suspicion of Austrian goals and with a confirmed belief
in the likelihood of Austro-Russian cooperation in case of war.
Though later developments moderated these views somewhat, the Austrian government had lost much of its leverage as a force for peace at
Constantinople. Finally, the issues involved in Bosnia-Hercegovina
and in Montenegro struck to the heart of the problems of centralization
and Christian-Moslem equality, and of the efforts made by the Tanzimat reformers to deal with them. When the Russian government
merged these questions with the dispute over sectarian rights at the
Holy Places and made them the burden of the Menshikov mission,
which was backed up with considerably more nerve and effective force
than the Leiningen mission, the result was bound to be dangerous for
the whole structure of the Ottoman Empire and the existing role of the
great power interests within it.

Yet despite "so many combustible elements" (to borrow Nesselrode's
phrase),[79] it is clear that no government consciously planned or sought
a major European war in 1853. Nicholas I did not shrink from a local
campaign: outraged by the untidiness of the Balkan power vacuum, he
was ready to contemplate an armed descent on Constantinople, but he

evidently hoped that a general—as opposed to a limited—war could be precluded by a combination of military agility and canny diplomatic bargaining. There were a number of people in the top levels of the Austrian military who indulged in drastic language; but their scenarios did not include Austrian provocation of a large-scale war. The Austrians and the Ottomans simply clashed head-on in their concern over revolution in the Balkans. Both powers wished hegemony in the western Balkans in order to control revolutionary movements that threatened their own survival; though the aims and approaches of the two powers were not dissimilar, the background of historical conflict made them competitive and distrustful of each other. Yet it is apparent in retrospect that responsible Austrian leaders of whatever political persuasion were not going to jeopardize in war with the Ottoman Empire the status quo that their counterrevolutionary policy was dedicated to sustaining.[80]

Britain and France contributed to the emergence of the crisis situation largely through inadvertence. The British failed to recognize how disruptive the humanitarian reforms they promoted might prove to be in the Ottoman context. (They made a similar mistake in India, where their abuse of power led in 1857 to the Mutiny.) The French did not foresee the implications of their demand for a review of the status of the Latin Catholics in the Ottoman Empire on the basis of the Capitulations. Like the British, their principal fault was ignorance of the Near East. It is perhaps for this reason that western historiography has so often emphasized the "bluffs and blunders" theory of the origins of the war—but the blunders were not peculiar to this situation; they were typical of the difficulties of cross-cultural communication and have also appeared in many situations that did not end in major wars.

Thus far, little or nothing has been said of the Ottoman Empire as a protagonist in the struggle. In the broadest sense, the Tanzimat reformers—men such as Reshid Pasha, Ali Pasha, and Fuad Efendi—had set in motion wide changes in Ottoman society, which created an unstable situation. Yet they certainly were not planning war; they were simply trying to devise a response to the problems posed for the Ottoman Empire by the still wider and more impersonal forces of revolution, nationalism, and shifting balances of trade—forces that simultaneously affected Europe through the 1848 revolutions and the Industrial Revolution. In the more immediate perspective, Ottoman ministers had tried to profit by episodes such as the revolutions in Moldavia and Walachia or the flight of the Hungarian refugees to improve the status of the Porte both in relation to its own subjects and to foreign powers. Yet the consistently patient and conciliatory policy adopted during the first three years of the Holy Places negotiations is evidence that most Ottoman statesmen shared a strong instinct for staying out of trouble. In fact—as the crisis over Moldavia and Walachia, as well as many other examples, illustrates—it was difficult to maintain a dynamic diplomatic stance in Constantinople. On several occasions after 1848, for example, the Russians had put pressure on the Porte; the reformers had tried to oppose concessions; appeals to Britain and France had been made, which either brought no real response or a response so hedged about with Western demands for further reforms as to be unacceptable domestically; and, as a result, the reform-minded members of the ministry would be eliminated and another group that would seek an accomodation with the Russians would be appointed. The surprise is that events in 1853 and 1854 did not follow this model. It was the Russians' error to lead off with a demand for dramatically improved status for the Christians and then to follow up this demand with a high-handed and humiliating style of diplomacy. In fairly short order, they managed to alienate the more conservative Ottoman leaders—who could generally be counted on to oppose overly close relations with Britain or France, but who disliked Christians and were actuated by a vigorous imperial pride. Once this group had decided that further concessions would be dishonorable, there was little any other Ottoman leaders could do except to try to make certain that, if the confrontation led to war, it was not fought on disastrous terms. This meant playing skillfully upon the ill-defined relation with the Western powers, Britain and France, until the tenuous bond could be hardened into a signed alliance. The highly subtle, limited yet responsive, diplomacy by which this was brought about was the catalyst that changed a limited Russo-Turkish tourney into a general European war.

Chapter II

Menshikov at Constantinople

WHEN the plans for the Menshikov mission were drawn up in the Russian Chancellery in January 1853, the opportunities for Russian policy appeared unusually great. The Austrians were sending the Leiningen mission concurrently; only Menshikov's unexpected illness prevented him from reaching Constantinople at the same time as the Austrian envoy and presenting his demands simultaneously.[1] The British, whose susceptibilities Nicholas had tried to soothe through his discussions with Seymour, seemed at least unlikely to oppose Menshikov's demands. Competent Russian evaluation of Napoleon III suggested that he was unlikely to go beyond hostile language and threats of action in any crisis situation. The Porte, in recent years, had generally yielded to the device of the special mission, which had been employed by the Russians with regard both to the revolutions in Moldavia and Walachia and to the Holy Places Question. The foreign minister, Fuad Efendi, was considered by the Russians to be their principal enemy at the Porte and the man responsible for recent pro-French decisions in relation to the Holy Places; otherwise the ministry, headed by Mehmet Ali Pasha, was composed of men who had relatively few ties with the West. By and large, the omens seemed propitious. Although Nesselrode wanted to send a diplomat, Nicholas selected Prince Menshikov, whose blustery personality, background in the naval administration, and proven loyalty to the tsar seemed to promise the decisive approach Nicholas had in mind.[2]

The instructions with which Menshikov was provided included both general surveys designed to brief Menshikov on the background of the problem and specific documents to be used in its solution. In a preliminary letter, Nesselrode exposed the origins and purpose of the mission. He castigated the Tanzimat reformers and accused them of using the Holy Places Question to foment a quarrel between Greek Orthodox and Roman Catholic millets in the Ottoman Empire. Their ultimate aim was to curtail the rights of the Orthodox millet and to extend those of the Catholics. In this, they were abetted by the French emissaries in the Ottoman Empire; to any representations made by the Russians, they would probably plead their promises to the French. He instructed Menshikov to demand full and immediate satisfaction on the Holy Places Question. But this was no longer enough. He continued:

After all that has passed recently at Constantinople and at Jerusalem and after the retraction of the solemn and reiterated engagements which the Ottoman government had made to us, the Imperial Cabinet will not be able to consider either the new firmans that will be published or the arrangement that will be agreed upon as sufficient guarantees until the totality of these measures, duly concerted and drawn up between the Ottoman ministry and Your Excellence, be converted into a separate act, public or secret, under the name of *Convention* or of *Sened* having the force and value of a *Treaty.*

In a second letter of the same day, Nesselrode considered Menshikov's course of action should his propositions be refused. The Prince was to draw up a note that would be given to the grand vizier in a formal interview and that would threaten the breaking off of negotiations and the departure of the mission. Three days later, Menshikov was to carry out his threat, and he was to direct Ozerov to follow with the entire diplomatic personnel of the embassy. Finally, if questioned about Russian troop movements, Menshikov was to admit that the Russians had been making "military preparations" and was to blame them on "the attitude" of the Ottoman government.[3]

In a third letter, headed "secret instructions," Nesselrode took up an alternative possibility: suppose Menshikov found the Sultan anxious about the French threat and ready for a "rapproachement" with Russia? In this case, Menshikov was authorized to propose a defensive alliance against France. This arrangement, which would be confirmed by a treaty, would be limited to a specific number of years and to the particular problem of French influence in Jerusalem. It would, of course, be kept confidential. As an additional inducement, Menshikov might point out that this treaty was highly advantageous to the Porte, since it committed the Russians to aid the Turks, but did not stipulate Turkish aid to Russia.[4]

After some more general briefing, Nesselrode reached the heart of the matter in three documents that were to be used directly in the negotiations. One was a letter from Nicholas to the Sultan, which introduced Menshikov and rehearsed the purposes of the mission. A second was the text for the draft treaty of alliance against France. But the most important and controversial was the project for a *sened*. The preamble made a link with the Treaty of Kutchuk-Kainardji of 1774.

In the Name of All-Powerful God, His Imperial Majesty the Very High and Very Powerful Emperor and Autocrat of all the Russias and His Imperial

Majesty the Very High and Very Powerful Emperor of the Ottomans, equally animated by the sincere desire to maintain the system of peace and of good harmony, fortunately established between the two Empires, have resolved to fortify the perfect friendship and full and entire confidence that prevails between them by the conclusion of a special convention, having the force and value of a treaty and designed to better elucidate and define the terms and the sense of articles VII, VIII, XIV, and XVI of the treaty concluded in the year 1774 at Kutchuk-Kainardji and confirmed by subsequent treaties and by that of Adrianople.

The key paragraph of the proposed convention was article 1, which put forward the demand for a special relationship with the Greek Orthodox millet.

The Imperial Court of Russia and the Ottoman Sublime Porte, desiring to prevent and to remove forever any reason for disagreement, for doubt, or for misunderstanding on the subject of the immunities, rights, and liberties accorded and assured *ab antiquo* by the Ottoman emperors in their states to the Greek-Russian-Orthodox religion, professed by all Russia, as by all the inhabitants of the principalities of Moldavia, Walachia, and Serbia and by various other Christian populations of Turkey of different provinces, agree and stipulate by the present convention that the Christian Orthodox religion will be constantly protected in all its churches, and that the ministers of the Imperial Court of Russia will have, as in the past, the right to make representations on behalf of the churches of Constantinople and of other places and cities, as also on behalf of the clergy, and that these remonstrances will be received as coming in the name of a neighboring and sincerely friendly power.

The remaining paragraphs spelled out other details of the special relationship: the Orthodox hierarchy was not to be hampered in the exercise of its functions by the Sublime Porte (article 2); the patriarchs were to be appointed for life and could not be removed except for offenses against religion or against their religious followers (article 3); further assurances were given as to the status of the Greek Orthodox missions at Jerusalem (articles 4, 5, and 6).[5]

These instructions were far more ambitious than anything the Russians had yet attempted in the Holy Places dispute. In a demand that paralleled the French use of the Capitulations of 1740, the Russians tried to interpret the Treaty of Kutchuk-Kainardji as giving them a special right of intercession on behalf of the Greek Orthodox millet. (Actually, neither Nicholas nor Nesselrode had a clear recollection of the text of the treaty, and both were somewhat embarrassed later when they realized how much they had stretched it.[6]) To prevent misunderstandings in the future, a specific agreement, or *sened,* was to guarantee Russian rights of surveillance, not only over the rights of the Orthodox at the Holy Places—the original subject of dispute—but also over the status of the millet as a whole, thus meeting the kinds of problems that the Austrians were raising on behalf of the Christians of Bosnia-Hercegovina and Montenegro.

From his very first contacts with the Porte, Menshikov adopted a high-handed and condescending tone. Arriving on the warship *Thunderer,* accompanied by a staff of military experts, he made his ceremonial visits on March 2, attired in a frock coat instead of the military uniform demanded by protocol.[7] Without warning, he omitted the expected interview with the Ottoman foreign minister, Fuad Efendi. Fuad, who had dressed for the occasion, found himself literally left standing.[8] Menshikov went directly to the grand vizier, Mehmet Ali Pasha. Their conversation was brief, since Mehmet Ali did not know any European languages; Menshikov limited himself to expressing extreme displeasure with Fuad.[9] Since Nesselrode had concluded that Fuad had been the prime exponent of a pro-French policy during the autumn and winter of 1852, the insult to Fuad was not mere caprice on Menshikov's part, but had been prescribed in his instructions. Fuad immediately resigned, as the Russians intended. The Sultan, Abdul-Mejid, in an unusual step, instead of simply dismissing Fuad, issued a firman stating that he had accepted Fuad's resignation upon the minister's own insistence. Some effort was made in British circles to see this as a compliment to Fuad;[10] in fact, it seems like a transparent attempt to lessen the humiliation of Menshikov's dictation of an apology.[11] Fuad was replaced by Sadık Rifat Pasha, a notable leader and theorist of the Tanzimat. Rifat, however, was not popular with the British: Stratford referred to him as "a beast" and declared that he looked for "truth at the bottom of his brandy bottle."[12] In fact, Rifat's formative European experience had been in Vienna; he had known and had been deeply impressed by Prince Metternich, and his political ideas, which emphasized balance and harmony rather than radical change, showed the mark of these early experiences.[13] In foreign affairs he had continued to be pro-Austrian; and it seems likely that the Porte hoped to capitalize on relations with Vienna, recently improved by the solution of the Leiningen mission, to build a bridge to the Russians.[14]

Possibly Menshikov hoped to shake up the ministry even more. On March 8, when he had an audience with Sultan Abdul-Mejid, he announced his intention of paying a formal visit to the elder statesman, Husrev Pasha. Conceivably, this was a hint that Menshikov wished Abdul-Mejid to substitute Husrev for Mehmet Ali in the post of grand vizier. Husrev, who had figured importantly in Sultan Mahmud's army reforms, was not attracted to the civil reform program of the Tanzimat.[15] He had had, and he continued to have, a rather bad press in British circles (Temperley, quoting the Prince de Joinville, refers to him as "the master-strangler"[16]), but he had won the approval of the Russians by signing the treaty of Unkiar Skelessi in 1833, and this time, Menshikov took pains to wear the required uniform. By now, however, Husrev was eighty-four years old,[17] and it is hard to imagine him as a serious candidate for the post of grand vizier. A more plausible reason for Menshikov's visit was the ample information Husrev was ready and able to give about the state of Ottoman politics.[18]

These preliminary encounters set the blustering tone that Menshikov had been ordered to adopt, and they irritated Turkish sensitivity and pride. As soon as Menshikov presented his specific demands, another dimension of the threat appeared. Menshikov's first *note verbale,* dated March 4 / 16, 1853, was devoted mainly to the Holy Places. Menshikov outlined the provisions of the Sultan's firman of January 29 / February 10, 1852, with regard to the privileges of the Greek Orthodox Church in the Holy Land; charged that the Porte had then made contradictory concessions on behalf of the Roman Catholics without informing the Russians; and demanded the conclusion of a formal agreement that would stipulate full implementation of the 1852 firman. In the last paragraphs of the note, Menshikov hinted at a larger mission. He declared that the Greek Orthodox had been subject to serious harassment in recent years. Events in Palestine were part of this, and the guilt here could be assigned to the Latins and to "the political support coming from the Occident." But beyond this, the Porte itself had shown "distrust and ill will" when presented with appeals from the tsar on behalf of his fellow believers. An example was the failure to listen to Russian admonitions in the Montenegrin question. Menshikov thus prepared the ground for the demand for a *sened.* He went on: "The ambassador has the mission to complain about these things to His Majesty the Sultan in representing to him, with all the respect due to his person, the necessity of removing the profound and justified dissatisfaction that his old and best ally feels about this by an act of confidence that will remove for the future every shade of disagreement between the two sovereigns."[19]

Menshikov's first *note verbale* was followed up by a second, given to Rifat on March 10 / 22, 1853. In this declaration, Menshikov confined himself to a call for action in the Holy Places Question. He affirmed the historical basis of the Russian claims and asserted, somewhat speciously, that the Russian government had shown courtesy in

deigning to discuss the implementation of the firman of 1852, rather
than making it the basis for a nonnegotiable demand. Finally he declared that the Imperial government now required "a solemn act." A
brief accompanying note introduced the text of the draft convention
that had been furnished in Menshikov's instructions. As Menshikov
described the scene, "during the perusal of these documents Rifat's
face grew visibly somber; he seemed to me deeply affected and could
not for some moments pronounce a word." Menshikov tried to rally
Rifat by minimizing the danger of international complications; he concluded: "I left him discountenanced and troubled, but not surprised
by this communication, for which he had been prepared for several
days."[20]

Rifat and his colleagues found that the brusqueness of Menshikov's
technique was matched by the extensiveness of his demands. But it
is impossible to understand fully the problems facing the Ottoman
ministers without a brief examination of the internal discontents of the
Empire and of Menshikov's effect on them. The Menshikov mission
could hardly fail to interest the more highly placed and politically
aware members of the Greek Orthodox millet. But though the prince
was lionized by the leading Greek Orthodox subjects of Constantinople[21] and quickly established a close working relationship with the
representative of Greece, Metaxas,[22] it is not clear that—in the long
run—his interests coincided with those of either group. The leaders of
the Greek Orthodox millet apparently feared that Russian supervision
would be more restrictive than Ottoman supervision; the strongest pro-
Russian feelings were to be found at the level of the lower clery.[23] By
the same token, official Russia was not necessarily favorable to Greek
political ambitions, though this was often overlooked locally. Greece,
as delimited in 1832, was a relatively small state that certainly did not
include everybody of Greek nationality, let alone everybody of Greek
religion. These circumstances gave rise to the *Megali Idea,* or the Great
Idea: many Greek patriots hoped to fulfill their country's destiny
through reunion with the fatherland of all Greeks. Since nationalist
ideas were still evolving, this ambition could take different forms: if a
religious basis were used, the true Greece could be taken to include
most of European Turkey in a reconstituted Byzantine Empire; even if
national identity were defined in terms closer to secularized Western
definitions, there was a strong claim to Epirus, Thessaly, Thrace, and
parts of Macedonia.[24] These ambitions kept the provinces bordering
on Greece in a semipermanent state of crisis that threatened to erupt
into war at the least shock from the outside.

Against this background came the events of the spring of 1853. Menshikov sent his staff member, Admiral Kornilov, to Athens in mid-March. Although the tour was billed as a pleasure trip, it included vists to King Otto; the premier; Paicos, as foreign minister; and other leaders; as well as to the Acropolis.[25] Although it is not known what was said, it is evident that Kornilov came at a critical juncture. Shortly before, the Porte had advanced a claim to two frontier villages that had long been occupied by the Greeks. Strong measures were threatened if the Greeks did not immediately recognize the Turkish right to administer the area. It seems unlikely that Kornilov was instructed to encourage the Greek government to immediate direct action;[26] however, he may have urged them to prepare to profit from an eventual Russo-Turkish breach.[27] The visit of a distinguished military man could hardly fail to have had a heady effect on the Greeks.[28] Paicos now appealed to the representatives of Britain, France, and Russia, the three protecting powers. He declared that the village in question had been ruled by Greece since the kingdom had been established and accused the Turks of unjustifiably threatening war on an issue that had never previously seemed important. He asserted that the Greek government wished to avoid war, but concluded that the Greeks must defend themselves if necessary.[29] The situation deteriorated rapidly as Greek troops gathered on the border. The Turkish authorities admitted that serious trouble could develop if there were any kind of local uprising.[30] As it turned out, Menshikov was not eager to second Greek claims; he accepted an overture from the British to settle the dispute through informal arbitration by the protecting powers. The two villages were awarded to the Ottoman Empire.[31] But this was scant comfort to the Turks, especially as the extra Greek troops remained stationed on the border.[32] The Kornilov mission underlined Russian influence at Athens and the whole affair confirmed convictions that any trouble with Russia was likely to unleash fighting in the provinces bordering on Greece.

This part of the Empire was, however, relatively distant from the main European theater—namely the Danube frontier—in case of war. Revolts in the Greek provinces could assume major importance for the Ottoman Empire only if they coincided with uprisings farther to the north, where there could eventually be a link with an invading Russian army. Unfortunately for the Porte, the situation did not look bright in the northwest Balkans either. Montenegro, Bosnia, and Hercegovina, whether despite of or because of Omer Pasha's recent pacification, remained potential trouble spots. More powerful and more unstable was the semiautonomous principality of Serbia.[33] As with the Greeks and the Greek Orthodox, the tendency in Serbia was for the people to be undiscriminatingly pro-Russian, while the ruling groups had strong reservations, based on their perceptions of Russian unwillingness to build up powerful rivals and on the likelihood that Russian supervision, unlike Turkish, would be relatively efficient. The reigning prince, Alexander Karageorgevich, was not considered pro-Russian; however, he had a rival in the heir of the opposing Obrenovich family. Michael, perhaps partly because he was not in power, seemed more pro-Russian; it was thus possible for Menshikov to threaten the Serbian Agent at Constantinople with a popular revolution against the Karageorgeviches.

Menshikov's main target was the Serbian premier, Ilya Garashanin, an able and dedicated nationalist who successfully resisted the running interference of the Russian consul general, Toumansky. Garashanin was also persona non grata to the Austrians, because in 1848–49 he had been one of the principal advocates of the Greater Serbia idea—a proposed union of South Slav peoples now under the Hapsburg yoke with the South Slavs of the Ottoman Empire. The Austrians accordingly joined in the campaign for Garashanin's dismissal.[34] The prince was quickly forced to yield, although the victory was somewhat marred by the fact that Alexander continued to consult Garashanin extensively in private. Still, the episode showed how Russia and Austria, when agreed, could manipulate this part of the Balkans—and in view of the Leiningen mission and the Hungarian Refugees crisis, there was no reason to assume that they would not be united, at least in the near future.

Both the trouble with Greece and the incident in Serbia occurred against a background of rising tension between Christians and Moslems.[35] It is easy to forget—in concentrating on negotiations between Constantinople and Europe, or between the European capitals—that this factor also influenced the attitude of Ottoman statesmen. They faced not merely the menace of Menshikov's high-handed methods and far-reaching demands but also the dangers of a deteriorating domestic situation that was only partially understood abroad. It is now necessary to see how they dealt with these staggering problems.

Mehmet Ali could take some courage from the Porte's recent record in dealing with pressure from the great powers. His own success as grand vizier in arranging the Montenegrin question with Leiningen doubtless bolstered his confidence. And the Hungarian Refugees crisis showed that the Porte could, upon occasion, stand up to the Russian government with impunity.[36] Mehmet Ali played a double game in the first weeks of the mission. Rifat was instructed to negotiate, in the hope that through his connections with Austria he could bring off an acceptable arrangement. But Mehmet Ali did not commit himself to this line: Rifat felt very isolated in the ministry, while the grand vizier continued to consult Fuad upon all occasions. It seems likely that, in case negotiations failed, Mehmet Ali intended to make Rifat the scapegoat.[37] Meanwhile, evidently without Rifat's knowledge,[38] he was preparing the Empire's military defenses.

First of all, he appealed to Britain and France for naval aid. His pleas were readily received by the diplomats. As it happened, both powers were represented in Constantinople at that moment by chargés d'affaires. Benedetti, of France, conscious of his limited mandate, immediately wrote Paris a full explanation of the situation. Colonel Rose, who had chafed under subordination to Stratford, yearned to play a larger role: he wrote directly to Admiral Dundas at Malta.[39] The reactions of the home governments differed sharply. Napoleon III was advised that too hasty a compliance with the Turkish request would look like petty vengeance against the tsar for the recent Recognition Crisis; but he decided that the circumstances were serious and gambled that, if the French moved, the British would follow.[40] The British, however, felt themselves bound by their conversations with the Russians and by the tsar's "assurances"; they also feared that Napoleon III, having involved them in eastern waters, might seize the opportunity for an invasion of England. So the French fleet sailed for the Levant alone, arriving off Salamis on the fourth of April.[41] Meanwhile, Mehmet Ali, who tended to oppose too close a relationship with Britain and France, had second thoughts about his request. When queried again by Rose in the middle of March about the need for the fleets, the grand vizier demurred.

Mehmet Ali, in retracting his demand for the fleet, was presumably motivated by practical considerations: the appeal to the fleets was certain to exacerbate relations with Russia and Austria and was evidently disapproved by Rifat. Furthermore, Mehmet Ali apparently decided that Turkey was in a position to defend herself.[42] Mehmet Ali had talked to Adolphus Slade, a British naval officer who had been attached to the Turkish forces in an advisory capacity at the time of the Hungarian Refugees crisis.[43] Slade had already spent a great deal of time in the Ottoman Empire and was close to Mehmet Ali Pasha. After consultation with Rose and Benedetti, Slade proposed to Mehmet Ali certain minimum defensive measures designed to forestall Russian capture of Constantinople. Slade found Mehmet Ali unreceptive; the grand vizier feared that any military action would anger the Russians and would impede negotiations. Since Mehmet Ali had asked for the French and British fleets, he presumably intended to put the burden, and the blame, for naval precautions on the two Western powers; with the city thus safeguarded, he could present the Porte in the ensuing talks as pacific and conciliatory. Slade, however, assured the grand vizier that it would be possible to put Constantinople in a state to resist attack without making moves that would be likely to attract the Russians' attention. From his wealth of information about the topography of the Bosporus, Slade made certain practical and relatively simple suggestions. Ships should be stationed at certain strategic points to intercept attack, and their equipment should be improved. Heavy guns should be mounted to command the harbors at Büyükliman and Tophane. Gun emplacements should be built and cannon installed on the hills above Büyükdere, as a second line of defense in case the Russians were able to run past the crossfire from the castles at the mouth of the Bosporus. These proposals were implemented,[44] which doubtless reassured Mehmet Ali.

It is interesting to note that, though Slade did not feel entire confidence in his plans,[45] the Russians were impressed. Admiral Kornilov, when he sent back reports from his subordinates, Butakov and Zheleznov, added a number of discouraging observations on Nicholas's plan to seize Constantinople. He showed far more enthusiasm for an alternate plan, which he also discussed, of an attack somewhere on the Black Sea coast to the north of Constantinople, perhaps at Burgas.[46] Menshikov, less deferential, termed Nicholas's Bosporus expedition "highly difficult or even impossible"; and seconded the proposal of a landing at Burgas or nearby Varna.[47] Accordingly, at the end of March and the beginning of April, Nicholas and Paskevich seriously considered a joint operation by land and sea, with Varna and / or Burgas designated as the point of junction and the base for a land campaign against Constantinople, perhaps via Adrianople. But this depended on the proposition that France and Britain would not send naval aid to the Turks and would not enter the Black Sea to dispute Russian control of those waters. Paskevich still preferred the plan he had originated, which was later adopted, for a temporary punitive occupation of Moldavia and Walachia, to be converted to a full-scale invasion should it become necessary.[48]

Meanwhile, negotiations between Rifat and Menshikov were proceeding. From the beginning, Rifat made a distinction between Menshikov's specific demands about the Holy Places and the proposal for a *sened*. The idea of separating the two questions, usually attributed to Stratford de Redcliffe, actually occurred to Rifat at the start of the talks. His purpose was similar to that ascribed to Stratford: he hoped that if the Holy Places affair could be satisfactorily terminated, the remaining Russian grievances would be too vague and all-encompassing to justify action.[49] The Russians evidently agreed in the hope that they might catch Britain and France off guard by introducing their most controversial demands late in a complex set of negotiations in which most of the other powers had not been involved.[50] On March 23, Rifat informed Menshikov that the Council of Ministers wished to settle the points concerning the Holy Places through joint sessions with the prince and with a representative of the French government. Menshikov, at first hostile to this idea, eventually agreed. Meetings got underway and continued throughout April.[51] The return, early in the month, of the French and British ambassadors—de la Cour and Stratford de Redcliffe—actually aided the process. De la Cour's instructions were specific: despite the many political ramifications of the question, the religious kernel of the problem was considered an anachronism that neither the French nor the Russians should wish to pursue. A following letter, although allowing for Nicholas's desire to impress the Turks, was optimistic about the tsar's readiness to patch things up with France.[52] Stratford, too, came with friendly inclinations; his was not "the angry return of a king whose realm had been suffered to fall into danger" described by Kinglake. Indeed, Stratford's instructions favored the Russians and enjoined him to use his influence to bring about an agreement as quickly as possible.[53]

The conciliatory nature of Stratford's instructions, drawn up during the brief Anglo-Russian rapprochement of the early spring, was reinforced by Stratford's own doubts about his previous championship of the Porte. A severe anti-Christian riot at Aleppo in 1850 had seemed to him a return to barbarism; it made him doubt the effectiveness of all he had done as the Turks' self-styled "mentor" in the preceding ten years.[54] In fact, it might be argued that it was progress, rather than lack of progress, towards Christian-Moslem equality that had touched off the disturbances; but the uprising did indicate profound disgruntlement on the part of the Moslem townspeople, who felt themselves victimized economically, politically, and religiously. Similar riots were to occur in other cities of the Empire in the 1850s, culminating in the famous riot at Damascus in 1860.[55] Stratford seems to have concluded that the dream of a reformed Empire under British sponsorship alone was impracticable; in the future, he was to emphasize, far more than in previous years, the necessity for combined pressure by all five great powers.

Stratford's pessimism about the efficacy of British influence at the

Porte was matched by his disillusionment with the reformers. Stratford
had undoubtedly overidealized his favorite, Reshid, and had certainly
refused to recognize his background. Stratford never recovered from a
conviction that Reshid, Westernized as he undoubtedly was, must be
Greek, and he invited Reshid's children to celebrate Christmas with
his own. The shock was correspondingly great when Reshid was implicated, during 1852, in a scandal involving corruption in the customs
collection at Constantinople. In Ottoman practice, Reshid's misdeed
was a mere pecadillo;[56] but Stratford insisted on judging him by nineteenth-century British standards of rectitude.[57]

So Stratford came prepared to mediate. Both Mehmet Ali Pasha and
Menshikov, to their surprise, found Stratford friendly. With such over-
whelming willingness to reach an arrangement, it is not surprising that
the questions concerning the sanctuaries were quickly resolved; the
definitive agreement was ready on May 5, 1853.[58] Meanwhile, the question of the *sened* had not been completely lost from view. When he first
transmitted the proposed draft on March 22, Menshikov made an important observation. Though Rifat was distressed by the project as a
whole, it seemed to be "the word Convention" that upset him most.
This impression was confirmed by Rifat himself the next day, after a
meeting of the Council of Ministers. He indicated that the Porte did
not find the contents of the draft particularly objectionable, but the
"form" of a convention was absolutely unacceptable. Some days later,
Rifat returned to the point in an unofficial talk with Argyropoulos, the
first dragoman of the Russian embassy. Argyropoulos reported: "Rifat
kept coming back to the convention. He begged that you would give
up the idea of a treaty and [said] that everything could be arranged."[59]
Evidently Rifat was exploring the possibility of salvaging what he could
for the Porte by limiting the binding quality of the agreement.

Menshikov accordingly decided to seek further instructions. In a
letter written early in April, he outlined developments for Nesselrode's
benefit, suggested that the *sened* was likely to prove the sticking point,
and asked for specific recommendations covering this part of his mission. If the Turks rejected the *sened,* should the Russian embassy leave
Constantinople? The answer, from Nicholas, was "yes." Would it be
possible to substitute some other form, such as an "exchange of notes,"
for the treaty? Perhaps Nicholas had not thought through this point,
for his marginal comments are ambiguous. Next to Menshikov's inquiry about an exchange of notes, the tsar wrote, "Treaty or convention
is all the same to me." At the end of the letter he noted, "I have nothing
to add to what I have marked down, the note I find clearly ordered in

the communication last sent and I insist upon its execution." Nessel-rode probably summed up the gist of the tsar's thinking in his reply; he minimized the novelty of the provisions contained in the *sened*, declared that the question of form was unimportant and could be arranged to suit the Turks, but emphasized that there must be no more procrastina-tion. Apparently the tsar was impressed by Menshikov's concluding comment, which he underlined: "I will permit myself to add here that without a crisis of coercion it may be difficult for the Imperial Mission to recapture the degree of influence that it exercised previously over the Divan." Returning to one of the features of Menshikov's original in-structions, Nicholas required that Menshikov present at least the gist of the *sened*, the demand for the protectorate, as a sort of ultimatum, with a specific time limit for acceptance.[60]

Meanwhile, Rifat was trying to drum up support from the other great powers for outright rejection of the *sened*. At the end of March, he invited Klezl to a meal at his home and sounded out the Austrian chargé about his views. The conversation revealed to Rifat that Klezl, far from cooperating with Menshikov, knew nothing about this dimen-sion of the Russian mission. Thus emboldened, Rifat asked specifically, a couple of weeks later, that Klezl write Buol for advice as to the re-sponse to make on the *sened*. Klezl, personally sympathetic to the Porte, wrote on April 18 an impassioned exposé of the danger inherent in the Russian proposals.[61] But it was far from clear how the Ballplatz would react.

Rifat also approached Stratford Canning, but with some hesitation—natural in view of the poor relations between the two men. Again, the results were not clearly encouraging. Although Stratford had arrived in Constantinople on April 5, it was not until April 9 that the Turkish ministers brought up the matter of the protectorate. Not until April 11 was Stratford able to send a copy of the Russian demands to London.[62] In line with his conciliatory instructions, Stratford was less hostile to the plan than might have been expected. In a memorandum written shortly after his return, he expressed disapproval of the Russian draft convention, but declared that he saw no objection to a *sened* that would merely confirm existing treaties. Later in the month, he suggested that the assurances the Russians called for might be embodied in a firman that would then be communicated to the Russian embassy.[63] Despite the Russians' reiterated firmness, Stratford seemed quite in earnest in assuring Ozerov that the Turks would produce a satisfactory formula.[64]

The test came with the solution of the Holy Places Question by the firman of May 5. In a note of the same date, Menshikov pointed out that only half of his mission had been accomplished. It was now necessary to conclude the *sened;* a proposed draft, similar to that suggested in March, was appended.[65] Although Menshikov had received the tsar's permission to meet Turkish requests for a less formal instrument, he presumably wished to start with his highest demands, in order to leave room for bargaining. The Porte's position was difficult. In addition to possible domestic troubles, the exterior military situation did not look good. Russian military preparations, which had been going on since the winter, were now virtually complete, and the Russian army seemed poised to invade the Principalities. There were disquieting rumors that the Russian consuls at Galatz and Brăila had been instructed to turn back travelers wishing to go to Bessarabia.[66] Menshikov offered the bait of a military alliance through the finance minister, Namık Pasha, as an alternative to the *sened,* but the overture was not successful.[67]

On the other hand, the aid of the Western powers was in doubt. The French fleet was at Salamis, but the British squadron had not moved; and Stratford, in conversations with the grand vizier and the Sultan, could not hide the fact that he was not empowered to do more than tell Admiral Dundas to hold the ships in readiness.[68] The Porte would have liked to threaten the prince with reprisals from Britain and France if he would not negotiate; but a communication from the British, while urging strong language, held out no hope of material aid.[69] Austria's acceptance of a visit from the Prince of Montenegro was hardly encouraging.[70] Nonetheless, there was considerable sentiment for a strong anti-Russian stand at the Porte. Menshikov's methods had been an irritant to Ottoman pride, and many of the more fervent Moslems were not disposed to favor interference on behalf of the Christians.[71] Under these circumstances, the Council of Ministers held an important meeting. Mehmet Ali spoke out vigorously against Russia. Rifat Pasha offered rather cavalier assurances of Western support. A proposal for further negotiations based on suggestions from Lord Stratford was considered: this plan called for a series of firmans that would guarantee the rights of all the millets and that would be communicated to the embassies of all the great powers, in the expectation that future protests on behalf of the subject peoples would be made jointly.[72] A substantial group under the leadership of Mehmet Emin Rauf Pasha, who was influenced by the Sultan, favored a peaceful policy; there is a story, which probably refers to this meeting, that when Mehmet Ali dramatically appealed to the sword against Moscow, Mehmet Emin told him brusquely to hush up.[73] The conclusion seems to have been a compromise: it was decided to negotiate on the basis of Stratford's plan, but this was seen as a pacific gesture; the sense of the meeting was opposed to Mehmet Ali's bellicosity.[74] In light of hints dropped by the Russian dragoman, this policy seemed likely to succeed.[75]

The influence of this discussion can be seen in the reply to Menshikov's note of May 5, which was sent by the Porte with the date of 2 Şaban 1269 / May 10, 1853. Rifat's text commenced with elaborate protestations of friendliness toward Russia. Strong assurances of the Porte's good intentions toward the Greek millet followed. It was, however, impossible for the Porte to conclude a special agreement with one power on behalf of a subject religion; an arrangement such as the Russians proposed would be a breach of Ottoman sovereignty. The note continued: "The Sublime Porte will devote all its attention to maintaining and to conserving for the future, in conformity with its rights of independence, all the religious immunities which have been spontaneously accorded and granted to its Christian subjects and particularly to the Greek subjects and monks."[76] The note continued, on lines similar to Stratford's proposal, with a promise of new firmans that would regulate the status of all the millets and would be communicated to all the great powers.[77]

According to one source, Menshikov was tempted to agree to some variant of this plan, but was dissuaded by younger and more militant members of the legation.[78] His reply mixed bitter and sweet: he seems to have decided to fall back on the supplementary instructions received during April. Accordingly, he began his note of April 29 / May 11, 1853, with a disclaimer of any intention on the part of the Russian government to infringe on Ottoman sovereignty. He alluded again to Russian grievances, but omitted another recapitulation. Avoiding such words as "*sened*," "convention," or "treaty," he now called for "an act emanating from the sovereign will of the Sultan, a free but solemn engagement." He finished, however, on a gruffer note: accusing the Porte of "systematic opposition" and rejection even of "the principles" proposed for agreement, he threatened to break off relations in three days' time (May 2 / 14) unless he had by that time received a different answer.[79]

Despite the virtual ultimatum contained in the last half of the note, Menshikov seems to have retreated from the unconditional demand for a *sened* to an implied willingness to accept a less stringent form, provided it met the criteria upon which the Russian government had insisted from the beginning. The desire for peace expressed in the Council of Ministers must have inclined Mehmet Ali and Rifat to welcome these signs of a thaw, confirmed through the Austrian representatives. In any event, Menshikov himself tells us that on May 12, Rifat contacted him and asked orally for further conversations the next day at the elegant waterside home of Mehmet Ali Pasha.[80] There is a story confirmed by the official protocol that Rifat and Mehmet Ali, basing their actions on the sense of the Council of Ministers, intended to resolve the crisis by accepting the substance of Menshikov's demands in the form of a note rather than a *sened;* Rifat's son Rauf Bey was accordingly sent to sound out Menshikov.[81] Mehmet Ali later claimed that he and the Serasker Pasha had reached virtually complete agreement with Menshikov about the terms of a note. Perhaps Mehmet Ali exaggerated the progress of the negotiations; he also glossed over the fact that he had been prepared to break with Russia and had only been talked into further conversations by pressure in the Council of Ministers. But be that as it may, on May 13, the grand vizier was eagerly awaiting the Russian prince at his country home, in the expectation of taking an important step out of this most difficult situation. Then came the great surprise. Instead of the prince, Mehmet Ali received a messenger from the Sultan, who bore in hand his dismissal from office.[82]

Mehmet Ali's dismissal was all the more puzzling and annoying because it soon turned out that it had been motivated by Menshikov himself. Since Reshid Pasha, the new foreign minister, was in Menshikov's own words an "honorable enemy" of Russia[83] and had been noted in the past for his close relationship with Stratford de Redcliffe, it might be logical to suppose that it was Stratford who had engineered his return to power.[84] Instead, overtures from Reshid to the Russians during the preceding winter had borne fruit.[85] Mehmet Ali's later revelations to Thouvenel permit us to reconstruct at least an approximate idea of the intrigue.[86] Apparently Menshikov's relatively dilatory and moderate conduct of his mission had displeased Ozerov and Balabin, two of his subordinates, who believed that a more warlike policy would further their careers.[87] They engaged in a conspiracy with Reshid and Nicholas Aristarchi Bey, a leading Greek. The first step was to consolidate their influence by getting rid of the first dragoman, Argyropoulos, who favored a peaceful solution. Up to now, Argyropoulos had been charged with most of the business of the negotiations, and he enjoyed a great ascendency over Menshikov. Indeed, one of Stratford's spies, concealed in a wardrobe, overheard two Russian secretaries saying: "the Prince was so wrapped up in Argyropoulo [sic] that there was no means of teaching him sense."[88] But Argyropoulos had a weak point; he longed for a yali on the Bosporus. This wish was to prove his downfall. The Sultan, who sympathized with Argyropoulos' pacific views, provided a beautiful home at fashionable Büyükdere. Aristarchi, acting as the go-between, gave Argyropoulos the keys and then went and told Menshikov. Menshikov, surprising Argyropoulos with the keys on his person, absolutely refused to believe that the dragoman had been framed. He was certain that the interpreter was in the Porte's pay and indignantly dismissed him. He was replaced by Aristarchi.

Aristarchi now told Menshikov (on May 2, according to Mehmet Ali) that Reshid Pasha, were he in power, would meet all the Russian demands for the *sened.* Menshikov still hesitated; he had negotiations in hand with Mehmet Ali's ministry, and he probably shared official Russian doubts as to Reshid's sincerity.[89] By May 10 (the date of the relatively unsatisfactory Ottoman reply), however, he had made up his mind to use Reshid in at least an unofficial capacity. Menshikov asked the ex–grand vizier to communicate with the Sultan directly and to explain to him "all the consequences that could spring from a rupture between the two states."[90] Then Menshikov wrote his carrot-and-stick note of May 11 to the Porte and waited for the official donkey to move. But Mehmet Ali and Rifat, though willing to go on talking, did not exactly hurry to placate the prince. Thoroughly disgusted, according to his own words, Menshikov now decided to see the Sultan. He asked for an audience on May 13, the date of his proposed interview with Mehmet Ali, but did not expect to be able to see the Sultan immediately. It was a Friday;[91] and the religious observance was compounded by Abdul-Mejid's mourning for the recent death of his mother.[92] Menshikov, in fact, was settled on his boat between Çirağan and Mehmet Ali's home, where he expected to keep his appointment, when he learned that the Sultan was ready to see him. When he reached the palace, Menshikov was informed that Mehmet Ali had just resigned.[93] Menshikov accordingly urged that Reshid Pasha be brought to power.[94]

Actually, it was not until after this audience with the prince that the Sultan sent a messenger to the grand vizier with news of his dismissal.[95] In accordance with Menshikov's wishes, Reshid was made foreign minister. His career up to that time qualified him eminently for the post. Reshid had been born in Istanbul. He had first distinguished himself at the time of the Greek revolt, but the bulk of his official training had been in the Translation Bureau and in embassies abroad; he had served in both Paris and London, and he spoke French well. These experiences had prepared him for his important role in the proclamation of the Hatt-i Sherif of Gulhane and for his emergence as the leading statesman of the early Tanzimat period. First appointed foreign minister in 1836, he had already served twice as foreign minister and twice as grand vizier.[96] His orientation towards Europe contrasted with the outlook of Mehmet Ali. Mehmet Ali had been born in Rize, on the eastern part of the Turkish Black Sea coast. He had been brought to Istanbul by his father, a hazelnut merchant and later a police officer; he had risen through the naval and military hierarchies, had not traveled abroad, and did not speak a foreign language. He was known for his many gifts to pious foundations.[97]   Although these two men's opportunities in 1853 were almost identical and their rivalry was correspondingly intense, they had reached their positions by very different routes—reflecting different values.[98]   Reshid, often criticized for undiscriminating faith in Western institutions, strove to reform the Empire along Western lines and believed that close relations with Europe, and particularly with Britain, would provide models for change and protection against foreign conquest. Mehmet Ali, though interested in updating the Empire's defenses, withstood intellectual, social, or economic change and therefore tended to oppose foreign entanglements, especially with the modern and industrialized West, whose social concepts clashed even more radically with time-honored Ottoman ways than did those of more traditional societies such as Austria and Russia.

The office of grand vizier in the new cabinet went to Mustafa Nâilî Pasha, an individual closer to Reshid than to Mehmet Ali in his outlook. He was to act as grand vizier through the rest of the crisis, and he proved an excellent choice. He was somewhat removed from the bitter factional intrigues of Istanbul because most of his official career had been spent outside the city. Born in 1798 in the village of Polyan, in what is now European Turkey, he had gone to Egypt with an uncle as a young man. After a creditable performance during these confused years in that province, he had ended up in the service of Mohammed Ali, the great reforming viceroy. As Mohammed Ali's dominions expanded, Mustafa Nâilî occupied a succession of important positions in various troubled outposts. He was in Aleppo for a time in 1838, when rebellious Maronites and Druses from the Lebanese mountains were attacking as far as Damascus; but his principal experience was in Crete—obtained by Mohammed Ali from the Porte as the price of his intervention in the Greek Revolt. Crete was recovered by the Ottomans after Mohammed Ali's unsuccessful bid for a larger role in 1840; but Mustafa Nâilî, who had risen to be vali, was confirmed in his post.[99] He had already had an impressive career in the service of the modernizing Egyptian viceroy, a background that produced a number of Ottoman reformers.[100] He had also had ample practice in dealing with the allied problems of modernization and Christian unrest. Incidentally, he was close to the Sultan, who had even spent an evening in his home in a visit to Crete in 1850.[101]

The other ministerial posts were distributed as follows: Mehmet Ali was transferred to the Ministry of War, Mehmet Rüştü Pasha, formerly Serasker (war minister), became president of the council (the *Meclis-i Vâlâ*); Fethi Ahmet Pasha, the finance minister, became director of the arsenal at Tophane; while his predecessor at Tophane, Namık Pasha, became the new minister of finance.[102] Given his personality and his position, Reshid was bound to be a key figure. During his intrigue with Aristarchi, Reshid had indicated to Menshikov that he would be willing to follow a pro-Russian policy, even to the extent of signing the *sened* in the form demanded by the prince. The Russians at first distrusted Reshid because in the past he had been, in embassy parlance, anti-Russian and pro-British. Actually Reshid was obliged to be an opportunist. Presumably, his first concern was to oust Mehmet Ali—whom he disliked and distrusted on both personal and political grounds—and to maneuver himself into a position of influence. Then it would be time to decide how to use that influence. A deal with the Russians might well be the best course, given the seeming indifference of the other powers. For there was no assurance that it would be feasible to work with Stratford, his previous ally; indeed it is said that when Stratford learned of Reshid's appointment, "he . . . went through an attack of fury that bordered on madness."[103] Furthermore, views in the Council of Ministers had been divided; it was not clear how official opinion was going to develop. There was strong sentiment in Constantinople, which Reshid probably shared, in favor of making an agreement to placate the Russians, with no expectation of fulfilling it afterwards.[104]

Reshid's first actions reflect these obvious uncertainties. Immediately upon the new ministers' assumption of office, on the evening of May 13, a meeting of the Council of Ministers was called to consider the situation. Unfortunately, the fullest evidence we have as to the tenor of the discussions comes from Menshikov, who was eager to believe that the Porte was about to meet his demands.[105] According to this account, Reshid began by outlining the Russian demand for a protectorate based on Kutchuk-Kainardji. He professed to accept the legality of the Russian claims, although his strong statement of their import was not designed to minimize opposition. He then went on to describe the result of resistance, in terms that show the breadth of his concern for the effects of the Menshikov mission on the Empire as a whole. He said:

> They have told you ... about the inconveniences that would result for us from the acceptance of the Russian claims, but have they made you see the consequences of a refusal? Let us suppose at first a simple cessation of relations with the populations in the interior of our country, whom this rupture would place in suspense awaiting more grave events, and do you think that there could be security for us in such a situation? Suppose now on Russia's part an imposing and hostile military attitude on our frontiers; do you think that this situation could be tolerable for very long with the prolonged perspective of an imminent catastrophe? Let us pass now to the occupation of the principalities; this would not yet be war, but would it not already be a very great misfortune for us? Finally, let us consider war: are you prepared for it; our fleet, our armies, are they in a condition to sustain it?[106]

Reshid was conscious of the threat posed by the Menshikov mission, both in terms of the extensive and embarrassing demands and in terms of possible uprisings within the Empire coinciding with Russian military action. As before, opinion in the council was divided. Some members, including Fethi Ahmet and the Sheikh ul Islam, the leading member of the ulema, declared themselves pleased by Reshid's speech and his relatively mild attitude; but a conciliatory policy was now "vigorously opposed" by "a party openly hostile to ... [Russian] claims." Spokesmen for this view were Mehmet Ali Pasha and Namık Pasha.[107] Although it is impossible to make a statistical breakdown, it would seem from the results of the two councils that anti-Russian feeling had increased greatly since the meeting that considered Menshikov's note of May 5.

Several reasons may be adduced for this change. To begin with, Mehmet Ali, as a devout Moslem, had never applauded the idea of an enhanced role for Christians in the Empire, although he had been willing to consider the expedient of an exchange of notes—if Rifat Pasha could bring about such a compromise—since it was the wish of the Council of Ministers. In any case, such an arrangement would have had only a minimally binding character, and it would probably have been less damaging than resistance with the help of the Western powers Britain and France—who would then undoubtedly demand concessions to the Christians as their price also. Ideas such as Christian-Moslem equality, a favorite of Lord Stratford's, found little favor in the circles in which Mehmet Ali moved.[108] His dismissal from the ministry, at the moment when he was making strenuous efforts to be reasonable and to meet Menshikov's demands, had "embittered" him.[109] There is no reason to suppose that he was alone in this sentiment. Menshikov's high-handed methods implied total contempt for the Ottoman government. His role in the change of ministry had been even more humiliating than his refusal to negotiate with Fuad Efendi. For that, there had been some possible justification; and there had been only a single victim. Now a shift in the entire ministry had been forced; and the fact that this crisis followed on the trouble over Fuad compounded the effect. It is true that Mehmet Ali's resistance was a dangerous policy that might well lead the Ottoman Empire into war with no firm allies. But Mehmet Ali, throughout the crisis, was to show more interest in what he conceived to be the justice of the Ottoman cause than in rational military predictions. Indeed this attitude was typical of many pious Ottoman officials, who felt that too much logical consideration called into question the power of Allah to give victory to the right.[110]

The meeting convinced Reshid that the Council of Ministers now inclined towards war. His next step was to try to gain time from Menshikov in order to explore the situation further. For it was not only Ottoman authorities who had to be sounded. It was imperative to find out the attitude of foreign powers as well.

On May 14, Reshid contacted Lord Stratford on the pretext of a consultation about the text of a note to Menshikov asking postponement of the break in relations, which was threatened for that very day. Apparently, Reshid attempted to frighten Stratford by insisting that the members of the council were not far from accepting the Russian proposals.[111] Stratford maintained a similar stand to that which he had adopted after Menshikov's May 5 note: he provided Reshid with a draft that met the Russian demand for confirmation of Greek Orthodox rights, but did so through unilateral action by the Porte rather than by a bilateral "guarantee" that might justify future Russian intervention.[112] Of course Stratford was not able to go beyond the tenuous hints at British aid that he had already offered. De la Cour, contacted on this subject at about the same time, was also cagey.[113] Reshid had been encouraged to believe that the British and French ambassadors were willing to work with him on a negotiated solution; but he was well aware that there was no firm prospect of material aid.[114]

Meanwhile, Menshikov proved willing to accept the delay.[115] As he explained to Nesselrode in his dispatch of May 4 / 16, this meant a departure from his original timetable; but he felt it justified by Reshid Pasha's exceptional situation. News of the council meeting and a report of Reshid's speech (quoted above) had reached Menshikov. He still believed that Reshid favored Russian demands and was engaged in an effort to convince recalcitrant colleagues. It seemed advisable to cooperate.[116]

But the meeting of the *Meclis-i umumî* that now took place did
not answer Menshikov's expectations. This body, whose origins go
back to 1838, was appointed from ministers, ex-ministers, and highly
placed members of the ulema. Its function, which was to prepare
laws for the Sultan's sanction[117] also included deliberation on declarations of war. Emboldened by the sentiment expressed in the
Council of Ministers and by his acceptance by Stratford and de la
Cour, Reshid now decided to use it in this manner. Some forty-eight
members, including old Husrev and the recently disgraced Fuad,
gathered on May 17 to hear a series of speeches that explored the alternative of war.[118] The director of the arsenal at Tophane, the Kaptan
Pasha, or naval minister, the minister of finance, Reshid himself as
foreign minister, and the minister of transportation discussed the
feasibility of war from the viewpoint of their various departments.
Favorable assessments were supported by various other dignitaries,
notably the Sheikh ul Islam; but dangers, including the possibility of a
Russian preemptive strike against the Straits, were also brought out.
Evidently the group that had spoken out for peace after May 5 had
dwindled into insignificance, for Abdurrahman tells us that nothing
more was heard "from silly Mehmet Emin Rauf Pasha and others."[119]
Nonetheless, in the absence of firm commitments from Britain or
France, the council decided to make a last offer, based on the compromise proposal that Lord Stratford had inspired. In terms roughly
parallel to the note of May 10, the council agreed to reaffirm the status
quo at the Holy Places; to confirm the privileges of the Greek Orthodox
millet by a firman to the patriarch; to send Menshikov an "explanatory
note" as the Porte's final word on the millet's position; and to offer
Menshikov a *sened* granting a location for a Russian church and hospital
to be constructed at Jerusalem.[120] A strong group evidently opposed
continuation of the negotiations, even on this restricted basis. Fethi
Ahmet Pasha spoke out against any agreement concluded with British
cooperation. He argued that the condition of British support would be
some kind of extension of the provisions of the Hatt-i Sherif of Gulhane. This would be a further blow to Ottoman traditions and would
not even give help in the short run, since further concessions would
make the Christians even more restive. Mehmet Ali Pasha, very bitter
against the Russians, argued for "aggressive measures on our frontier."
One may surmise that the argument against this was the lack of firm assurances of aid from Britain and France, despite widespread hopes;
Mehmet Ali suggested a "defensive alliance with Sardinia." This proposal stemmed from a letter from Arif Efendi, the Porte's ambassador

at Vienna, and from overtures from Tecco, the Sardinian minister at Constantinople. Mehmet Ali and Arif believed that this combination would worry both the Austrians and the Russians; but it was ridiculed by Reshid and others,[121] who were primarily interested in great-power support.

Accordingly, the council decided to offer Menshikov the program originally suggested by Stratford; but it seems likely that they regarded this as a mere tactical step in the progress towards a war to which many of them were not averse. Reshid paid a visit to Menshikov on May 18 to outline the council's decisions. Menshikov rejected the plan, but asked to see the individual documents. Reshid demurred, on the grounds that the final texts would not be approved by the council until later that morning. By this time, Menshikov was thoroughly disillusioned; he decided that he had been duped and laid most of the blame on Lord Stratford. He believed that Stratford had personally persuaded most of the forty-eight council members to reject the Russian demands, while keeping in constant touch with Reshid.[122] Undoubtedly Stratford's activity had followed the general lines Menshikov suspected. Acquiescence to the *sened* as proposed by the Russians was no part of his instructions. But Stratford had not been responsible for the humiliation meted out to prominent Turks by Menshikov; and the militants' view of the dangers of foreign interference was diametrically opposed to Stratford's own assessment of Turkey's needs.

Meanwhile, Menshikov decided to break relations immediately, without waiting for further communications from Reshid. Perhaps he hoped to influence the Porte by making this drastic step coincide with the final council meeting. At any rate, the note was given to Reshid during the debate. But it did not have the effect intended. The *Meclis-i umumî* met in no mood to retract. The proposals discussed the day before as the Porte's last offer were confirmed by a vote of forty-two to three. As corollary measures, the Empire's defenses were to be improved. It was decided to put the army, the reserve (redif), and the navy on a war footing, a process that would require about three months.[123] Steps were to be taken to insure that the Christians were not victimized by Moslem fanaticism aroused by the crisis.[124] The Porte had taken a stand and had accepted the risks. Menshikov's note did not alter the situation.

It was now the turn of the four great powers to intervene, in an attempt to bring agreement before Menshikov left Constantinople. Klezl contacted Reshid and suggested that he get in touch with Menshikov through a trusted person, perhaps his son Ali Ghalib, in an attempt to

revive the negotiations for an exchange of notes that had occupied
Mehmet Ali and Rifat. This plan merged on May 19 with a call from
Stratford for a conference of the four representatives.[125] They decided on "offering their good offices," in the hope that they could keep
the negotiations alive by acting as a channel of communication between
the two sides. Since Stratford was hopelessly compromised with
Menshikov, it was decided to send Klezl. Menshikov, aboard his
yacht, was still at Büyükdere waiting for a thunderstorm to clear before
he set out into the Black Sea.[126] Klezl and a companion "rowed up the
Bosporus to make a final appeal to the prince's feelings."[127] Menshikov
was somewhat impressed. He now sent another note, which incorporated substantial concessions and brought the negotiations back to
the position before Reshid's entry into office. The form of a *sened* was
dropped in favor of a note, and though the agreement was likened to
previous treaties, it was not actually stipulated that it had the force of
a treaty. The protectorate was reiterated in a special paragraph.

> The orthodox cult of the Orient, its clergy, its churches, and its possessions,
> as well as its religious establishments, will enjoy in the future without any in-
> jury, under the aegis of His Majesty the Sultan, the privileges and immunities
> that have been assured to them *ab antiquo,* or that have been granted to them on
> different occasions by Imperial favor, and in a principle of high equity will
> participate in the advantages accorded to other Christian rites, as well as to the
> foreign legations accredited to the Sublime Porte, by convention or particular
> arrangement.

The following paragraphs called for the observance of the firman of
May 5 and for providing the Russians with a site for a Russian church
and a hospital at Jerusalem, should they so wish.[128]

Stratford apparently opposed the resumption of talks on this basis,
although he hoped that some means might yet be found of averting the
rupture. He objected to Menshikov's May 20 note on two grounds.
First, he believed that the agreement called for was to be "an official
note having the force of a treaty." Second, he believed that it still preserved the concept of the protectorate.[129] Certainly his own solution, as
it had been adopted by the Porte on May 18, would have given the
Russians less excuse for future intervention. There is some evidence
that Reshid was willing to accept the Russian proposals,[130] but in view
of the growth of war sentiment at the Porte and the general readiness
to consider a war even without allies, it seems impossible that he could
have carried such a policy.[131]

And so the Porte refused to budge beyond the program approved by
the *Meclis-i umumî* on May 18. The draft note conveyed to Menshikov

by Reshid Pasha's son on May 8 / 20 closely followed the explanatory note drawn up according to the council's decision, but not delivered after Menshikov initially broke diplomatic relations.[132] Stratford's objections were incorporated in the careful verbal distinction between religious privileges as they were strictly interpreted in the West, and the phrase more generally used in the Ottoman Empire, which had a broader implication.[133] Needless to say, this was unacceptable to Menshikov. News that the Porte intended to implement another part of the May 18 plan, the firman confirming Greek privileges, brought a final menacing note from Menshikov. Then, at midday on May 21, the prince "steamed away up the Black Sea."[134] Next day, the eagles were taken down "from the gates and façade of the Russian embassy." A silent "crowd of Greeks" had gathered to watch and "blessed their descent."[135] They, like most people in Constantinople, believed that war was imminent.

Chapter III

The Vienna Note

IN THE weeks following the failure of the Menshikov mission, the chances for peace diminished rapidly in Constantinople. Not only Russia and the Ottoman Empire, but also Britain, France and Austria began or continued military preparations that left them in a poor position to retreat. Simultaneous diplomatic negotiations raised hopes, in France and Britain, for a peaceful solution to the crisis; but in actuality, the peace initiative was deeply flawed from the start. Although Nicholas gradually began to realize the dimensions of the opposition to his policy and, by the end of the summer, was willing to accept a graceful exit, the Ottomans had been correspondingly encouraged and undertook negotiations mainly in order to gain time to complete their cumbersome military mobilization. To compound the problem, Britain, France, and Austria impaired their best opportunity for mediation by a faulty understanding of the way things looked from Constantinople; instead of allaying outrage at the Porte, they exacerbated the irritations.

Though Nicholas had rejected the alternative of an immediate full-fledged attack on the Ottoman Empire, he was not prepared in June to retreat further. Nesselrode drew up a note dated May 19 / 31, which reiterated Menshikov's last demands. Formal notification was given that Ottoman refusal would be the signal for occupation of the Principalities, not as an act of war, but "to have a material guarantee" during further negotiations.[1]

This plan, originally proposed by Paskevich, grew out of considerable debate concerning how to fight the Ottoman Empire. Reports from the Menshikov mission had cast doubt on the feasibility of a coup de main against the Ottoman capital. Reluctantly, Nicholas was obliged to consider alternatives. An attack on the Varna-Burgas area by land and sea, to be followed by a march on Constantinople, held his attention during the spring, but this obviously assumed the absence of Anglo-French naval opposition in the Black Sea, since the Russian fleet was no match for the two Western squadrons. After mid-June, when the British and French fleets took up stations in Besika Bay (as discussed below), this approach became highly risky. The other possibility, the occupation plan, demanded the benevolent neutrality or active cooperation of the Hapsburgs, but in June this seemed plausible. In a letter of April 20, Nicholas had outlined the occupation plan to Franz Joseph and had hinted that the Austrians might move into Serbia and Hercegovina in the western Balkans.[2] Franz Joseph in May made plans to dispatch Count Gyulai to Saint Petersburg to urge against seizure of Moldavia.[3] But Nicholas continued to elaborate his scheme through a series of "epochs," or stages, that would maximize the flexibility afforded by Paskevich's proposals. The "first epoch," the response to Ottoman refusal of the demand of May 19 / 31, would be occupation of the Principalities as a bargaining counter. If the Porte did not yield, the next stage would bring Russian blockade of the Bosporus; hopefully, an Austrian move into Serbia and Hercegovina; and finally threats by the tsar to declare Moldavia, Walachia, and Serbia independent. As a last resort (the "third epoch"), Nicholas would carry out these menaces, in the expectation of causing the fall of the Ottoman Empire.[4] Baron Meyendorff, Russian ambassador at Vienna, was instructed to inform Franz Joseph of these projects. Meyendorff was given a version of the "epochs" plan, complete with a tentative timetable. The ambassador evidently judged it best to communicate only an attenuated outline to Franz Joseph, in a memorandum of May 26 / June 7, 1853. He gained merely a promise of diplomatic support;[5] and in a comprehensive dispatch of June 18 / 30, 1853, Meyendorff analyzed with much insight the reasons why all factions in the Austrian government wished to avoid war. Even those Austrian leaders who advocated vigorous cooperation with Russia did so because they believed that a united front was the best means of making the French and the British back down—thus avoiding war. Others maintained that war was simply not an option for Austria while finances were lamentable and the domestic situation continued troubled in Hungary, in Transylvania and Galicia, and worst of all in Italy, where revolution was bound to break out at the first sign of international complications, perhaps even with French aid. Nicholas had foreseen some of these worries and offered a corps of the Russian army in case of difficulties in Italy.[6] He was unable to believe that the Austrians would resist the temptation to join in the spoils of a Balkan war and continued to angle for Austrian support. He also endeavored, with more success, to win over the Persians, eventually offering a subsidy of ten million pounds sterling.[7]

Another question raised by the occupation plan concerned the Russians' relation to Balkan revolutionary movements. Despite his authoritarian policies in Russia, Nicholas was tempted to ally himself with the malcontents of the Ottoman Empire.[8] Considerable anti-

Ottoman sentiment did exist in the peninsula: Moldavia and Walachia were already tied to Russia by an informal protectorate; Russian influence was significant in Serbia and Montenegro; and the Greeks, still in occupation of the villages in dispute during the spring,[9] were ready to move. War would exacerbate tensions, for the withdrawal of troops on garrison duty in the provinces would give free rein to local grievances, both Christian and Moslem. Indeed, ever since 1848, certain Rumanian revolutionaries, such as Balcescu, Brătianu, and Ghica, had been plotting a general Balkan uprising. They had established contacts with Hungarian radicals, notably Kossuth and Klapka, and plans were discussed in Paris, London, and Constantinople for some kind of Danubian federation comprising Rumania, Hungary, the South Slavs of the Hapsburg Empire, Serbia, and perhaps Bosnia, Hercegovina, and Montenegro. The stumbling block was Kossuth's unwillingness to relinquish Hungarian control over the minority groups within the borders of the Kingdom of Hungary in favor of a federal solution;[10] but there were hopes that, as the possibilities of action increased, Kossuth might become more flexible.[11]

It was not clear, however, whether the revolutionaries would make common cause with the tsar or whether they would simply seize the opportunity for an independent rising. Though the Russians had at times appeared as liberators and modernizers—for example, in their initial impact on Moldavia and Walachia—and though they allowed, in this instance as in others, more liberal regimes than were tolerated at home, close acquaintance with the "colossus of the north" generally bred disillusion.[12] And Russian policy during the 1848 revolutions had hardly enhanced the tsar's image in revolutionary circles. Indeed, there is evidence to suggest that there was some hope of an anti-Russian revolutionary movement in the Danubian Principalities, the ubiquitous Polish refugees were trying to organize an anti-Russian legion to fight with the Ottoman army,[13] and some radical Americans suggested that the Porte place Kossuth in command of an army against Austria.[14] What seemed certain was that a full-fledged Russian campaign in the Balkans would precipitate political and social change—much of it inevitably at the expense of the Porte, as the government with the strongest stake in the status quo.

Meanwhile, the British had also become militarily involved. Reshid's immediate response to Menshikov's departure had been to request aid from the French and British fleets. Clarendon, in supplementary instructions to Stratford dated May 31, declared that Russia's intentions were now open to serious doubt; although the British government wished to be conciliatory, it was prudent to put the fleet at Stratford's immediate disposal, with the proviso that he should call it up to Constantinople only if the Russians went to war or took any obviously aggressive steps.[15] Behind this move lay a strong sentiment in the British press in favor of associating the country with Napoleon III's naval gesture of March; as Clarendon wrote Aberdeen, it was "*the least measure that will satisfy public opinion.*" The decision was communicated to the Turkish ambassador, Musurus Bey, unofficially by Palmerston, and later, in an official interview, by Clarendon.[16] The fleet reached Besika Bay on June 13, where it was joined by the French squadron on June 14. And the French apparently went so far as to convey the impression that they were ready to offer outright military aid to the Turks in the event of a Russian invasion.[17] Extensive Ottoman military preparations further raised morale at the Porte.[18]

Accordingly, the Ottoman response to the May 19 / 31 note was not conciliatory, and the Russian government decided to proceed with the occupation of the Principalities. Drouyn de Lhuys had declared in an official circular that the French government would consider the Porte justified in considering this move an act of war,[19] but the British attitude was not encouraging. As early as June 3, in response to a direct question from Reshid, Stratford had counselled that the Turks should withdraw without fighting until such time as Constantinople was in danger. A few days later, he advised the Porte not to remove its hospodars in case of a Russian occupation of Moldavia and Walachia, since this would give the Russians an excuse to nominate their own governors and thus consolidate control of the provinces. Musurus, who argued the case with Clarendon for regarding the occupation as a casus belli, received a shower of sensibly presented discouragement. He did learn, however, that Stratford would have the power to call up the fleet from Besika Bay to Constantinople if the Russians crossed the Danube. Stratford himself gave this information to the Sultan on June 16; but he accompanied it with a vigorous plea for reform, especially in the status of the Christians.[20]

All these developments worried Mehmet Ali Pasha and his associates. When Reshid decided to let the occupation pass with mere diplomatic protest, it was too much. The Porte had been dishonored. Mehmet Ali and Fethi Ahmet Pasha, who was closer to the Sultan, decided to use their influence. It was the holy month of Ramazan, and the conspirators were invited to the palace for a banquet on the *Bayram,* the holiday that breaks the fast. Waiting until everyone had had a good deal to drink, they approached Abdul-Mejid and persuaded him to change his ministers. Cleverly, Mehmet Ali did not demand a key post. Instead, the grand vizierate went to Mehmet Rüştü Pasha, while the foreign ministry was given to Ali Pasha. The choices were ambiguous. Mehmet Rüştü was closely associated with Mehmet Ali, but Ali Pasha had a considerable reputation in the West—especially in France—as a reformer. Perhaps more important however, he had recently made himself persona non grata to the Austrian government by his handling of the Koszta Affair as vali of Smyrna (discussed below). Neither minister seemed likely to appease the Russians.

The news of the change provoked consternation among the diplomats. In Saint Petersburg, Nesselrode threw up his hands; in disgust, he wrote Meyendorff that Nicholas's anti-Ottoman policy had been right after all, "for an empire governed by a sovereign who gets drunk every night and who, in a fit of intoxication, dismisses his ministers, will not be capable of growing old bones. It is a sorry candidate for conservation that France and England are supporting." [21]

The decisive reaction was Stratford's. When he heard the news, he rushed off to the palace and demanded information. Abdul-Mejid, who could hardly explain to the British ambassador the doubts that Reshid's Anglophile policy inspired, told the angry Englishman that the change "was exclusively attributable to personal causes." Stratford told the Sultan that it was his job to "control" such "personal jealousies" and that the essential thing was not to upset the negotiations by "an untimely and injudicious change." [22] The Sultan yielded; the old ministry was reinstated with, according to Mustafa Nâilî, substantial pledges to protect them against a repetition. [23] But the biggest guarantee was Stratford's support; and this must be borne in mind in studying the later stages of the crisis, particularly the negotiations surrounding the Vienna Note. Reshid Pasha and the colleagues who shared his relatively moderate views had been imposed at the Porte because they were willing to accept the humiliation that the British seemed determined to mete out. Their room for maneuver was correspondingly circumscribed.

Against this unpromising background, several diplomatic plans circulated during June and early July that were calculated to compose Russo-Turkish differences. Each of these plans was a little more anti-Russian than the last, a sure index of the direction of "neutral" opinion. The Aberdeen plan, designed to complement the Turkish proposals of June 16, assumed that the Turks would accept Menshikov's last note, with the addition of certain "stipulations." [24] This proposal immediately foundered on the tsar's refusal to enter into anything that might be construed as further discussion with the Turks. Meanwhile, another plan was mooted at Vienna in talks between the French ambassador Bourqueney and the Russian ambassador Meyendorff. [25] According to this proposal, the Porte would send its ambassador to Saint Petersburg with Menshikov's last note, which would be accepted without negotiation, but Nicholas, in acknowledging the note, would issue a declaration in which he would limit Russian rights by explaining his understanding of their extent.[26] This arrangement was favored by the Russians but was not satisfactory to either the British or the French. Neither government, by this time, was prepared to accept a Russian statement without international consultation or supervision.[27] Accordingly, an international conference was suggested. Drafts were proposed by Clarendon and by Napoleon III. Clarendon ultimately withdrew his draft in favor of the French one.[28] Although the Russian government was not enthusiastic about such a conference,[29] Buol took up the plan. At the end of June, Bruck, the new internuncio at Constantinople, was instructed to approach the Porte about a "fusion" of Menshikov's and Reshid's last notes, to be worked out with international consultation.[30] Stratford, though unenthusiastic, called together the representatives of France, Austria, and Prussia to consider the proposal. They agreed to recommend it to the Porte. Stratford seems to have been actuated more by the desire to prevent Bruck from acting alone than from any high hopefulness as to the plan's success. Indeed, according to Bruck's recollection, it was the Bourqueney plan that absorbed most attention at Constantinople.[31] Then came the Russian occupation of the Principalities, the bitter reaction in Constantinople, the ministerial crisis. It was only on July 9 that Mustafa Nâilî and Reshid were reinstated.[32]

On July 12, the *Meclis-i umumî* met to consider a response to the Russian invasion. The alternatives were clearly presented in a form that facilitated discussion. One possibility was that the Ottoman Empire could "go it alone," eschewing foreign aid and advice; in the event that bilateral negotiations with the Russians proved impossible, as was expected, the result would be war. As the other alternative, the Ottoman government could accept great-power mediation, but would then be bound to heed the powers' counsel. It is obvious from the protocol of the meeting that many members present preferred the alternative of war, and in fact, much of the session was devoted to an effort to find a way to make this course of action feasible. The numbers of troops available on both sides were calculated, and attention was given to problems of supplies, munitions, and money; but there was no way around the simple fact that Ottoman preparations were not then complete and could not be concluded for another twenty to twenty-five days. In this situation, there seemed no practical alternative to playing along with the mediation, at least as a means of buying time. Further arguments in favor of this course were the presence of the allied fleets in neighboring waters and the danger of revolution in the Balkans in connection with a campaign. But the protocol suggests that the agreement on internationally sponsored negotiations was taken with reluctance and with the express understanding that it did not preclude continued military preparations and recourse to war at a later date.[33] In light of this discussion, it seems evident that all of the negotiations mounted during July faced severe obstacles to success. Indeed, Reshid supposedly admitted that he was beginning to doubt that it would be possible to gain the consent of the Ottoman authorities to a peaceful formula, should one be worked out.[34]

At this stage, Bruck submitted to Reshid a revised version of the Bourqueney plan: the Ottoman protest against the Russian occupation should be accompanied by further documents, including a letter from Reshid to Nesselrode, which would convey the hint that further negotiations might be initiated. Reshid Pasha, in the wake of the council meeting, showed sufficiently strong interest that Bruck felt obliged to plead the necessity of consulting his colleagues before entering into detail.[35] Stratford now announced that he favored some such discussion. Information from the Prussian envoy, Wildenbruch, indicated that Nicholas was prepared to accept a solution worked out through Austrian good offices.[36] So the four diplomats met on July 16 at the British Embassy. They agreed that the protest should be accompanied by a letter from Reshid to Nesselrode in which Reshid would communicate the June firman confirming the privileges of the Greek Orthodox millet (which, owing to the rupture, had never been formally given to the Russian government); on this basis, Reshid would ask whether the tsar would be willing to receive a special mission.[37] The recommendations of the conference were conveyed to Reshid that evening by memorandum. Next morning the representatives met with the Ottoman foreign minister. Reshid made it plain that the Porte could not reverse the decision "never to make a diplomatic engagement with Russia relative to the privileges of the Greek Church"; such action he termed "a death sentence for the Ottoman Empire." Within these limits, Reshid professed himself pleased with the plan.[38] Some discussion centered around the Russian presence in the Principalities; Stratford and de la Cour insisted on early withdrawal, in return for which Bruck demanded the recall of the French and British fleets. The idea of a simultaneous retreat was generally accepted.[39] In a later exchange without Reshid, the envoys decided to suggest excision of the special mission proposal from Reshid's letter. The idea was mentioned in the Ottoman protest[40] and would be brought out again in the recommendations of the conference. This airing should be sufficient and would spare the Porte the embarrassment of a rebuff.[41] With these considerations and changes, Reshid professed himself satisfied; and he prepared to lay the plan before the council of ministers. But already Bruck was cautioning that the Turks were reaching the limit of their concessions: "to desire more means to call for war, for no Turkish minister would dare to support such a demand."[42]

The Council of Ministers reviewed the progress of the deliberations on the evening of July 17 and in a further session on July 18.[43] The decision was favorable, for on July 19 Reshid met again with the diplomats to consider the text of the documents proposed. The discussion was apparently heated. According to Bruck, the debate centered on whether the démarche should entail the Porte's acceptance of Menshikov's last note, virtually unchanged, in return for a Russian counterpledge or whether the idea of a Russian declaration should be dropped and the note offered by the Porte rewritten in consultation with the conference. Bruck capitalized on Ottoman distrust of the Menshikov text and managed to win agreement on a revision of the proposed note. The other matter hotly discussed was the text of appeals that Stratford and de la Cour were to direct to the British and French ambassadors at Saint Petersburg, asking them to support the Turkish démarche. Bruck felt that the versions proposed called for too harsh an interference, and a number of minor changes were made.[44]

After the results of the July 19 meeting had been communicated to the council by Reshid,[45] the conference met again on July 20 to draw up final copies for communication to Saint Petersburg by way of Vienna. The protest had already been issued under the date of July 14; and the text of Reshid's letter to Nesselrode did not bring difficulties. A courier bearing these papers was dispatched to Vienna that evening.[46] The major problem was presented by the text of the note that the Porte was to propose to Russia as the solution of the dispute. To avoid delays, as de la Cour euphemistically put it, the representatives had drawn up a draft, which they communicated to Reshid with a plea that the Porte act on it as soon as possible. Apparently the general tenor and even the main section had been provided by Lord Stratford.[47] Reshid took the text for referral to the Porte, but it was becoming clear to all that the Ottoman government was reaching the limit of concession: as Bruck put it, "farther may they not go, whatever may come of it."[48]

The Porte's intransigence was stimulated by bad news which apparently came in during the day on July 19.[49] In occupying the Principalities, the Russian commander, Gorchakov, assured the Turks that existing arrangements would not be disturbed. It now developed that the Russian government did not interpret this statement as literally as had the Turks. The hospodars were ordered to have no further contact with Constantinople and were forbidden to send tribute. De la Cour heard rumors in Constantinople that Gorchakov had exceeded his authority; but it soon became evident that the command had issued from Nesselrode.[50] Nesselrode later defended the decision with the argument that it was impossible to permit that "supplies of money . . . be sent to the enemy."[51] But the Turks, who had justified their pacific response to the occupation by the presumption that the Russians would avoid hostile acts, now felt that they had been outmaneuvered; and, in fact, the Russians did systematically try to use the hospodars as a focus for resistance to the Ottoman Empire.[52] The Turks had reason to feel that they had been badly advised, by Britain especially. All these points contributed to the difficulty of the negotiations.

In no very pleasant frame of mind, then, the diplomats reassembled at Reshid's yali on July 23 to learn of the council's action on the draft note. Reshid communicated the approved text. Stratford's version had been rejected. The note accepted seemed tough to de la Cour, but he gathered that a large faction within the Porte favored an even harsher formulation.[53] The note, immediately dubbed the Turkish Ultimatum, explained the firmans to the heads of the millets and promised to maintain rights expressed in them "in perpetuity," with the qualification that the Porte "reserved the sacred rights of sovereignty in relation to its own subjects." The Porte also promised to extend any new rights granted to other millets to the Greek Orthodox. The note concluded optimistically that these arrangements had "inspired confidence everywhere" and trusted that they would be received with "satisfaction" by the Russian government as well.[54] In order that there should be no misunderstanding of the Porte's position, Reshid signed a memorandum that summarized his remarks at the meeting. He emphasized that the Porte would not make further concessions. He reiterated Ottoman willingness to send a special ambassador to Saint Petersburg with the note, as soon as the Russians should have signified their readiness to accept it, and on the assumption that the Russians would immediately start withdrawal of their troops from the Principalities. If these arrangements did not work out, and if war resulted, the Sultan wished it to be understood that the "independence" of the Ottoman Empire was at stake.[55] The foreign representatives agreed that the mood in the Turkish capital was as strained as Reshid's declaration suggests. Bruck wrote: "If Russia wants to demand more, then war is unavoidable." De la Cour judged that the ministers were deeply divided, and that a Christian revolt might break out "from one moment to another," while many Ottoman leaders were coming to believe that Turkey must fight, even if alone, and that it was better to die with honor "on a battlefield" than "to succumb without a sound."[56] The first definite word about the Turkish Ultimatum, in the form of the documents sent on July 20, reached Vienna on the 29th.[57] Much had happened in the Austrian capital since Buol first proposed the démarche. As negotiations in Constantinople seemed stalled, Buol had grown increasingly impatient. On July 24, he called together the representatives of the four great powers (Russia being excluded) and divulged his fears, based on the news from Constantinople up to July 14. It was not until July 18 that Bruck reported Reshid's renewed interest in the Austrian plan. Buol had meanwhile suggested (on July 14) that the ambassadors at Vienna should assume the task of drafting a formula in the form of a note that could be sent by the Porte to the Russian government.[58] Although Buol's idea proved disastrous, there seemed sound reasons in favor of it at the time.

Probably one motive for Buol's move was the distrust he felt for the internuncio. Bruck, who had made a fortune as a founder of the Austrian Lloyd's shipping company, had gone on to a government career as minister of commerce and most recently as negotiator of an important tariff treaty with Prussia; he was chosen for the post at Constantinople because of his unusual knowledge of Austria's commerical needs and of the economic potential of the Middle East.[59] But on matters of diplomacy, he and Buol represented opposite extremes within the Austrian government. Buol was deeply anxious about the stability of the Hapsburg empire in the aftermath of the 1848 revolutions; he was worried about anything that smacked of adventurism in the Balkans; he feared possible French reprisals in case of war and wished to work closely with France and Britain. Bruck, although ready to push for peace at Constantinople as instructed, was fascinated by Georg Friedrich List's ideas of an economic Mittel-europa and foresaw an important commercial role for Austria in the Balkans.[60] He was not above suggesting that the government profit from Russian ambitions by extending Austrian territorial bases for action.[61] Although some authors have played down this disagreement between Bruck and Buol, it was probably of great significance, for it presumably contributed to Buol's unwillingness to make full use of the Constantinople delegation and it must have influenced Ottoman uncertainty as to Austria's real objectives.

A final reason for Buol's suggestion was related to a purely technological factor: most of Europe was now linked by telegraph, but the lines stopped at the Austrian border. Vienna was therefore the diplomatic center closest to Constantinople that was in speedy communication with the other European capitals;[62] the advantages for consultation are obvious.

In any event, the ambassadorial conference, meeting under Buol's chairmanship, quickly agreed upon a draft note in two sessions on July 26 and 27. The text followed the same broad lines as the Turkish Ultimatum, but several important differences seemed to promise wider influence for the Russian government. While the Turkish Ultimatum had stated in very vague terms the Sultan's general desire for amicable relations with Russia, the Vienna Note declared: "If in every age the Emperors of Russia have testified their active solicitude for the maintenance of the immunities and privileges of the Greek Orthodox church in the Ottoman Empire, the Sultans have never refused to sanction them anew by solemn acts that attest their traditional and constant benevolence with regard to their Christian subjects." Then, while the Turkish Ultimatum was limited to the communication of the firmans and the promise to extend new rights granted to other Christian sects to the Greek Orthodox, the Vienna Note preceded these pledges by a commitment to honor "the letter and the spirit of the stipulations of the treaties of Kutchuk-Kainardji and of Adrianople relative to the protection of the Christian cult." Since the Russian government claimed that Kutchuk-Kainardji gave them a protectorate over the Greek Orthodox millet, this passage was not likely to inspire confidence at the Porte. Finally, after noting the recent settlement of the Holy Places Question, the note continued in a passage that could be construed as applying to the entire document: "The Sublime Porte, moreover, promises officially that no modification will be made in the state of things that has just been adjusted, without a previous understanding with the governments of Russia and of France."[63] This specific pledge to the great powers contrasted with the Turkish Ultimatum, where the communication of the firmans to the diplomatic conference was not a condition, but simply an attendant circumstance, designed to manifest the Porte's sincerity. While the Turkish Ultimatum would permit the reformers to continue their program of secularization under a general promise of solicitude for Christian rights, the Vienna Note seemed to open the way to an enlargement of the role of the millets through running Russian interference on behalf of the Greek Orthodox.

The text of the Vienna Note was not likely to satisfy the Porte. Furthermore, the procedures envisioned in the Turkish Ultimatum were preferable: the Ultimatum emphasized the Porte's unilateral action through the firmans, which would be voluntarily communicated to Russia through a note drawn up by the Porte, not dictated by foreign powers. The European representatives appeared as advisors, rather than as parties, to the agreement. The Vienna Note looked like a specific pledge to the Russians that admitted much of their case and was forced on the Turks from abroad. This impression was heightened by tactlessness during the negotiations in Vienna. The Russian ambassador, Meyendorff, was asked to sit in on the meetings. He refused, but was kept closely informed of developments. According to Westmorland, the British ambassador to Vienna, the Turkish ambassador was in Baden at the commencement of the negotiations: he was informed of their progress on his return, but while Meyendorff reported in detail to Saint Petersburg, Arif Efendi evidently concealed the developments from Constantinople.[64]

Unconcerned, however, by the objections that might be raised to the Vienna Note at the Porte, the conference proceeded to adopt it in preference to the Turkish Ultimatum. Probably the consideration that persuaded Buol to this course was the virtual certainty that the tsar would accept the Vienna text.[65] The Turkish Ultimatum seemed less likely to please. Indeed, Nesselrode later expressed his gratitude for the decision in strong words: "Please thank Count Buol. That letter is really too bad a joke, and one cannot conceive how Bruck made himself the instrument of its transmission." But Nesselrode had little use for Bruck; he exclaimed on another occasion: "How can one choose a merchant from Trieste for a diplomatic post of that importance?"[66]

In addition to this practical consideration, both Buol and Aberdeen opposed the Turkish Ultimatum because they felt it implied an international guarantee of the Ottoman Empire.[67] Actually, the international involvement in the Ultimatum was somewhat tenuous, but perhaps such an interpretation could be made from the text of the protest against the occupation of Moldavia and Walachia, in which the Porte suggested that the Russians had violated the internationally signed Straits Convention of 1841.[68] And certainly such an idea was a favorite plan of Reshid's. The Vienna Note, which assigned the follow-up to Russia and France alone, was perhaps less ambiguous, though Clarendon would later propose a supervisory role for all the members of the Vienna conference.[69]

The news of the substitution of the Vienna Note reached Constantinople on August 9.[70] Stratford at first refused to believe it. He built his hopes on the fact that the telegram from Westmorland in Vienna urged him to stand behind the Vienna Note "*if no other arrangement has been already made.*" Stratford's calculations showed him that the Turkish Ultimatum had been worked out before the Vienna Note; he therefore decided to wait until the *Caradoc* brought him definitive instructions from London.[71] De la Cour, though less outspoken, announced that he was awaiting word from Paris on the *Chaptal*.[72] Meanwhile, Nesselrode accepted the Vienna Note, with the understanding that the Russian government would not be obliged "to examine or to discuss new modifications and new projects, elaborated at Constantinople."[73] News of the acceptance caused a sensation at Constantinople, where it was learned almost at the moment the *Caradoc* arrived.[74] Perhaps the most critical moment of the months before the war approached, as the ambassadors pressed the Vienna formula on the Porte.

Obviously, the Porte was not going to welcome the Vienna Note. Yet, despite the flaws in the text from the Ottoman point of view, and despite the high-handed way in which the plan had been presented to the Porte, the Vienna Note did represent the best chance for resolution of the crisis by international mediation. The ambassadors of the four great powers had tried to intervene between Russia and the Ottoman Empire in the last stages of the Menshikov mission, in hopes of preventing a rupture. But their efforts were improvised, and did not carry the weight of an appeal from the home governments. In the later months of 1853, and even into 1854, proposals were to multiply until the story indeed became a romance of "Mille et Une Notes."[75] But by this time distrust had deepened and the very failure of previous attempts encumbered the negotiating process and diminished optimism about the success of plans which generally incorporated features of projects already rejected. The Vienna Note came with the full backing of the European Concert before disillusion had had time to grow.

Since the Russian government accepted the Vienna Note, the principal interest attaches to the Porte's decision. The obvious course was to turn down the Vienna Note and to declare war on Russia. The Turkish Ultimatum had been acceptable to the Ottoman government, for it consisted of a reiteration of the existing privileges of the millets, issued by the Sultan on a unilateral basis and communicated to the representatives of all the powers as a matter of courtesy. It emphasized tradition and the status quo in a manner pleasing to conservatives, while it did not really tie the hands of the reformers in any significant new way. The Vienna Note strengthened the millet system by basing the position of the Greek Orthodox millet on Russian intervention and by stipulating that any changes must be sanctioned by Russia and France. It implied that the Greek Orthodox millet might benefit from an exclusive status that would clash with the historical standing of the Christians and would, in theory, bar further progress towards secularization. No Ottoman statesman, whatever his views on Christian-Moslem equality, was likely to find the note acceptable.

In any event, the strength of the so-called "war party" had been growing by leaps and bounds. Even Reshid was becoming bellicose, although de la Cour judged that his power had diminished so drastically that he was the captive of his warlike adversaries.[76] These sentiments were increasingly shared by the public at large, and rumors flourished, sometimes with the encouragement of members of the government. The Sultan was paying the British and French navies to fight for the Porte, clear evidence of Moslem superiority. Nicholas was about to yield: he had sent his wife in disguise to Constantinople to negotiate a settlement; he was prepared to indemnify the Turks for the cost of their mobilization; he would return the Crimea.[77] The Sultan, though he had hoped for peace, did not favor the Vienna Note; but it seemed possible that he might achieve peace by the dismissal of Reshid and Mustafa Nâilî and appointment of a new ministry pledged to direct bilateral negotiations with Saint Petersburg.[78] As early as July 20, Bruck had learned from Reshid that Argyropoulos and other pro-Russian notables were constantly hinting in this direction.[79] Early in August, there were tales of a letter from Gorchakov to Reshid Pasha, intended to bridge the way to new talks.[80] On August 8, through the intervention of the Prussian representative, Wildenbruch, the Sultan decided to send a special emissary to Saint Petersburg, carrying his apologies and instructed to follow through on Gorchakov's overture. This decision was withdrawn;[81] but some such project remained a possibility.[82] Many of the more bellicose ministers seemed to favor it: it is uncertain whether their motives were to promote rumors that would compromise Reshid by portraying him as pro-Russian, or to preclude further European exploitation of the Ottoman Empire as a surrogate against Russia, or to initiate negotiations that would quickly fail and would lead to war on the Danube.[83]

The confusion of the official world was visible at a grand banquet and reception held at the French embassy in Therapia on August 15. The occasion was the birthday of Napoleon I; de la Cour had been ordered to spare no effort. Significantly, the officer corps of the French fleet was brought to the capital for the ceremonies of the day. The gathering of many Turkish dignitaries offered a splendid chance for politicking. Even Bruck, though he omitted to mention the reason for the entertainment in his report, profited by the opportunity to urge the Vienna Note. Stratford de Redcliffe was very much in evidence; it was particularly noted that he chatted with Mehmet Ali, not usually a favorite with the Great Ambassador—to give Stratford his complimentary title.[84] Unfortunately we do not know whether he encouraged or discouraged the principal advocate of war at the Porte.

On balance, the evening probably changed few opinions. The next few days were passed in anxiety and confusion by the foreign representatives. On August 18, de la Cour noted that there had been a slight thaw. The meeting of the *Meclis-i umumî,* originally scheduled for August 17, was put off to allow the ministers to draw up specific proposals.[85] It was determined that the Vienna Note could not be accepted without certain changes. The following day, the matter was laid before the decisive meeting of the *Meclis-i umumî.* A strong group still favored complete rejection of the note. The Sultan, however, had now come around to favor acceptance of the note, with modifications[86]—indeed the policy that offered the best remaining hope for peace. Alison from the British Embassy was present, with Stratford's injunctions as to possible amendments should the council turn decisively against adoption pure and simple.[87] Finally, a version of the changes was passed and was approved as soon as possible by the Sultan. Official word of the decision was in the diplomats' hands by August 20 and was on the way to Vienna by special courier.[88]

The modified version of the note was accompanied by a letter from Reshid Pasha to the members of the Vienna Conference, in which he explained the amendments. The thrust of the changes was to remove any suspicion that the Vienna Note sanctioned a Russian protectorate over the Greek Orthodox millet. The original note had declared: "If in every age the emperors of Russia have testified to their active solicitude for the maintenance of the immunities and privileges of the Greek Orthodox church in the Ottoman Empire, the Sultans have never refused to consecrate them anew...." A strategic rearrangement rendered the sentence essentially innocuous: "If in every age the emperors of Russia have testified to their active solicitude for the cult of the Greek Orthodox church, the Sultans have never ceased to watch over the maintenance of the immunities and privileges...." In a second change, the Vienna Note's insistence that the Porte "remain faithful to the letter and spirit" of Kutchuk-Kainardji was weakened to a pledge simply "to remain faithful to the stipulations of the treaty"; Russian attempts to interpret the treaty in a favorably broad sense were thus undercut. Finally, the Sultan, in promising to extend future privileges given to other sects to the Greek Orthodox, referred to those privileges as "granted" (*octroyés*) rather than "conceded" (*concédés*). The modifications were subtle, and, as will be seen, were at first dismissed in the West as mere verbal fiddling; but they did assure the Turks, and the Russians also, that the position of the Christians would depend on the Sultan's benevolence rather than on the intervention of a given foreign power and that all the millets would be treated equally, with no special position for any one group.[89]

The rejection of the unamended Vienna Note represented a long step towards war. It came as a shock to many Europeans, especially those not present at Constantinople. The whole procedure by which the Vienna Note had been drawn up presupposed that, while the tsar's susceptibilities must be appeased, the Ottomans could be forced to "put up and shut up." When the Ottomans did not meekly accept the Note, Europeans immediately scented foul play, and suspicion soon centered on Lord Stratford.

The accusations against Stratford originated among Europeans in Constantinople. Stratford was a difficult and overbearing colleague; both Bruck[90] and de la Cour testified to the problems of working with him. One cannot take de la Cour's accusations on this point at face value, however—especially as he made them, not while the negotiations on the Vienna Note were taking place, but only after their failure had become apparent.[91] De la Cour's suspicions reached Lord Cowley, the British ambassador in Paris, and Cowley in turn reported them to London,[92] where—to judge from many informal comments—doubts were already entertained about Stratford.[93] Aberdeen, Clarendon, and Sir James Graham were all inclined to believe, at one time or another, that Stratford had outmaneuvered them.[94] Similar stories circulated among Russian diplomats, and Nesselrode's distrust of Stratford predisposed him to accept them.[95] From such official sources, the story passed into international gossip through diaries and memoirs such as those of Greville and Vitzthum von Eckstaedt.[96]

The thesis of Stratford's "guilt" has become a hardy perennial of Crimean War scholarship. A strong tradition in Russian historiography has clung to the thesis of Stratford's "guilt," and scholars specializing in French history have generally agreed with this thesis. An eminent Turkish historian has followed suit in a recent history of nineteenth-century Turkey.[97] Stratford has found supporters in a small group of British historians who, led by H. W. V. Temperley, have concentrated on his work.[98] They have emphasized Stratford's own statement that he did his "official best" and his many descriptions of Turkish intransigence.[99] Indeed, it is true that, in a letter to Musurus Bey, Reshid himself formally "absolved" Stratford of blame.[100] Nonetheless, perhaps all these supporters are too close to Stratford for comfort. In any case, even their best efforts have failed to dispel all questions concerning his guilt, despite their confident assertions.[101] Most recent work has left the question open, but one suspects that this may be more from a distaste for simplistic "villain" theories than because of any major new arguments justifying Stratford.[102]

In any case, if one seriously attempts to reconstruct the Porte's viewpoint, it becomes clear that the Vienna Note, in the form in which it was drawn up, had scarcely a chance of acceptance. Stratford's own assessment of the situation was on the mark: "the Turks are altogether on their high horse;" "the Porte is to all appearance ready for anything."[103] Indeed, it is evident that for years scholars have been asking the wrong question. The problem is not, why did the Porte refuse the Vienna Note? The real question is, why was the Porte ready to accept the text with comparatively mild amendments?

Fortunately, it is possible to reconstruct the thinking at the Porte in some detail. In addition to the text of the Note and the fashion in which it had been drafted, several other considerations combined to stiffen resistance. Reshid himself echoed the assessment of the war party when he commented to de la Cour that the Vienna Note was "a brainchild of Austria, who is proceeding in this whole affair hand in glove with the Russians, either out of deference to them, or out of the desire to take her part of the spoils of the Ottoman Empire."[104] Several incidents during the summer lent plausibility to this cynical evaluation of Austrian motives. One example was the so-called Koszta Affair. Martin Koszta was a Hungarian revolutionary who had escaped briefly to the United States. He returned to Turkey, evidently with the intention of fomenting revolution in the Hapsburg Empire, and was arrested by the Austrians at Smyrna, whereupon he claimed American protection, a claim that was honored. The confrontation was resolved by the French consul, who arranged that Koszta should be sent back to the United States. But the Austrians, somewhat illogically, made scapegoats of the Turks. The dismissal of the vali of Smyrna and of the minister of the interior was demanded and obtained. Furthermore, Bruck made this affair, which occurred in June,[105] the point of departure for a renewed campaign against the presence of refugees in the Ottoman Empire. After several angry exchanges, Bruck sent a note, dated July 30, in which he demanded a definitive solution of the refugees question, urged the danger that revolutionaries presented for the Porte as well as for neighboring states, and concluded that the present situation was "sooner or later incompatible with the peaceful relations between the two empires." In an interview with Reshid at about the same time, Bruck made the same point verbally: "I concluded with this, that it would be very unpleasant to me if, from these recent things, highly disagreeable developments with the Imperial regime should spring, and this must unfailingly be the case, unless something decisive happened soon."[106] As Paul Schroeder has pointed out, this kind of proceeding had a harmful effect on the diplomatic situation. The Koszta Affair created strains between Austria and the other European powers. It weakened any hope of moral pressure on the Russians; Nesselrode was disgusted that Saint Petersburg alone was accused of attacking Ottoman sovereignty when other states disregarded it with impunity. And certainly it did not serve to convince the Ottomans that the Austrians were their friends in court.[107]

But the most important area of conflict between Austria and the Ottoman Empire was the principality of Serbia. As early as July 19, Reshid Pasha inquired why Austrian troops had been concentrated on the Serbian border. The Ottoman foreign minister declared that he could understand why the Austrian government would feel it necessary to assemble troops as a counter to the Russian presence in Moldavia and Walachia; but he did not see why those troops should be stationed in the vicinity of Serbia, rather than in the Banat and Transylvania. Bruck, mindful that the talks on the Turkish Ultimatum were at a crucial stage, determined to stall about Austrian intentions until the courier had left with the text of the Ultimatum.[108] By the beginning of August, there was general anxiety in Constantinople over reports that the Austrian force was prepared to occupy Serbia—with or without the Serbian government's consent—should any revolutionary disturbances occur. Reshid demanded an explanation. Bruck insisted that, at a time when the British, French, and Russian governments had all brought up military forces, Austria was obliged to do likewise. But he took the opportunity to read Reshid a lesson from the antirevolutionary text: "The Porte should especially take care not to turn the country into an arena for all sorts of revolutionaries; it is the having called such into the ranks of the army . . . that has created the belief in a highly ambiguous attitude towards Austria." One can credit de la Cour's conviction that Reshid was not "completely" satisfied by this conversation. The French ambassador concluded: "the extreme distrust he is in, along with many of his compatriots, with regard to the Cabinet of Vienna—distrust that so many motives and so many persons contribute, at this moment, especially, to excite even more—has not diminished."[109]

Reshid's disquiet seemed justified by a series of threatening coincidences that led many observers in Belgrade to believe Austrian occupation imminent. General Mayerhofer paid a visit to Serbia during a tour of the western Balkans; rumor had it that the Austrian general had come to demand Prince Alexander's abdication. Alexander's rival for the throne, Prince Michael Obrenovich, published an open letter to the Serbian Senate from his exile in Vienna in which, though disclaiming any desire to reign, he professed himself willing to take up the burden should he be legally chosen by the Serbian people.[110] It was noted that Prince Michael concurrently celebrated his marriage to a young Austrian noblewoman and that Russian as well as Austrian dignitaries were conspicuous at the ceremony. Fonblanque, British consul in Belgrade, believed that the Russian and Austrian governments were preparing Michael as Alexander's replacement.[111] In fact, Michael's actions were an embarrassment to the authorities; the Russian ambassador, noting with relief that Michael was about to take a wedding trip to the Tyrol and Italy, drily urged him to stay "rather a long time."[112] But Fonblanque's reports during late July and August testify eloquently to Serbian terror of an immediate Austrian occupation, perhaps in conjunction with the Russians. Despite the limited consular budget, Fonblanque retained the service of a special courier to carry the first news to Constantinople.[113] The arrival of Fonton, the Russian Commissioner Extraordinary, from Vienna in mid-August—when the atmosphere was most charged[114]—naturally reinforced these suspicions: Fonblanque believed that Fonton had been sent so that the Russians would have a man on the spot when the Porte's decision on the Vienna Note was publicized. Should the Porte refuse, Fonton would announce military measures against Serbia.[115]

Reshid was determined that the Porte should make some show of resistance to Russian and Austrian pressure on Serbia. He found support from Stratford. It was decided that the Porte would station a force near the Ottoman border with Serbia, while a special commissioner would be sent to Belgrade. Later, additional troops were earmarked for the garrison at Belgrade. These steps were communicated to Bruck. Meanwhile, the Serbian Agent was not pleased either by the commissioner or by the extra troops,[116] both of which might be used for interference in Serbia, where the Turks were most unpopular. In fact, the Turkish commissioner's departure for Belgrade was held up for some weeks.[117] Though the Austrians now offered reassurances, particularly disclaiming the Obrenovich letter to the Serbian Senate,[118] they do not seem to have been entirely convincing. In view of these elements of strain, it is not surprising that the Porte considered it possible that, in case of war, Austria might attack the Ottoman Empire simultaneously with Russia.

When in mid-July the *Meclis-i umumî* had considered the alternatives of negotiation through international good offices or immediate war, many members had accepted further diplomatic steps only to buy time, since careful discussion of the military situation offered no solution to the inescapable fact that the Ottoman army could not be put in anything like a state of readiness for at least another month. By mid-August, excellent and visible progress had been made, adding fuel to the pressure for rejection of the Vienna Note. British experts agreed that the Ottoman army was in good shape. Reports reaching Stratford from the Danube front were quite optimistic. Slade pointed out that Turkish artillery was "excellent" and that the key fortresses of Şumla, Silistria, and Varna had been strengthened. A numerous force was concentrated on the eastern frontier, although Slade was not impressed by its commanders.[119] These positive factors were offset by some less encouraging aspects. Even early in the summer, money had been a problem; Consul Longworth reported to Stratford from Monastir at the end of June that the army was owed five months' pay, that the Albanian irregulars refused to fight without advance wages, and that brigandage was on the rise.[120] This was serious, since the Porte had sent all the regular troops ordinarily garrisoned in Thessaly, lower Albania, or Macedonia to the front.[121] Omer Pasha, top commander in the Danube theatre, accordingly urged prompt termination of the armed peace; Omer praised the morale of the troops under his command; but, citing inadequate supplies and lack of activity, he called for a vigorous stand and prompt recourse to war to get the best performance from the army.[122]

In addition to its normal resources, the Porte had requested reinforcements from the Pasha of Egypt. Fourteen thousand soldiers were sent to Constantinople in August. They camped at Unkiar Skelessi in transit for the Danube. Joined with other recruits, they made a colorful sight. Alison wrote: "'Tis a pity you can't see the Bosphorus about Therapia, swarming with ships of war, and the opposite heights crowned with the green tents of the Egyptian camp. Constantinople itself has gone back fifty years, and the strangest figures swarm in from the distant provinces to have a cut at the Moscov. Turbans, lances, maces, and battle-axes jostle each other in the narrow streets, and are bundled off immediately to the camp at Shumla for the sake of a quiet life."[123] The presence of these reserves encouraged the Porte, but added to the pressures for action of some sort.

In light of all these motives for rejection of the Vienna Note, it would have been difficult for the original text ever to have won acceptance; indeed Stratford admitted, "Reshid told me candidly that no personal influence could have induced the Porte to give way." However, Reshid had few illusions about the consequences if the Porte fought alone; he showed his real concern when he asked de la Cour repeatedly if France would abandon the Porte to its own devices if war broke out as result of an Ottoman rejection of the Vienna Note. De la Cour's reply was equivocal.[124] If the British attitude had been unencouraging as well, Reshid might have felt obliged either to accept the Note or to propose merely cosmetic changes. Stratford later said he had done his "official best" in this sense; and (as mentioned above) Reshid bore him out. On the other hand, if Reshid had not had confidence that the British could be induced to help, he might have given up on negotiations entirely and surrendered to the war party, or he might have been the victim of a new attempt to force him from office. But in fact, Reshid had received reassurances of British support from a source other than Stratford. He had benefited from a series of interesting and highly colored reports from the Ottoman minister to London. Constantine Musurus (known in Ottoman circles as Costaki Bey) was a Greek who had opted for the Ottoman Empire and had served in a series of high diplomatic posts. His reports during the summer of 1853 emphasized the increasing enthusiasm for the Ottoman cause emerging in Britain. One might be tempted to lay this to a desire to please the Porte, but really a comparison of his reports with the dispatches of other ambassadors in the same period suggests that Musurus's exaggerations reached an extent that sets them apart.

Musurus's analysis of the intentions of the British Cabinet was cautious early in June but quickly became enthusiastic. On June 4, he reported the orders to the fleet to move to Besika Bay, as communicated by Clarendon. He also described a conversation with Palmerston that was rather discouraging: Clarendon had emphasized that Britain and France expected Turkey to be able to defend herself; Palmerston added that it was important that the Porte should avoid any appeal to religious fanaticism in the course of preparing for war. He also emphasized further reforms, as the best means of insuring the loyalty of the Christians.[125] On June 7, Musurus sent another rather tepid report. He gave more information about the sending of the fleet, which had been communicated to him unofficially by Palmerston even before Clarendon's disclosure. A further conversation with Clarendon on June 4 had been used by Musurus for an impassioned explanation of the injustice of the Russian claims. The impression seemed to be growing in British circles though that Nicholas would back down. On June 17 Musurus wrote that, despite his urgings, Clarendon did not feel that the prospective Russian occupation of the Principalities should be considered as an act of war either by the Turks or by the British. Musurus gave an accurate summary of the Cabinet's position: the British government would emphasize international efforts to bring Russia and Turkey to agreement; only if Russia crossed the Danube or ordered the fleet out of Sevastopol would Britain send ships to Constantinople. Subsequently, however, Musurus rather distorted the situation. On June 27, he announced that, with regard to potential Russian occupation, Clarendon advised an appeal to the other great powers and again stated that the fleets would not leave Besika Bay. But Musurus continued:

> Whatever may be the weight of this counsel of the British Cabinet, it is evident that the entrance of the fleets depends entirely on the manner in which the Sublime Porte will envision this aggression of Russia, for the reason that it is permissible for the Imperial Government either to protest against that act of open hostility by fixing, according to my advice, a term for the evacuation, or to consider that invasion as authorizing the Sublime Porte to declare, on its side, war against Russia, and to call, from that time, immediately the two fleets to Constantinople. In any case, the Sublime Porte can reach an understanding, on anything that relates to that eventuality, with the Ambassadors of England and France who, I am positively certain, have unlimited powers in this respect.[126]

In other words, Musurus was guessing that the Cabinet's pacifism was not borne out by the instructions to Stratford; and he believed that, if the Turks pressed ahead, the British would send the fleet, not to enforce negotiations, but to support the war effort. Further hopeful news was conveyed in Musurus's letter of July 2. Musurus had announced dramatically at the Queen's Ball that the Russian army had been ordered across the Prut; What, he asked, did Britain intend to do about it? Musurus's own solution, evidently suggested by instructions from Reshid of June 25,[127] was a new treaty of guarantee based on the Straits Convention of 1841. Musurus declared that this project won a favorable hearing,[128] although British sources suggest that Aberdeen and Clarendon never liked it.[129]

The impact of Musurus's overoptimistic descriptions of British readiness to help was greatly enhanced by the great number of newspaper clippings that he enclosed in his dispatches. There has been some doubt as to the influence of these articles, since English was not widely known at the Porte. Still, there is evidence that Reshid was familiar with the views of the British press.[130] In any event, the clippings reinforced the message of Musurus's despatches. The *Times,* rumored close to Lord Aberdeen, reflected the anxiety that plagued him and contributed to his hesitations.[131] Britain was sliding into the stance of Turkey's protector against Russia. Did not this mean that Christian Britain was supporting Moslem oppression of millions of fellow-Christians against the efforts of another Christian power? The *Times* concluded, sententiously: "whatever may be the ultimate condition of the territories and the tribes which now constitute the Ottoman Empire, we are not prepared to admit that Russia has the right to conquer or to hold them against the will of all Europe." More typical was the attitude of the *Standard*, which charged that the average man was better off under Ottoman rule than under either Russian or Austrian rule. "By the edict of Gulhane the first great step in civil liberty has been secured—the pure administration of justice; and the wholesome authority of independent and unexceptionable courts of law has been made paramount to that of the sovereign himself. No subject can be put to death or otherwise severely punished but by sentence of judges selected for their learning, intelligence, and good character. We need not say how favourably such a constitution contrasts with deportations to Siberia, or the military executions at Milan." An equally astonishing description of life in the Ottoman Empire was offered a few days later by the *Sun*. "The SULTAN, in conclusive testimony of his good-feeling towards the Christian population in his empire, has issued a remarkable and humane series of firmans, according to them a perfect equality in all the national rights, privileges, and immunities. By these memorable documents, not only have the Rayahs been formally emancipated, but all classes of Christians without distinction—Latins, Greeks, and Armenians—have been placed upon precisely the same footing with the mass of their Mahometan fellow-countrymen."[132] Such impressions fitted in with deep prejudices in the Liberal British outlook;[133] they later helped to justify some potentially embarrassing actions and they could hardly fail to gratify the Porte.

In fact, Musurus reported growing popular pressure for a still more overtly pro-Ottoman position. The clippings sent with Musurus's dispatch of June 7 showed general confidence that Nicholas would back down as soon as he realized that his course was disapproved internationally. By June 17, the tone of the clippings was more warlike. Considerable excitement was aroused by rumors that some, at least, of the ministers had known of Menshikov's demands and had approved them; the *Sun* queried: Will Clarendon and Aberdeen be impeached?[134] The bundle of clippings with the June 27 dispatch conveyed several appeals for transferring the fleets to Constantinople should the Russians occupy the Principalities. The *Sun* predicted that, if Clarendon and Aberdeen refused to go to war over the invasion, the Cabinet would fall. Musurus further sent information about interpellations in Parliament, which he judged were designed in part to stir up public opinion.[135] The rumor of a change in ministry took root in Constantinople, for de la Cour gathered that this hope was a fairly important consideration in Reshid's calculations in August.[136]

What conclusions can be drawn from this survey of Musurus's correspondence? First, Musurus distinctly exaggerated the willingness of the British Cabinet to help the Porte. Second, his contacts were not designed to give him a balanced view. When he was not talking to Clarendon, he was in touch with Palmerston, or with Lord Lyndhurst, an opponent of the government's policy in Parliament.[137] There is no record of confidential conversations with Lord Aberdeen who—given his low opinion of the "crapulous barbarians,"[138]—was not likely to have cultivated the Ottoman ambassador. Third, there is no need to suppose that Stratford gave the Porte an unduly favorable impression of British policy; Musurus's reports suffice to explain the Porte's confidence on this point. And finally, the aggressive groundswell of British public opinion—which Kingsley Martin has ably described as a key factor in moving the government towards war in the following winter and spring—made an earlier contribution to the crisis. Without the reassurance of popular support in Britain, the Ottomans might conceivably have felt obliged to accept the Vienna Note as it stood. Or if even without such reassurance they had rejected negotiations and opted for an immediate declaration of war (as seems more likely), they would have fought under circumstances that would have made it easy for the British to have washed their hands of them.

More than almost any other incident in the period immediately before the outbreak of war, the negotiations concerning the Vienna Note lend themselves to the historical game of "if only." "If only" the British and French had scrutinized the text of the Vienna Note more closely! Later, when the Russians revealed that they understood the Note as conceding the protectorate, London and Paris were horrified. Could they not have forced a more careful drafting of the original words, so that the safeguards the Ottomans wanted would have come from the Vienna conference and would thus have been less humiliating to the tsar than stipulations formulated at Constantinople? "If only" Buol had been more prescient about the impression Bruck was making in Constantinople; "if only" he had insisted that Bruck present Vienna's demands in a more muted tone, in order to build the climate essential to mediation. "If only" Buol had not reversed himself concerning the site of negotiations. Allowing the Turkish Ultimatum to be drawn up, if it was not to be used, was a very serious mistake. Negotiations held either entirely in Constantinople or entirely in Vienna would have had more chance of success than the parallel procedures that inadvertently emerged. "If only" Musurus Bey had not exaggerated British readiness to help the Ottoman Empire. Perhaps Reshid might then have won the Porte's acceptance of the unamended note; or, if the war party had won out, the Porte would have appeared in the wrong in Western eyes, and an easily containable Russo-Turkish war would have been the result.[139]

It is this sort of analysis that has fed the "bluffs and blunders" school of Crimean War origins. Yet, as much as any other episode, the Vienna Note negotiations show the weakness of this interpretation. Although the Russians had become more conciliatory during the summer, they reacted with shock to the terms of the Turkish Ultimatum. And the original Vienna Note was totally unpalatable to many Turks, for a variety of sound reasons. Some differences in international affairs are unbridgeable; when (as in this case) the "last position" of each party to a quarrel is totally unacceptable to the other, inability to produce a compromise may not reflect on the competence of the mediators—it may simply show that the differences were irreconcilable. In Paris and London, the mediators regretted the virtual failure of the Vienna Note; from the viewpoint of Constantinople, the negotiations had been surprisingly successful.

Chapter IV

The Declaration of War

THE summer of 1853 was crucial in the drift towards war in the East. With the rupture of relations between Russia and the Ottoman Empire, mediatory action by the other great powers seemed essential to break the deadlock. The Vienna Note was the fruit of the four powers' attempt to perform this role through the conference of ambassadors at Vienna. But the negotiation of the Vienna Note seemed to confirm Ottoman objections that Russian aims and Russian sensibilities were carefully considered, while the Turks were supposed to accept whatever Europe, in its wisdom, decreed. In fact, diplomatic developments during the summer months could hardly fail to exacerbate Ottoman pride and to intensify factional differences within the ruling elite. Mustafa Nâilî Pasha and Reshid attempted to meet the Russian government's recall of its mission and the subsequent march into the Principalities with reasoned reiterations of the Porte's willingness to negotiate; this posture was easily caricatured as weakness, and it led (on the insistence of Mehmet Ali Pasha and Fethi Ahmet Pasha) to the Sultan's dismissal of their ministry. Stratford forced their reinstatement, in the belief that they were best qualified to work with Britain and against Russia. But the fact that they had been imposed by foreign pressure robbed Mustafa Nâilî and Reshid of a strong base; any diplomatic solution they sponsored would be portrayed as a sellout to foreign interests. The limits on their powers were very evident during the following weeks, when the Turkish Ultimatum was drawn up. The diplomats' suggestions were rejected at a number of points in favor of phrasing believed to be more favorable to the Porte. The final proposal was accepted by many Ottomans as an expedient to buy time; still, it represented a hope of conciliation. The Vienna conference's unwillingness to take it seriously was an insult to the Porte. Further, the diplomats at Vienna seemed oblivious to the very real differences implied in the terms of the Turkish Ultimatum and the Vienna Note. They were not, as they seemed to imagine, choosing the more acceptable of two formulas; rather they were choosing between two different lines of development for the Ottoman Empire. Finally, their cavalier assumption that the Turks would gratefully accept their decision was not likely to enhance the Vienna Note's popularity in Constantinople. What is surprising is, not that the original text of the Vienna Note was refused, but that it was accepted even with amendments. It is clear that many factors, as described above, made an immediate recourse to war highly tempting. But rational calculations, for what they were worth, discouraged such action without more explicit indications of support from Britain and France. Yet the price of continued negotiations under international sponsorship might come high. It would possibly entail a closer relationship with Britain and France, which might be useful if the talks broke down and war resulted, but which also might lead to increased influence for the two powers at Constantinople and to increased Westernization of the Ottoman government.

During the six weeks that separate the vote on the Vienna Note from the Turkish declaration of war on Russia, a confusing struggle continued between different factions. At the end of August, Argyropoulos —the Greek translator who had formerly been first dragoman to the Russian legation—had a number of unexplained conversations with high Ottoman officials, including Reshid Pasha, Mehmet Ali, and the commander of the guards, Mehmet Rüştü Pasha.[1] Argyropoulos suggested that it might be possible to solve the crisis through negotiations between Saint Petersburg and Constantinople based on the amendments. Argyropoulos indicated that the Russians might agree to the first two amendments but would certainly demand changes in the third; the details might be made the subject of discussion.[2] The inspiration for Argyropoulos's démarche was mysterious: de la Cour reported a widespread impression that the ex-dragoman was not acting on his own initiative. Yet he could not have received word from Saint Petersburg or even from Vienna so soon after the amendments had been drawn up. Perhaps he had had some sort of hint either from Gorchakov in Bucharest or from Odessa. But subordinates would have been unlikely to interfere in a matter so important in the tsar's eyes. More probable is de la Cour's guess that Argyropoulos was incited by pro-Russian elements in Constantinople.[3]

Argyropoulos's overtures received short shrift from Reshid Pasha, though Reshid took good care to see that Stratford[4] and de la Cour heard of a possibility they were sure to find disquieting. But apparently Argyropoulos was relatively pleased with his conversations with Mehmet Ali and Mehmet Rüştü. They might have had good reasons to consider the proposal. As de la Cour pointed out, Ottoman statesmen were aware of the fact that the four great powers might decide to force the unamended Vienna Note on the Porte. In that case, a direct agreement with the Russians might be a better bargain.[5] Or it might be possible to cut through the complications by initiating negotiations that would quickly fail and lead to war.[6]

Meanwhile, diplomacy at Constantinople was stalled. Until word arrived from the Vienna conference, the future of negotiation was cloudy. But at the Porte there was an increasingly strong undercurrent of belligerence. The diplomatic corps had received the amendments with some sympathy and many had expressed their own hope that the changes would be favorably considered.[7] But such remarks were influenced by professional politeness and by empathy with the Porte during days of crisis in which they had shared. The reports that gradually came in from the Ottoman representatives abroad accurately reflected a soberer evaluation of the Ottoman modifications. The British were at first not pleased by the independent action of the Ottoman Porte, their supposed protégé. Clarendon, like Buol, was very much opposed to Reshid's idea of a four-power guarantee of the Ottoman Empire, a proposal that accompanied the amendments.[8] And Clarendon's first reaction to the amendments themselves was hostile. He wrote Lord John Russell on August 27: "The enclosed which came last night and contains fresh conditions clearly shews [*sic*] that the Turks are determined not to have any settlement. If they had sent their ambassador to Vienna he might have waited there till proper arrangements were made.... I have read the Note again and again and can discover nothing in it derogatory to the dignity or the independence of the Sultan, and all the important parts are taken verbatim from Reshid's own note to Menshikoff."[9] This letter exemplifies Clarendon's inadequate grasp of the state of affairs at Constantinople. He was inclined to patronize the Porte: Turkish ministers were not equal partners in the negotiation, but should be glad to have Britain speak for them. Clarendon could only explain their reluctance by a desire to sabotage the whole démarche. Furthermore, he had no awareness of the implications of the Vienna Note for the Ottoman Empire and could not see how it differed from the Porte's own wishes. Finally, he had a very peculiar notion of the powers of Ottoman emissaries abroad: the diplomatic corps was of very recent date in the Ottoman Empire and Ottoman representatives still suffered under the handicap that the Sultan feared delegating authority and always kept his diplomats on a very short leash. If an ambassador had gone to Vienna, he would have been so hampered by requirements that the affair would have been complicated rather than expedited.

In any event, Clarendon's initial reaction to the amendments was definitely not favorable. Likewise, the popular press was at first lukewarm—unready to abet the Porte in revising Britain's own proposals.

But gradually a more bellicose sentiment prevailed, and "for the first time there was complete unity," which centered around the opinion that the Turks had, after all, been right in proposing the amendments. The government, too, changed its stand. For example, Lord John Russell, who had at first echoed Clarendon's disapproval of the amendments, came to believe that "to have held out such encouragement to the Turks as we have done and afterwards to desert them, would be felt as deep disgrace and humiliation by the whole country." This complex and varying pattern of reactions was faithfully and fully reported to Constantinople by Musurus in his dispatches of August 26 and September 10.[10] The upshot was that the British government determined to recommend acceptance of the amendments to Saint Petersburg, on the rather specious basis that they really changed nothing and were to be construed as a meaningless concession to Turkish susceptibilities.[11]

Reactions in France were, on the whole, more favorable to the Porte than those in Britain. Drouyn de Lhuys regretted the amendments, since they retarded a solution, but he did judge that the Turkish proposals improved the Vienna text by clarifying certain passages and thereby preventing possible future misunderstandings.[12] Veli Pasha, the Ottoman representative in Paris, traced this relatively friendly response in his report.[13]

As it turned out, the prospect of forcing the Turks to agree to the letter of the Vienna text was dispelled by reawakened anxiety as to the Russians' real aims. The Russian victory in the neighborhood of Khiva doubtless stimulated British fears of an eventual attack on India.[14] And the excitement of Indian Moslems, reacting to the pressure on their coreligionists in the Ottoman Empire, touched off a near panic on the upper Indus and suggested possible troubles to come.[15] But the decisive factor was a lengthy "Examination" of the Vienna Note and the proposed changes in it, drawn up by Labenski, a subordinate in the Russian State Chancellery, and leaked to a Berlin newspaper. This document explained Russian rejection of the amendments by making it clear that the Russians interpreted the unamended Note as allowing the protectorate over the Greek Orthodox subjects of the Porte.[16] This, of course, was precisely what Britain and France had thought was being prevented; and after this so-called "violent interpretation" was published, there was no question of insisting on the original Vienna draft. On the other hand, unless the tsar chose to accept the amendments of his own free will, there way no way to make them stick, short of a war for which the European capitals were as yet physically and psychologically unprepared. So the diplomats found themselves obliged to start over just as the situation in the East threatened to get completely out of hand.

Reshid and his colleagues lived through the first three weeks of September in uncertainty as to the fate of the Vienna negotiations. Although the slowness of communications made it impossible for them to follow in detail the developments sketched above, enough information reached them in the reports dated late August to convey the likelihood that the discussions would break down. Meanwhile, the news of the imminent meeting at Olmütz between Franz Joseph and Nicholas I reinforced expectations of an Austro-Russian attack; the so-called "war party" began to fear a "peace at any price" movement.[17] War sentiment mounted impressively among the public. Particularly affected were the ulema and the *softas* (students in the *medreses*, or religious schools) of Constantinople; and they in turn used their functions to press for war through the mosques.[18] Placards began to appear mysteriously on the walls, exhorting the people to a holy war.[19] This movement was immediately blamed by Reshid Pasha on the advocates of war within the ministry.[20] There is ample testimony to the effect that Mehmet Ali, Mehmet Rüştü, and others were deeply involved in the later development of this movement. To what extent they were responsible for its initiation is conjectural. It is important to remember, however, that the religious profession in Constantinople formed an impressively large group with its own reasons, both specific and general, for discontent. The *softas* were particularly numerous: Kovalevsky estimates their numbers at about forty-five thousand.[21] Although certain of the high ulema had favored the early stages of reform in the Ottoman Empire,[22] by mid-century there was a growing movement among the lesser ulema and the students to oppose change, particularly Westernization. Şerif Mardin, in his admirable study, suggests that this trend must be seen in the context of the worsening opportunities of the group as a whole. For several centuries, the ulema, as the educated class, had held many high state positions. Now—as many offices were secularized and as schools such as the school attached to the Translation Bureau at the Porte were opened—this control was broken. In fact, the students trained in the more modern institutions generally had an advantage, since their curriculum, secular in inspiration and organized around language studies, fitted them for office more adequately than did the study of the Koran in an age when the bureaucrat's prime function was to mediate between European—particularly Western—culture and traditional Ottoman ways. To make matters worse, at the moment when the access of the ulema to government positions

was curtailed, the opportunities within the Moslem Institution were
diminished by the government's expropriation of the wakf, or the prop-
erties belonging to Moslem foundations. These holdings had traditionally furnished the revenues from which most ulema were supported;
now a large proportion of this income went to the state. The result
of these changes was a serious dislocation within the learned profession.
The course in the *medreses* was still long and exacting, and students
continued to nourish expectations of achieving a position commensurate with their efforts at the end of their studies.[23] Indeed, as the social
background of the students declined, these results become more important.[24] But the realistic prospects of upward mobility had greatly
lessened. There was a natural tendency on the part of people caught in
this process to strike out against an unjust society. These feelings
were exacerbated by the conspicuous Westernization caused by the
Tanzimat reforms, which was hard to reconcile at many points with
Moslem teachings and attitudes.

The Tanzimat became increasingly unpopular with this group because of the emphasis on raising the status of the Christians, and, at
least as a theoretical goal, on achieving some kind of Christian-Moslem
equality. This policy led to a series of anti-Christian outbreaks in the
fifties and sixties. The first such riot was the massacre of Christians
at Aleppo in 1850. In these disturbances, religious objections mingled
with the economic dislocation that resulted as European manufactured
goods flooded into the Ottoman Empire and displaced local crafts—
thus benefiting Christians and Jews, who were better qualified by outlook, and often by language, to act as middlemen, at the expense of
Moslem craftsmen.[25] It is, of course, hard to establish just who was
involved in these riots, but it seems clear that the disturbances attracted
at least tacit support from a broad spectrum of groups, from impov-
erished ne'er-do-wells, to declining artisans, to ulema and notables.[26]
The agitation in 1853, promoted through the mosques and the craft
guilds,[27] falls into this general pattern.[28] It is ironic that this excitement was touched off by Russian moves, for most of the time this kind
of feeling made a pro-Russian policy easier than a pro-British policy.
The Russians, although they demanded concessions for specific provinces such as Serbia and Moldavia and Walachia in 1829 or Moldavia
and Walachia in 1848, did not, as a rule, demand the kind of structural
change in Ottoman society to which the British were committed by their
sponsorship of the Tanzimat reforms. It was the mistake of the Russian government in this particular instance to lead with the one demand
most likely to lose them their natural support. A Russian protectorate
for the Greek Orthodox millet suggested to the popular mind constant

Russian interference to better the status of this largest group of Christians, and this concept was totally unacceptable. The leaders who advocated war shared in many ways in these popular prejudices. It is significant, for example, that Mehmet Ali grew up in the provinces, near Rize, rather than in Constantinople; that he did not learn any European language; and that he was noted for his piety.[29] At the same time, this popular agitation, with its anti-Western, anti-Tanzimat, and anti-Reshid overtones, formed a perfect instrument for Mehmet Ali and his associates in the factional struggle with Reshid and his friends. And the factional struggle beneath the obvious, and often seemingly dominant, level of personalities had ideological implications. Though it is not possible to speak of a conflict of ideologies in the sense of two clearly opposed platforms supported by two sharply defined groups, it is important to recognize that even such imperfectly articulated perceptions could create tendencies that must be taken into account when attempting to sketch political events.

In any case, it seems evident that Mehmet Ali Pasha, Mehmet Rüştü Pasha, and the Sheikh ul Islam were behind the major disturbances of September 9–12.[30] The campaign of placards culminated in a petition that was given to Reshid and to Mehmet Ali and was formally presented to the Sultan during his procession to the mosque.[31] The petition—as Stratford later pointed out—was signed by only thirty-five of the ulema,[32] but it doubtless represented the sentiments of the large crowd of students who turned out to support the presentation. The petition called for a holy war and sharply criticized any policy that entailed the granting of further rights to the Christians: this was considered to be a "sacrilegious violation" of the Koran. Any ministers who could suggest such a course were traitors and should be dismissed in favor of a more correctly oriented leadership. The content of the petition and the agitation that accompanied it led some of the ministers to fear a coup d'état aimed at deposing Abdul-Mejid in favor of his brother, Abdul-Aziz, who was believed to be more conservative.[33]

Opinion varied as to the seriousness of the riots. Reshid immediately called together the diplomatic representatives and gave them a gloomy briefing. But Bruck reported that, under questioning, Reshid admitted that energetic measures by the Porte would suffice to contain the movement. Still, there was considerable anxiety at the Porte, for Stratford boasted that one of the ministers had asked to confide him his jewels. Stratford himself discounted the gravity of the situation, however, as did Slade.[34] Much of the fear related to what might happen rather than to what actually had happened: September 13, a festival, would be the occasion for the Sultan's procession to the Old Palace in the heart of Stamboul, and this public appearance might bring a disaster of some kind.[35]

In fact, as Bruck pointed out, Mehmet Ali and Reshid were rather evenly matched. The Sultan could not disgrace all the ministers who advocated war and who were suspected of complicity, for they controlled the entire military force of the country. Their ranks included Mehmet Ali—the Serasker Pasha, or minister of war; Mehmet Rüştü Pasha, the captain of the guards; the Kaptan Pasha, or naval minister; the minister of police;[36] and Omer Pasha, the commander-in-chief on the Danube front. The Sheikh ul Islam, who previously had seemed to mediate between factions, had come round to support of war at the end of August;[37] his cooperation was of great importance to the war party, because he had the power to issue a *fetva* officially deposing the present sultan and proclaiming a new one. On the other hand, Reshid and Abdul-Mejid had the confidence of Britain and France; it was not likely that those powers would give the same support to Abdul-Aziz as Sultan and Mehmet Ali as grand vizier. There was some room for doubt as to whether Mehmet Ali, despite his many anti-Western statements, would really destroy the only chances for foreign alliances;[38] there was much reason to believe that Britain and France would not permit such a loss of influence at the Porte.

In any case, Reshid's briefing was not designed to calm the representatives' anxieties, and de la Cour, who had spent a relatively short time at Constantinople, was particularly upset. He asked Reshid straight out what he intended to do. Reshid pointed out that, since the war party controlled the entire military apparatus of the Empire, there was no possibility of calling out the troops to quell riots. The only hope was the French and British fleets. But Reshid admitted that he hesitated to ask for foreign naval support, for this would lend credence to rumors that the European powers were going to force a settlement.[39] Apparently, though, the seriousness of the situation had overcome his objections: de la Cour indicated in a coded dispatch that Reshid some days before had doubted the wisdom of an appeal to the fleets, but in two recent council meetings had spoken out for it. Evidently Reshid thought this course would strengthen his position and would destroy the argument of the war party that, since Britain and France were not going to help, the Ottoman Empire must go it alone.[40] It might be the only means of maintaining Reshid's position and of keeping the Porte committed to diplomacy.

De la Cour, joined by Bruck, immediately contacted Stratford. They found the British ambassador little disposed to share their worries.

Stratford, although he claimed to have been warned "of personal danger," refused to get excited; and one senses a certain secret triumph in this old Turkish hand's phlegmatic pose. He was very much against the idea of calling up the fleets, for he felt that it was very important to avoid "an air of intimidation." He suggested bringing up a few more steamers "under cover of the steam-communications continually plying between the Squadrons and the Capital." This would be sufficient to "protect us from any immediate attack, and enable us to assist the Government in case of an outbreak threatening its existence, without attracting any unusual attention."[41]

It is essential to a correct understanding of Ottoman policy to bear in mind the circumstances of this appeal for reinforcements. In the first place, as de la Cour made clear, it was the group pledged to diplomacy, not the group pledged to war, that was eager to see French and British ships anchored in the Bosporus.[42] And the entire maneuver was carried out in the context of fear lest the advocates of war see this as an attempt to suppress their views. Though the presence of the squadrons ultimately emboldened the Porte after their call-up was completed in November, there is no basis for Temperley's charge that the war party brought about the demonstration in order to force the moving of the fleets to Constantinople.[43] It is also evident that the motive behind the appeal for reinforcements was fear of trouble in Constantinople, not fear of a Russian offensive.[44] Though the long-term effect of the buildup of the fleets was to involve France and Britain more heavily and strengthen the Turks, it is unfair to Stratford to present this as his motive in mid-September;[45] rather, he seems to have been trying to preserve a situation and a government that would make further negotiations possible.

But Stratford was guilty of serious miscalculation. In the first place, he misjudged the distance by which opinion at home had outstripped him. Drouyn de Lhuys had been eager for some time to move the two naval detachments at least into the Dardanelles: he argued that it was impossible to bring them home while the problem was unsettled, but it was also impossible to leave them in Besika Bay, in danger from autumn storms.[46] Aberdeen hypocritically produced manufactured testimony to the effect that the winter storms were not imminent.[47] Now, with de la Cour's graphic descriptions of the situation in Constantinople in hand, Drouyn could not resist trying to scare the British Cabinet into authorizing the moving of the fleets.[48] The Cabinet concurred, without even waiting to see Stratford's version of events; but this precipitate action probably shows, not that the government "had lost its composure," but that it anticipated that the French would act alone[49] and feared the increasingly violent excitement of British public opinion.[50]

The British were backing into an awkward position vis-à-vis the Porte. British rhetoric claimed that the British government was always the supporter of "liberal," enlightened rule in the Ottoman Empire. Now, however, the British ambassador had moved up ships in order to maintain a minority clique in power against the wishes of an important and vociferous section of the populace. And meanwhile, in London, the British Cabinet had authorized the dispatch of the entire fleet, against the express judgment of the ambassador on the spot. It was not likely that the British could extricate themselves easily from this predicament; but it was not Stratford who was the most warlike.

Indeed, Stratford apparently underrated the pressure for war at Constantinople. The news that additional British and French ships were on the way to the Bosporus irritated the militants without overawing them. A highly plausible rumor recounts that a group of leaders, themselves unimportant except as representatives of the chief of the demonstration, came to the Sultan, evidently on September 12, and delivered an ultimatum: he must decide, within one day, whether to abdicate or to declare war. The events of the rest of the day suggest that the Sultan hinted at his readiness to go to war.[51]

At any rate the Sultan instructed the Sheikh ul Islam to call together the ulema on September 12 and to put the case for cooperation with the ministry. At the meeting, the Sheikh ul Islam's presentation was reinforced by appeals from other ulema who were close to those ministers who desired further diplomatic steps. The propaganda was astonishingly successful; indeed, Bruck claimed that the ulema even expressed regret for their opposition.[52]

On the same day, September 12, a meeting of the Council was held. The Council, the main center of Reshid's strength, did not decide on an immediate declaration of war, perhaps because of the dubious international situation. The British and French stand was not encouraging and argued at least a pause to see the formal results of the amendments plan.

Finally, on the evening of September 12, the Sultan called together his principal advisers on both sides, Mustafa Nâilî Pasha, Reshid Pasha, the Sheikh ul Islam and Mehmet Ali Pasha. Mustafa Nâilî and Reshid reported on the anxiety felt by the British and French representatives at the prospect of an explosion in Constantinople and emphasized the decision to move additional ships to the Bosporus. The Sheikh ul Islam reported on the success of his meeting with the ulema.

Mehmet Ali, the most warlike, was isolated. Probably a compromise was reached: war would be declared, but to improve appearances and curry favor with possible allies, the declaration would be held up until the Russian reply to the amendments, almost certain to be negative, was known.[53] Meanwhile, as result of the agreements reached at this conference, a series of arrests was carried out during the night. By the morning of September 13, the day so widely feared as the occasion for revolution, the opposition was broken and the Sultan's procession passed without incident.[54]

For the moment, Reshid had stayed in power; but it is not possible to see this as anything other than the most tentative solution. Communications with Vienna, always unreliable, were maddeningly slow in this instance, and the definitive textual answer to the amendments was delayed. But by September 19, word had reached Constantinople that the tsar had refused the amendments. On the night of the 18th, Bruck received notice from the Austrian consul-general at Belgrade that such a communication was coming; the next morning, he made the rounds of the Porte and the diplomats with his information.[55] That same morning, an even more discouragingly worded message reached the Porte from Arif Efendi, the ambassador to Austria. While Buol held out hopes that a diplomatic formula might soon be found, Arif gave the impression that Nicholas's refusal was categoric. In either case, a speedy recourse to war now seemed inevitable.[56]

The four great-power representatives, very much concerned, still considered methods for avoiding the debacle. But plans for concerted action foundered on Lord Stratford's unwillingness to participate. Not until September 25 was he ready to agree to a meeting of the diplomats. By then, a special meeting had been convoked at the Porte, and it was clear that a formal declaration of war was imminent.[57] Stratford has been criticized for dragging his feet, and his slowness to respond has been taken as evidence that he really wanted the war. But some of the suggestions—for example, that he see the Sultan and forbid the war— were unrealistic at best. The moral ambiguity of Britain's current position at the Porte has been noted. There is much merit to Temperley's suggestion that Stratford feared that any attempt to prevent war would lead to revolution and that he accordingly preferred to try to keep the war on a "phony" basis during the few weeks before the onset of winter prevented campaigning and gave the diplomats another chance.[58]

Meanwhile, the Ottoman government was rushing into war. On September 21, de la Cour had reported sporadic exchanges of shots on the Danube.[59] On the 23rd, the Sultan spoke to the ministers and announced plans for calling an extraordinarily large session of the

Meclis-i umumî; it was plain that he expected a declaration of war.
On the 24th, Reshid was instructed to take a still harsher tone towards
Russia. On September 25, more formal notification of the refusal of
the amendments reached Constantinople.[60] The representatives of the
four great powers, meeting at Stratford's home a few hours before the
council was to come together, found themselves so split on the issues
that they finally had to send two notes to the Porte rather than adopt-
ing an identical text. The burden of the Austro-Prussian and the
Anglo-French notes was the same, however; they recommended that
the Porte accept the unamended Vienna Note on the condition of a
guarantee by the four neutral powers that would preclude any later
Russian claims to a protectorate.[61]

The complexion of the council has been colorfully described by
Temperley: "Its members, mostly unemployed pashas and *softas,*
passed to their deliberations through the streets crowded with soldiers
flourishing modern weapons and with bravos flourishing ancient ones,
with dervishes praying aloud for vengeance on the infidel. It was a fit
preparation for an assembly unknown to the law, free from rules of
procedure, and given over to bigotry and prejudice."[62] Though Temperley was certainly right to emphasize the concerns of public opinion,
one might comment that bigotry and prejudice rarely announce themselves so conveniently. Actually the council was well-behaved and professional. Bruck praised the bearing of the members, with one possible
exception, while Alison, the British embassy secretary, likened it to
"a meeting of the Commons."[63] The reference to "unemployed pashas
and *softas*" is hardly justified. The Sultan called together everyone
who held, or had held, ministerial office, plus the higher levels of the
bureaucracy, the ulema, and the military officer corps resident in
Constantinople,[64] in a procedure not inconsistent with the consultative
practices in vogue during the Tanzimat.[65]

The decision on war was almost irreversible when the council met.
Schlechta's account of the proceedings to his superior, Bruck, as well
as other contemporary diplomatic descriptions, emphasizes the parts of
the debate most comprehensible to European observers, namely, the
discussion of the Vienna Note and of the supporting memoranda presented by the representatives of the four great powers and the attempts
to determine the probable future policies of the great powers.[66] But it
is clear from the official protocol of the meeting that, during most of
the session, Reshid, Rifat, Ali Pasha, Fuad Efendi, and the other
"Europeanized" ministers faced a stinging attack from the more traditionally oriented ulema and *hocas.* Many of the *hocas* did not have a

realistic idea of the position of the Ottoman Empire in the international community. The Sheikh ul Islam, supported by the mufti of the *Meclis-i Vâlâ,* argued that, in the present state of the negotiations, recourse to war was a religious duty. As one *hoca,* Yahya Efendi, put it, it was not up to the government to ask the meeting whether the Porte possessed the capacity to make war against the Russians. It was the government's business to create that capacity; and if they had not been able to do so, then explanations were in order. By implication, any flaws in the Ottoman military establishment were not the fault of diminishing power in relation to other, more modernized, states but were to be blamed simply on official mismanagement. Efforts were made to introduce a rational scale of comparison—for example, the precedent of Napoleon's disastrous Russian campaign was introduced to show that even a world conqueror might hesitate before attacking Russia—but these arguments were lost in a welter of discussion. The situation was complicated by the impossibility of reaching any firm estimate of the size and strength of the Ottoman forces in relation to the Russian forces: the Serasker Pasha, the Kaptan Pasha, and those military officers still resident in Constantinople gave conflicting opinions. Supplies and finances were considered, but again many of the members were obviously thinking in terms of a bygone age—it was even suggested that the campaigns be financed by the booty to be captured.

Evaluation of the diplomatic situation was also difficult. Many of those present rejected the very idea of European alliances: this line of thought was stigmatized as blasphemy against the nation. Evidently, if an ally were to be sought, the only acceptable candidate was the Moslem state of Persia. Reshid gave short shrift to this notion by pointing out that the Persians were definitely not inclined towards the Ottoman side. Despite some objections, Reshid did analyze the Porte's relations with Europe, and although his conclusions were ambiguous, he held out tentative hope that the neutral powers were less firmly set against a Russo-Turkish war than before; he assured the council that he was working to solidify support. Despite the scorn of many *hocas,*[67] it seems likely that Reshid and other Westernized ministers scrutinized the situation closely; indeed, Schlechta suggested that the Turks hoped that in taking drastic measures they could force the European powers to adopt a more vigorously anti-Russian stand on the basis of their particular concerns.[68] Some Turks were forcing the pace in an attempt to win commitments abroad. In fact, there was reason to trust that they would not have to fight alone, and for the historian considerable interest attaches to the proceedings of the Austrian, British, and French emissaries in the Ottoman capital. It is now possible to reconstruct these dialogues with a fair degree of accuracy.

Austrian policy had been a matter of doubt to the Porte throughout the summer, but by this time the Turks probably felt reassured. Since the crisis over Serbia in August, the Austrian government had worked to smooth away some of the irritants in Austro-Turkish relations that, though they looked insignificant from Vienna, might loom fairly large in Constantinople. The fact of the Olmütz meeting between Franz Joseph and Nicholas, held September 26–28, was known in Constantinople, but as yet there was no information as to the content of the discussions.[69] But the anxieties that such a rendezvous at such a time might be expected to awaken were doubtless mitigated for the Porte by Buol's telegram concerning the amendments to the Vienna Note, which hinted that the Olmütz meeting would be dedicated to renewed search for a diplomatic solution.[70] In fact, the Olmütz meeting was to prove a failure. Nicholas apparently grasped the likelihood that he had involved Russia in a general war without firm pledges of support from anyone. Although he was not willing to accept the Turkish amendments, which would have been a gross humiliation at this stage, he did reject the "violent interpretation" and suggested that the four neutral great powers guarantee Russian good faith.[71] He did however try to interest Franz Joseph in an alliance, much as the Turks had feared, through wildly generous terms: if the Ottoman Empire were partitioned, Austria would receive the western sections of the Balkans and might even participate with Russia in a protectorate over Moldavia and Walachia. But all these proposals proved abortive. Franz Joseph was not impressed with the prospect of adding Balkan problems to the domestic difficulties of the Hapsburg empire.[72] Although Napoleon was somewhat interested in the tsar's proposals for a diplomatic solution,[73] the British government was completely unwilling, in the aftermath of the "violent interpretation," to have anything more to do with any formula based on the Vienna Note.[74] And in any case, the Porte had turned down an arrangement along similar lines contained in the notes of the great-power representatives.

At the Porte, Austrian plans were really less important than French and British. As early as 1919, Bernadotte Schmitt would speculate that the Porte was "confident" of French and British aid in case of need.[75] Suspicion has inevitably centered around Lord Stratford and his close relationship with Reshid, but the documents now available suggest that neither the French government nor Lord Stratford was responsible for Ottoman faith in such support. Veli Pasha reported from Paris that the French government was displeased by the recent turn of Ottoman policy and intended to leave the Ottoman Empire to its lethal obstinacy. When this report reached Reshid, he questioned de la Cour on the subject with great care on two separate occasions. De la Cour was cautious in his replies but felt that he was not making much of an impression. He blamed Lord Stratford, whom he suspected of giving a different evaluation.[76]

In fact, Stratford claimed to be behaving most discreetly. When he learned of the council's strong inclination towards war at the September 25 meeting, he immediately visited Reshid on the morning of the 26th and stayed with him until he went to the meeting. Stratford, according to his own story, emphasized that the Porte must not have "confidence" in "active cooperation from without" and he painted a gloomy picture of the adequacy of the Empire's military preparations and resources should it be necessary to fight alone.[77] In fact, Stratford's expressed bellicosity was lagging behind that of his colleagues in London, for on September 23, Clarendon declared that, though Britain would regret a Turkish declaration of war, the British government could not counsel the Porte to act against its own "interests" even if that involved military action against Russian presence in the Danubian Principalities before the onset of winter.[78] Musurus, the Ottoman ambassador in London, was exposed to this more favorable climate. Possibly decisive to the Porte's conclusions was a letter written by Musurus on September 7, in which he reported a highly interesting conversation with Lord Palmerston. Musurus, in a conscious attempt to flatter Palmerston, told his lordship that the Porte was counting on his aid with the British Cabinet. He even showed Palmerston a letter from Reshid in this vein. Musurus continued: "His Lordship was very conscious of the confident appeal of Your Highness to his friendship, and authorized me to give Your Highness on his part the assurance of an aid all the more efficacious because the present Cabinet counts in its numbers influential members, equally devoted to the cause of the Ottoman Empire, such as Lord John Russell, Lord Lansdowne, Lord Clarendon, and others." Palmerston's remarks continued along lines that could not fail to gratify Musurus. The powers should have shown the Vienna Note to the Porte before it was submitted to Russia; Pam hinted that the British had wished to do so, while the French had objected. Palmerston declared that he believed the Ottoman amendments were justified and judged that, if the tsar refused to accept them, he would lose credit with international opinion. Palmerston denied that the Russian government should have a right of intercession on behalf of the Greek Orthodox millet but conceded that the Russians were within their rights in invading Moldavia and Walachia; he argued, however, that the Turks, in turn, had the right to go to war on the pretext of the occupation. Musurus now brought the conversation around to the Egyptian crisis of 1839–41; he felt that Palmerston seemed to favor the idea, emphasized by Reshid, of some more extensive guarantee, modeled after that allegedly contained in the preamble of the Straits Convention of 1841. In any event, Palmerston promised "his support and his concurrence, insofar as circumstances may lend themselves to it." Though, as Musurus noted, Palmerston was not foreign secretary, these assurances, and the many expressions of friendliness with which the discussion closed, could hardly fail to have a heady effect in Constantinople.[79]

There is some evidence that the hope of support from Britain was an important factor in bringing the Porte to the long-contemplated decision on war.[80] Other considerations pointed in the same direction: the fear of revolution and the belief that acquiescence in a Russian protectorate over the Greek Orthodox millet would make the existence of the Ottoman regime untenable.[81] Although the "violent interpretation" was not known in Constantinople until October,[82] the Turks had already guessed its substance. They had believed to begin with that the Vienna Note really assured the Russian protectorate. Now the tsar's objection to changes designed to prevent such a construction of the note seemed to confirm their original intuition.[83]

Other motives for the decision on war included bitterness over the ambiguous stand of Britain and France, patriotic pride, and a serious overrating of Ottoman military capacities—plus the wish to gain something from the effort of mobilization.[84] One has the feeling that, by September 26, nothing less than the tsar's full acceptance of the amendments—and probably not even that—would have sufficed to preclude a Turkish declaration of war. The *Meclis-i umumî* concluded that "accepting these proposals would be like drinking deadly poison and simply dying": whatever the outcome, it was more honorable to die in battle than standing still.[85] The natural intransigence of many Ottomans had been rendered widely persuasive by European clumsiness. Dislike of the Christians' position was very deep in many sectors of the Moslem public. The cavalier treatment accorded Ottoman proposals and the feeling in the West that the Porte should wait on the convenience of Britain and France had further embittered many members of the ruling elite. Some felt that an independent stand by the Porte was the only acceptable course. Others, more calculating, were ready to move at the slightest indication of support from the West.

Once the decision on war was taken, the Porte moved very rapidly to implement the details. On September 29, Abdul-Mejid issued a *hatt-ı hümayun* (imperial order) accepting the council's recommendation for war.[86] On the same day, the Council of Ministers met to consider new levies for the army[87] and the possibility of a foreign loan.[88] On October 4, the manifesto containing the declaration of war appeared.[89] Six months of the diplomats' best efforts had served to define the deep gulf between the Russian and Ottoman positions, rather than to bridge it.

Chapter V

War Begins

ON OCTOBER 4, 1853, the Porte's manifesto declared war on Russia. On October 6 Omer Pasha summoned Gorchakov to evacuate the Danubian Principalities within fifteen days or face "hostilities."[1] Although many factors were weighed at the decisive Council meeting and such considerations as the dispositions of the great powers (especially Britain and France), the morale of the army, and the need to get some benefits from a costly mobilization were brought out, it is impossible not to see the unanimous vote as the response by the members, some frightened and some delighted, to rising popular agitation. Recent studies of Ottoman society in the mid-nineteenth century give interesting perspectives on this and similar outbreaks in the fifties and the early sixties. In light of this work, we must recognize that the movement was much more broadly based and much more closely related to structural stresses within Ottoman society than we might gather from Temperley's colorful portrayals of leering fanatics. Only exceptionally rapid diplomatic footwork could have staved off a recourse to war. Such diplomatic action was impossible in the international disarray evident when the publication of the Turkish amendments and of the Russian "violent interpretation" indicated how far apart the two sides really were. The diplomats at Constantinople did their best to find some way of reviving the Vienna Note through great-power guarantees, so as to maintain the idea of negotiation as a credible alternative to the Porte. But the Vienna Note had aroused such distrust by this time that, as Stratford apparently recognized, too much insistence was likely to alienate the Turks further without winning any useful result. This did not mean, however, that the diplomatic game was over. It was already late in the season. Nicholas—witness his overtures at Olmütz—was apparently turning away from a war policy. There seemed to be a good hope that, if only the Turks could be restrained, the war might be kept on a "phony" basis until winter gave the diplomats a second chance to reach a solution. In October, there was pretty general agreement on this approach in Europe—where Buol sponsored efforts to find a new formula—and in Russia, where Nesselrode was particularly hopeful.[2] That these plans came to nothing was again the result of the activities

of the Ottoman government. The pressures that had led to the declaration of war continued, in modified form, as pressures for its vigorous
prosecution. The military, diplomatic, financial, and domestic situation
of the Ottoman Empire, which we must now examine, seemed favorable
enough for the risks of an aggressive policy. And once a few engagements had taken place, it was difficult for the Russians to stay quiet,
especially as the first skirmishes were Turkish victories. By the beginning of December, the Russo-Turkish war was a reality.

A survey of the Porte's situation at the beginning of October shows
some grounds for hope. One of the Porte's first concerns was to try
to pin down British and French aid. Early in October, Reshid again
approached Stratford and de la Cour with a request for the approach
of the fleets. A formal demand followed on October 8; in this Reshid
limited himself to asking that some more of the combined fleet should
enter the Dardanelles. Meanwhile, Reshid had already instructed
Musurus to ask Clarendon for Britain's armed support.[3] Veli Pasha in
Paris apparently had similar orders.[4] Reshid talked to Stratford and
de la Cour about a naval agreement. De la Cour was very much opposed to this, though Stratford's reaction was more favorable; but
Stratford was outweighed by Clarendon, who regarded the terms of
the proposal as highly unusual.[5]

But although the Turks did not at once get what they requested,
they were not entirely rejected. Stratford had received the command
from London to call up the British squadron on October 4, but he put
off the step. Probably his main reasons were the fear of encouraging
the Turks by seeming to commit Britain to their cause and the hope
that something might yet come of the Olmütz meeting.[6] He also adduced the legal argument that, as long as hostilities had not actually
begun, the Porte was not technically at war and the Straits were theoretically closed to warships.[7] But de la Cour was receiving pressing
orders from home[8] and finally undermined Stratford by telling Reshid
that he was prepared to bring up the French fleet alone.[9] The collapse
of the Olmütz proposals was known by October 15, and Stratford
agreed "in principle" to the transfer. Even so, it was October 20 before
he sent word to Dundas and October 22 before Dundas was able to act
on the instructions.[10] And even then only part of the fleets was moved;
as we shall see, some ships remained outside the Dardanelles until well
into November.

Puryear has argued that all this maneuvering was irrelevant. The
ships brought up in September were sufficient to secure Constantinople
against Russian attack, and the disposition of the rest could be decided according to other criteria.[11] But the number of ships at Con-

stantinople was reduced immediately after the danger of revolution seemed to have passed.[12] And, as has been shown above, the motive in moving the ships had been to create an effect on opinion in the Ottoman capital rather than an effect on the Russians. Stratford seems to have been doing his best to exercise a restraining influence on the Turks, in accord with his announced policy of keeping the war phony.

Reshid himself, though unwavering in his search for a commitment from Britain and France, was not inflexible on the station of the fleets. He eventually concurred in Stratford's desire to keep a part of the fleets outside the Bosporus and opposed de le Cour's idea of uniting them. Apparently his motives sprang from qualms similar to those he had felt in September: he feared that some ministers might oppose the presence of the fleets and that doubts might arise as to whether their purpose was supportive or comminatory.[13] A further difficulty probably influenced him as well: he wanted the Turkish squadron to join with the British and the French, an arrangement that would certainly be more acceptable to Ottoman pride; but in this case, there would be too many ships for the Bosporus, and it would be necessary to divide the forces, perhaps even leaving some in the Mediterranean. Reshid suggested a convention to regulate naval cooperation, a device that, incidentally, would insure the maximum of commitment from the Western powers with the minimum of physical pressure. Reshid was fairly frank in his explanations of Ottoman war aims as he saw them. He wrote de la Cour and Stratford on October 19:

> The unique object of the Sublime Porte, the salutary aim that she entertains, is to come to the end of this war completely protected from any exterior anxiety, in order to busy herself solely with interior regulations to assure the well-being of the Empire by the perfecting of her progressive system of administration, by the just amelioration of the condition of all classes of her subjects, and by the development of her commerce and industry without any impediment; and as we have obviously just seen that the treaty of the year 1841 doesn't suffice to give her security in the foreign quarter, the Sublime Porte believes it her duty to submit, as of now, to her allies, the necessity of making another treaty to serve as a complement to that one.[14]

In addition to the guarantee in international law, Reshid suggested that Russia and the Ottoman Empire be separated, in the future, by a series of autonomous buffer regions: these would be Serbia, Moldavia, and Walachia in the west and Circassia and Dagestan in the east.[15] The program was an ambitious one: although Serbia, Moldavia, and Walachia had functioned essentially as buffers for some twenty-five years (longer in the case of Serbia), Circassia and Dagestan had been for-

mally ceded to Russia in 1829. The Porte would be conceding little
in the west (or would even gain there if Moldavia and Walachia became genuinely autonomous) and would be rolling back Russian power
in the east. Indeed, Clarendon, when he heard of the proposal, was in-
credulous: he spluttered: "All this is very wild and founded upon convictions of great military triumphs & complete Russian humiliation,
very desirable both of them certainly if they can be achieved, but in the
mean while selling one's chickens before they are hatched & requiring
that they shd be paid for is not the best way to do business or inspire
confidence."[16]

Clearly, all these plans went far beyond the decisions made in London
and Paris in response to the original Ottoman request for formally
pledged assistance. In this case, as in the ambassadors' decision
about the fleets, it is evident that the British especially were trying to
set limits to their role, in order to prevent escalation of the conflict.
At the same time, however, both parties felt an obligation to "honor"
their commitments that led them into steps that to the Turks were encouraging—if only moderately so.

From Paris, Veli Pasha reported a moderately heartening response to
Turkish proposals. Officially, the French government rested on the
naval support afforded by the presence of the fleet. Veli's request for
the loan of French officers to the Ottoman army was refused, although
Veli was allowed to consider this a delay rather than an outright rejection.[17] Drouyn emphasized that the French government still hoped for
a negotiated solution. Apparently, however, Veli had received secret
information indicating that the French and British would send troops
to defend European Turkey if the Russians broke Omer Pasha's line
on the Danube;[18] but if Veli sent a report containing such information,[19]
it was misleading, for as late as November Napoleon had done nothing
to build up France's military strength. Nonetheless, the fantasy of
frantic French preparations was widely held.[20]

From Vienna, Arif Efendi described a relatively friendly talk with
Buol, in which the Austrian foreign minister approved Ottoman policy
and promised to observe complete impartiality. Buol did take the occasion to urge Arif to transfer any Hungarian refugees serving in the
Ottoman army away from the Danube frontier.[21] But despite this
point, which was also taken up by Bruck in Constantinople, Reshid
seemed considerably reassured about Austrian intentions.[22]

More important than Austrian or French plans was British policy.
Opinion in Britain was becoming increasingly polarized. A series of
mass meetings in October, and on into the winter, favored the Turkish

cause; other groups, notably the Peace Society in its Edinburgh meeting under the influence of Cobden and Bright, condemned the recourse to war.[23] The split in the country was beginning to affect the Cabinet as well: Palmerston and Russell supported the Ottoman Empire, while Clarendon spoke of "the beastly Turks" and Aberdeen chimed in, "their whole system is radically vicious and abominable." Nevertheless, Aberdeen admitted the proposition that the maintenance of the Ottoman Empire was "a . . . necessity" for the European balance of power,[24] albeit a distasteful one. In phrases that curiously foreshadow Neville Chamberlain, some eighty-odd years later, he wrote to Princess Lieven: "The relations of England and Russia are so unexpected, so incredible, and indeed so unintelligible, as to make it very difficult to form any clear notion of what they really are."[25] There was, in some quarters in the British government, a suspicion that the Turkish tail was wagging the British lion.[26] Any positive steps taken in response to the Ottoman plea for aid were bound to deepen the ambiguities and the dangers of the relationship; but a strong party in the Cabinet believed that Britain must increase her support of the Empire during a period so dangerous for the Porte.

These conflicts surfaced at a Cabinet meeting held on October 4. The French and British fleets had already been ordered to Constantinople, though—due to slow communications and Stratford's dilatoriness—they were not to anchor in the Bosporus for some weeks. Nonetheless, the Cabinet faced the question, What would the fleets do once they were at Constantinople? Lord John Russell wanted to send ships immediately into the Black Sea—not so much to forestall Russian attack as to discourage the Turks from any outbreaks against the Christians. Palmerston wanted to go ahead with a naval convention with the Porte, which would lay down the terms for cooperation and would permit British subjects to enroll in the Turkish "forces." As part of the combined action, Palmerston suggested immediate entry into the Black Sea and detention of any Russian vessels met in those waters. Aberdeen, reduced to consternation, put all his energies into combatting the idea of action in the Black Sea.[27] In this, he was supported by the opinion of Brunnov, the Russian ambassador, that the Russian government would consider any such action as equivalent to a "declaration of war."[28] The upshot was a compromise. The fleet would remain within the Straits unless "the Russian fleet were to come out of Sevastopol" or unless it was a matter of "defending the Turkish territory against direct aggression." Stratford was to instruct Dundas to notify the Russian command at Sevastopol of these conditions.[29]

This half measure had a harmful effect everywhere. Britain's attempt to set limits to Russian maneuvers on the high seas enraged Nicholas and incited him to tell Menshikov, now commander at Sevastopol, to act as vigorously as would be possible this late in the season. And Saint Petersburg formally gave notice that Russia could never accept such conditions unless Britain were legally at war. Yet Clarendon, consoling himself that, though the Russians had complained, it was "apparently not with anger," still seemed to believe that entry into the Black Sea, under the right circumstances, might not provoke reprisals.[30] The correspondence ended with each side confident that the other had been scared off. But the Turks were not likely to let matters rest with the fleets in the Bosporus. All through November, there was pressure from the Porte to undertake action, on one pretext or another, in the Black Sea. Queen Victoria summarized Britain's false position very shrewdly:

> As matters have now been arranged, it appears to the Queen, moreover, that we have taken on ourselves in conjunction with France all the risks of a European war without having bound Turkey to any conditions with respect to provoking it. The hundred and twenty fanatical Turks constituting the Divan at Constantinople are left sole judges of the line of policy to be pursued, and made cognisant at the same time of the fact that England and France have bound themselves to defend the Turkish Territory! This is entrusting them with a power which Parliament has been jealous to confide even to the hands of the British Crown.[31]

Clarendon agreed: "The Supreme Council inspires me with supreme distrust," and, unwittingly showing his bias, he had confided to Stratford, "I can't help saying that the tone in wh [*sic*] Rechid replies to your advice is somewhat new & by no means as deferential as it ought to be to one who understands the true interests of Turkey *quite as well* as the Supreme Council. If I am wrong in this pray correct me as I don't want to do injustice to Rechid."[32]

To make matters worse, even the French—who, according to the British view, were to join in the action in the Black Sea—were less than enthusiastic. In a conversation with Cowley early in October, Drouyn de Lhuys made it plain that France was chiefly worried about the defense of Varna and Burgas, as part of the overall plan to block a Russian move against Constantinople; extension of the mission to the eastern waters of the Black Sea did not figure in these calculations. In a confidential communication to de la Cour, Drouyn revealed a suspicion that the British might force the French into protection of British interests in the whole sensitive band from the Caucasus east to Khiva—scene of a recent Russian expedition. The British government—constantly preoccupied with supposed threats to India—might try to use support of the Ottoman Empire to their advantage, and discourage the Russians in that area as well. But to such an enterprise Drouyn's response was categorical; it was not something in which the French should participate.[33]

Perhaps Drouyn was influenced by the French tendency to sympathize with Russian efforts to pacify the Caucasus, an enterprise often compared in France to the *mission civilisatrice* in Algeria;[34] this attitude contrasts sharply with British glamorization of the brave mountaineers of the Caucasus.[35] In any event, Drouyn's instructions about the use of the fleet, although uniformly unclear, decidedly discouraged action in the Black Sea, especially in the eastern part. Since the British were simultaneously ordered to act in conjunction with the French,[36] a fertile field for disagreement was opened.

It is important to dwell at some length on these discussions concerning the conditions of Franco-British aid to the Porte, because they had a large influence on the war. The Turks had set their sights on unrestricted Western aid through some kind of convention or alliance. This they were not able to get. In the hope that the war could be kept "phony" until winter permitted a negotiated solution, the French and British governments limited their aid to the minimum believed suitable with the previous encouragement to the Ottoman Empire and the dangers presented by Russia's military superiority. And disagreements over action in the Black Sea made it unlikely that even this aid could be utilized to the full extent envisioned in London. All this was disappointing for the Porte. But at the same time, the Ottoman government was given a weapon. If the fighting involved an attack on Ottoman territory, Britain—and probably France too—would be obligated to participate, and the result could hardly fail to be the full alliance that the Turks had sought. As Victoria recognized, the Turks were placed in a very strong position. A predicament inherent in great-power commitments to client states was, in this case, enhanced by the sloppiness of the arrangement—a sloppiness designed to plaster over disagreements in London and Paris, but ill suited to realities on the Bosporus.

The encouragement to action built into the terms of Anglo-French aid was confirmed by the view the Porte took in October of the Empire's financial, military, and domestic readiness for war. It is probably true (as Kovalevsky states), that financially the Ottoman Empire had never been in worse shape at the start of a war with Russia. Desperate expedients—such as collecting certain taxes in advance, demanding special contributions,[37] requisitioning goods and services, and printing a new issue of paper money—were no more than stopgap measures to

improve the state of the treasury.[38] Reshid, Mustafa Nâilî, and other
top officials offered a patriotic gift of horses from their own stables for
the artillery.[39] A leading financial expert, Musa Saffetî Pasha, was
chosen as finance minister to preside over the chaos.[40] What was
needed was a new approach to Ottoman governmental financing, and
this at last seemed possible. After much discussion, the Sultan had
agreed that the Porte should seek a foreign loan.[41] While recent, unsuccessful projects had been designed to strengthen Ottoman currency
through a loan that would permit the Porte to retire some of the *kaimes,*
or paper money,[42] the present plan was to borrow money, to the sum of
fifty million francs, to take care of current extraordinary expenses. The
loan would be negotiated by a special emissary, who would be sent to
Paris and London.[43] Preparations at first pushed forward rapidly:
Namık Pasha was chosen as envoy, and Stratford provided an intro-
ductory letter, dated November 5.[44] By early December, Namık had
reached Paris, and though contradictory rumors flew, the negotiations
seemed to be going well.[45] Later, however, problems arose: European
bankers were ready to make a loan for peacetime development, but
they did not want to underwrite the cost of a war without extensive
guarantees.[46] It was not until after France and Britain had formally
entered the war that the loan was finally arranged.[47]

Financial difficulties, of course, had a bearing on the military strength
of the Porte. De la Cour reported that due to the embarrassments of
the treasury, the soldiers were receiving one month's pay out of four.[48]
This was especially serious at a time when the Porte was planning to
raise the number of men under arms to three hundred thousand,[49]
which meant the recruitment of an additional seventy-five thousand
men.[50] Still, the war seemed to be very popular with the public, judging
by the enthusiasm of the volunteers, and a Russian authority judges
that the Turkish "army was ... better organized and better armed,
than ... earlier."[51] There was no doubt that the Russians could smash
the Ottoman army in open battle any time they chose. But the Russians
believed that the Turkish artillery was, at some points, superior to
theirs, and they were impressed by the line of fortresses along the
Danube frontier.[52]

Neither on the western front nor on the eastern, however, could the
Russo-Turkish war be viewed solely in terms of the two armies. On
both fronts, the dispositions of the populace played a considerable part.
The Porte entered the war determined to play down religious differences
and the divisions they might bring in their wake. Thus, the Porte's
manifesto carefully avoided anything that might be interpreted as a call
to religious war; in contrast, the Russian reply (which followed on

October 28) asked for "fervent prayers to the Most High, that his hand deign to bless our arms in the holy and just cause that has found at all times ardent defenders among our pious ancestors."[53]

Further evidence of the Porte's determination to emphasize the political and nonsectarian aspects of the struggle can be seen in other official documents. A proclamation of October 8 from the grand vizier to the inhabitants of the Ottoman capital explained the Council's decision on war and cautioned against any outbreaks of Moslem fanaticism with the words: "the life, the honor, and the property of the *râya* (non-Moslem subjects) must be as sacred as our own," and the official announcement of the beginning of the war given in the *Takvim-i Vekâyi* emphasized the unity of all the peoples of the Ottoman Empire in the face of the Russian threat.[54] Wide publicity was accorded the addresses given by the Christian millets to testify "their loyalty, gratitude, and devotion" at the start of the war;[55] during the winter, the full texts submitted by the Greek Orthodox, Armenian Catholic, Roman Catholic, and Protestant millets were published in the *Takvim-i Vekâyi*.[56] Though one must doubt the sincerity of such pro forma declarations, it is significant that the Porte tried so hard to capitalize on them.

The Porte was also able to make good use of a coincidental occurrence. At the end of September, the Greek Orthodox Patriarch, Germanos, died. Apparently, there was no question of foul play, as he succumbed to a spinal ailment that had been troubling him for some time. At this juncture, the Russians were not able to play a role in the choice of his successor;[57] rather, it was Stratford who recommended the only man who seemed to him suitable. Stratford's candidate, Anthimos, was duly elected, and at Stratford's suggestion, the formal ceremony of investiture, which had been in abeyance for over two hundred years, was revived in an effort to flatter the susceptibilities of the millet.[58]

But official gestures from Constantinople are obviously less important, though easier to observe, than the state of feeling in the provinces. A quick survey of the Balkans suggests room for anxiety everywhere, but disaster certain nowhere. Among the most agitated regions were Thessaly and Epirus, both bordering on Greece. When the regular army was removed from these provinces, they were turned over to the bashi-bazouks (Moslem irregulars), and incidents between the latter and the pro-Greek sympathizers—or even the *pallikares* (freedom fighters) from Greece—were inevitable. The Greek government now reinforced its detachments on the frontiers[59] and reorganized the command in such a way as to bring prominent nationalists to the fore.[60] Fervent propaganda was circulated, through the new journal, *Spectateur de l'Orient;* through the *Aion,* which expressed the views of pro-Russian elements;[61] and through pamphlets that were sent over the border.[62] The Greek government asked for a public loan, ostensibly "to intensify the cultivation of cereals." Serious efforts were made to interest the European powers. The Greek Committees were in full flower; delegations went to Europe, especially to the German states, to ask money and weapons; the Greek queen made a visit to Oldenburg. The Bavarian government, not unnaturally, sympathized with King Otto of Greece, a Bavarian prince by origin; the Greeks found it easy to believe that Austria and Prussia would support them too.[63] Although France and Britain were clearly opposed to Greek ambitions, King Otto thought that they would not be able to bring an effective force to bear on Greece, given their involvement against Russia; and he was convinced that, unless the Greek provinces rose before some kind of settlement was negotiated between Russia and Turkey, the Greeks would come away empty-handed.[64] Certainly this situation was one of the most menacing faced by the Porte.

Farther to the north, there were other signs of unrest. Stratford had been exercised during the summer by conditions in the Albanian countryside. The son of Meyendorff (the Russian ambassador at Vienna) had made a disquieting visit to Montenegro. (Actually, his visit to Prince Danilo had been directed towards calming the Prince's ambitions.)[65] A group of Bulgarians sent the tsar a petition declaring that Ottoman rule was "intolerable" and asking his "protection."[66] But all these circumstances were more or less endemic. It was the state of Serbia that was crucial. The approach of war forced the revolutionaries, who had been debating fruitlessly on combined action since 1848, to submerge their differences. In the fall of 1853, conversations in London and Constantinople brought agreement on a plan for a confederation of Rumania, Serbia, and Hungary. Each national group would be given local autonomy for internal matters, but the regions would be united by a single administration for military affairs and foreign policy. The project was significant as the first occasion on which Kossuth brought himself to agree on a formula that implied the loosening of Magyar control over Croatia and Transylvania. But it depended on a Hungarian revolution, which could succeed—if at all—only in the event of Austrian participation in the war.[67]

Austria's role was also basic to another attempt to persuade Serbia to an active policy. In the middle of October, a Russian emissary, Muchin, arrived in Belgrade. His mission had not been cleared with the Porte,[68] and quickly aroused the distrust of the French and British consuls. After a stay of some weeks, he was told to leave.[69] Reports to

Constantinople from Ottoman authorities in Belgrade asserted that the Serbs were basically well-disposed towards the Empire, but proposed that the Porte attempt to conciliate them by confirmation of their privileges.[70]

Doubtless basic to the Serbs' good intentions was the stand of the Austrian government. The observation corps mustered on the Transylvanian border and around Vidin was maintained and even strengthened by the addition of artillery.[71] And Vienna was to make it perfectly plain that the prerequisite for obtaining any aid from Austria, such as arms, was absolute neutrality towards both Russia and the Ottoman Empire.[72] The Austrian attitude, in turn, forced a modification of Russian policy. Nicholas decided to test Austrian intentions by requesting permission to send ten thousand guns across Austrian territory into Serbia. This was judged such a hot issue by Meyendorff that he did not even want to present it to the Austrian government. He suggested, instead, that the Russians should build up their strength in Little Walachia, across the Danube from Serbia. It would then be possible to send supplies directly.[73]

Russian intentions of sending troops into Serbia were reported to the Porte from Belgrade.[74] Developments in this quarter dictated important changes in the Ottoman command's strategy for the Danube front. The obvious and basic plan was to hold the line of the Danube fortresses, in the hope of preventing an advance towards Constantinople. But Omer Pasha was now tempted by the situation in Little Walachia. The Russians were less strongly entrenched there than in other parts of the Danubian Principalities. In fact, Paskevich's original plan had called for a short line of one hundred versts on the Danube between Bucharest and Hîrşova. Little Walachia would not be occupied at all, and the main effort would be concentrated on the campaign towards Constantinople through Sofia.[75] But there were objections to this blueprint. First, though Paskevich tried to combine it with cooperation with the Christians, it was obviously not so well designed for that purpose as a more westerly route. Second, it would pit the Russians against major fortresses such as Varna. Although Paskevich argued that Varna could be taken by land, this was doubtful. And a combined land-and-sea attack would risk intervention by the French and British fleets.[76] As Nicholas continued to harp on the idea of a Christian uprising,[77] and as the British and French became more deeply involved, a campaign through the central Balkans seemed more and more attractive, and the failure to occupy Little Walachia, ill-advised. As early as the beginning of October, troops were sent west to make good Russian control in that area.[78]

It was not hard to figure out Russian intentions at Constantinople.[79] Omer Pasha and other Turkish leaders believed that the Russians would strike at Vidin towards Serbia; once they had joined forces with the Serbs, they could move south over the Niš-Sofia road, to link their efforts with those of the discontented Greeks of the border provinces and with the Greek government. With so much unrest, the Bulgarians would almost certainly revolt also, since there had been trouble there as recently as 1850; and the result would be a general Balkan conflagration at the expense of the Ottoman regime.[80] To forestall this danger, Omer wanted to attack the Russians first, in their positions in Little Walachia.[81] Apparently, he had hopes of going on to a successful campaign to drive the Russians out of the Danubian Principalities.

In fact, there was considerable unrest in Moldavia and Walachia. As hostilities started and relations with the Porte deteriorated, the hospodars decided to follow instructions already received from the Porte and withdraw.[82] General Budberg was appointed commissar and plenipotentiary extraordinary to rule the two provinces under the general "direction" of the Russian army commander, Gorchakov.[83] Thanks to the acquired expertise of the Russian consuls at Bucharest and Jassy, Budberg's regime worked well.[84] But there were some built-in problems. One was the question of payment for the goods and services exacted by the occupation forces. In 1848, the Russian army had estranged public opinion in the Danubian Principalities by forcing the Moldavians and Walachians to pay the costs of occupation. Naturally, the sum was not immediately obtainable, and it remained as a debt owing to the Russian government. In 1853, the Russians made a great point of paying for what they received; but as Seymour pointed out, the claim was deceptive. The payment was made in bills or *bons,* paper notes that were to be subtracted from the total owed to Russia.[85] What was lacking was hard cash in the pocket of the Rumanian merchant or farmer.

Another difficulty also went back to 1848. At that time, the Russians had intervened to stamp out revolutionary disturbances. The Turks, whose policy towards the revolution had been somewhat more equivocal, had emerged with a better image. Many Walachians, who had fled from the Russians across the Danube, were now able to give the Turks superior intelligence about their native region.[86] This also opened the possibility of organizing fifth columns within the Principalities.[87] Indeed, Gorchakov was obliged to deal firmly with dissidence in Bucharest.[88] This unrest might have facilitated a drive into Walachia, such as Omer Pasha advocated. But that plan carried many dangers, as was recognized by the Ottoman council. If the Russian army were superior in the field, it would be safer to make a stand on the line of the Danube forts and to avoid pitched battles, even if conditions seemed relatively favorable.[89]

Despite the hopes of Omer Pasha and Mehmet Ali Pasha, there was general agreement at the Porte on the principle of resting on the defensive on the Danube and concentrating offensive operations on the eastern frontier, where the advantage seemed definitely to lie with the Turks.[90] In part, this was a matter of geography. The remote mountains of eastern Turkey were not very important to the Ottoman Empire as a whole. As General-Adjutant Berg pointed out early in the war, the most fantastic Russian successes—the capture of the fortresses of Kars, Ardahan, Erzurum, Bayezit, Van, Muş and Sivas—would hardly affect the regime in Constantinople. On the other hand, if the situation were reversed, Turkish successes might bring Persia into the war and raise the mountaineers of the Caucasus, and Russian rule might crumble.[91] The Caucasus had not been long under Russian rule; the southernmost strip had been acquired as recently as 1829, and it was far from pacified. Russian rule meant greater centralization under the direction of Vorontsov, the military governor; the mountain tribes looked back with nostalgia to the days of virtual autonomy under Ottoman power. Indeed, many of them were to flee eventually into Anatolia. In leaders such as Sheikh Shamil, the mountaineers found attractive and wily commanders, who were able to prolong the guerilla conflict for many years. The Russians were seriously worried about military prospects in this area, especially as it was believed in Saint Petersburg that both the Turks[92] and the British[93] had been stirring up trouble. In fact, these fears were not to be realized; impressive numbers of the inhabitants actually fought as irregular troops cooperating with the Russian army.[94]

In addition to the geographical conditions that favored the Turks, certain circumstances added to their advantage at the beginning of the autumn. Paskevich's plans had concentrated on the occupation of the Danubian Principalities and on the Danube front. At the beginning of September, the Caucasus was not adequately defended. The problem was whether it would be possible to transport adequate reinforcements across the Black Sea before French and British naval activities interfered with that process. In fact, the maneuver was successfully carried out—and Western opposition was largely imaginary. But the Russians felt more confident after the thirteenth division had been brought to Anaklia, before the Ottoman declaration of war.[95] Although the immediate danger was over, however, the Caucasus remained an obvious target for the Turks and a sensitive point for the Russians.

Implied in the preceding résumé is the observation that, as of

October 1853, the Turks and Britain and France had substantially different aims. While, in the interests of further negotiations, the great powers wished to prevent shooting, the Porte had good reasons to begin the fighting. It was believed that important gains were possible on the eastern frontier. Omer Pasha was eager to safeguard, at the very least, the Ottoman position in the strategic area around Vidin. And the conditions laid down by Britain and France for their help made it seem likely that extended hostilities were the best means of bringing them into the war. As the fifteen-day term for the evacuation of the Principalities ran out, the British tried to get a further abstention from fighting for a reasonable time, freely translated by Stratford as meaning to "the end of the month." The *Meclis-i umumî* considered Stratford's proposal in a thirteen-hour meeting, from five in the afternoon until six in the morning of October 21 and adopted it, despite the likelihood of great popular opposition. Reshid, however, had asked Stratford what would happen if the fighting had already started.[96] Reshid's own orders to Omer to begin fighting had already gone out, on the 18th or the 19th, and we may surmise that the council fully expected that it would prove too late to countermand the decision. This, in fact, was the case: the new instructions arrived at Varna on the 22nd, but could not be brought to Omer's headquarters at Şumla until very late that day, after Omer had authorized an attack over the Danube at dawn on the 23rd on Tutrakan.[97] Even before this, hostilities had begun on the eastern frontier, with the Turkish capture of the fort at Saint Nicholas.[98] This was the first Turkish success of the war and a psychological blow to the Russians, who identified the fort with Saint Nicholas's namesake, the tsar.[99]

Omer moved quickly to safeguard the critical Bulgarian border area around Vidin and to prevent a Russian breakthrough towards Serbia. In mid-October, he had ordered the occupation of an island in the Danube between Vidin and Calafat. Then, on October 27, he dispatched ten thousand troops across the river against Calafat itself. The operation was successful in the sense that the Ottoman forces remained in possession of the town, but they were not able to extend that foothold further into the countryside.[100]

On November 4 a more important engagement took place at Olteniţa.[101] The Russian troops under Paulus had received confusing orders: on September 30 / October 12, Dannenberg—pursuing the policy of avoiding serious hostilities—had commanded that, if Turkish troops crossed the Danube, the Russians were not to fight but were to contain the Turks and to keep them from moving inland. When a substantial body of Turks crossed the river on November 1 and occupied the quarantine house at Olteniţa, Paulus felt obliged to communicate with Dannenberg and to ask for further instructions. Time was lost through a misunderstanding concerning the size of the force involved. When the Russians finally received the order to advance, the Turks were well entrenched.[102] The Russians went forward under heavy fire—they left 970 dead or wounded, at a conservative estimate[103]—but they seemed, despite their losses, to be succeeding and to be on the point of storming the quarantine house when the order to retreat was given. Much controversy surrounds this decision. Supposedly, the Russian command feared Turkish artillery dug in on the island and on the opposite bank of the Danube. But as Bogdanovich has pointed out, this danger was one that must have been foreseen, and if it were really serious, it should have prevented the whole attack. Bogdanovich blames Gorchakov for not sending reinforcements; Tarle places the blame at an even higher level—criticizing the strategy of a light concentration in Little Walachia, insufficient to hold the balance against superior Turkish artillery on the right bank.[104] Nonetheless, the Turks had been so discouraged that they now withdrew. This did mean renunciation of Omer Pasha's hopes for an offensive operation against Bucharest.[105]

Both sides claimed victory at Olteniţa. The Russians pointed out that their retirement had been voluntary and that the Turks had eventually been frightened into giving up their position. Still, Nicholas's comments on the handling of the battle were severe.[106] The Turks harped on the Russian retreat and heavy Russian casualties—one thousand dead and two thousand wounded, according to an official announcement.[107] The real significance of these engagements, mere skirmishes from the military point of view, lies in their psychological effects. The Russians' pride was pricked, and they felt that they could not accept a solution without somehow teaching the Turks a lesson first.[108] The Turks, on the other hand, came to entertain exaggerated hopes. Rumors flew after Olteniţa, and even reached Europe, that Omer Pasha was already at Bucharest.[109] And Slade tells of a quaint encounter in Constantinople. "A pasha inquired of the author if he thought the Turks would be allowed to march to St. Petersburg the following year? Certainly not, was the reply. He mused awhile, then said: 'I see how it is; Europe will not allow the Russians to come to Constantinople nor the Turks to go to St. Petersburg.'"[110]

News of the battles was particularly unfortunate for the cause of peace, because it came as the Porte was considering new plans of action and as the nonbelligerent powers were pushing new proposals for a diplomatic solution. The collapse of the Vienna Note negotiations in

September had dealt a blow to common European action for peace; during October and November, different efforts, only loosely related to each other, were going forward. When Western objections to the Olmütz proposals became clear, Buol contacted Nesselrode (October 6) with a suggestion for a new approach: the neutral powers would ask the Porte to send an emissary to Gorchakov's headquarters to negotiate peace, working on the basis of the Vienna Note. Nesselrode, although skeptical about the Porte's readiness to accept such a plan, put no obstacles in its path. On October 25, Buol laid the scheme before the Vienna conference. He felt obliged to modify it somewhat, in view of British and French qualms about bilateral negotiations between two such unequal parties. He enlarged upon the powers' communication to the Porte—which became a collective note based on the Porte's amendments as well as on the tsar's revelations at Olmütz. He also changed the place of the negotiations from Russian headquarters to Vienna, in order to ensure a preponderant role to the conference.[111] Britain and France proved slow to take up this initiative: privately Clarendon huffed: "Such a note as Buol has sent to Mr. Bruck for delivery to Reschid Pacha merely shews his utter ignorance of the state of things at Constant. & the feelings of the Turkish Govt & nation."[112] But Buol, alarmed by the outbreak of fighting, had instructed Bruck on November 11 to urge it on the Porte unilaterally. Not surprisingly, this overture was quite unsuccessful.[113]

No better result attended the concurrent efforts of Britain and France. At the end of September, Stratford had been busy with a project for a new draft note that the Porte would send to Saint Petersburg, on the model of the Vienna Note.[114] Largely in order to forestall a text from Stratford that would certainly not recommend itself to the tsar under present circumstances, Clarendon and the cabinet drew up a proposal.[115] Stratford was given the hint to prefer it to his own.[116] The Clarendon note was communicated to the French, who made some changes. Clarendon at first wished to see these as purely stylistic. The Ottoman ambassador, however, insisted on seeing both drafts and expressed a strong preference for the British formulation.[117] Musurus's objections were instrumental in persuading Clarendon to base his instructions to Stratford on his own draft, although Drouyn de Lhuys communicated the French version to de la Cour.[118] Musurus at first was loath to consider any proposals for negotiations. According to Lady Clarendon's account of her husband's trials, "Musurus, the Turkish minister, had found objections and difficulties in everything proposed; so much so that George said he would have discovered some danger in an invitation to dinner. At last George seems to have lost patience and told him that he was *digne représentant de son pays.*" Finally, after this fairly heavy pressure from Clarendon, Musurus in his report counseled acceptance of the British plan, as a necessary gesture to world, and especially British, public opinion.[119] He admitted that Russia stood to gain, and the Porte to lose, by immediate negotiations, and expressed the hope that, before the plan could be put into execution, the Ottoman army would have won a few victories in Moldavia and Walachia that would make it possible for the Turks to raise their terms to something more commensurate with their sacrifices. If this were not the case, Musurus counseled reliance on wily diplomacy.

The Sublime Porte will always know how to profit by that same desire of the Powers to preserve the peace. But, in any case, it is important for the Imperial Government to show itself, insofar as possible, consistent in Its policy of moderation, in order not to appear irrevocably resolved on war, a task that will be very easy, to judge by the line of conduct that the Sublime Porte has so skillfully followed since the beginning of this disagreement, as well as by all the diplomatic papers emerging from the pen of Your Highness, which have obtained universal approbation.[120]

Musurus did let Clarendon know that he felt the proposal was fairer to Russia than to the Porte,[121] and he stated the Ottoman war aim as "an end, once for all, to the encroachments of Russia and specially to any intervention on her part in the affairs of the Principalities." As Clarendon recognized, this went beyond the provisions of a simple note, to a "revision of treaties."[122]

Even the insincere acceptance counseled by Musurus did not find favor in Constantinople. Stratford wrote sadly that "Reshid is as hot on war as the most military of his colleagues," for, as Thouvenel noted shortly afterwards, "The little successes on the Danube and in Asia have turned everybody's head at Constantinople."[123] The combined fleets had been brought to the Bosporus, and Reshid had become far more popular with the public and with the Sultan. Basking in this new approval, he seemed ready to work with Mehmet Ali in the vigorous prosecution of the war policy.[124] To make matters worse for Stratford, de la Cour had received his recall, and although initially he had added his representations to Stratford's, he did not feel able to continue with the negotiation.[125]

When Stratford approached Reshid with the new text, he discovered that Reshid already knew of the démarche through Musurus's reports, and that the Council of Ministers had already expressed itself as "decidedly unfavourable." Nonetheless, Stratford and de la Cour formulated a list of reasons for acceptance, which they duly laid before

the Ottoman authorities.[126] Stratford also made individual representations and was so pressing that both de la Cour and his successor, Baraguay d'Hilliers, reported that Stratford had threatened British abandonment of the Porte if compliance were not forthcoming.[127] Reshid
told Stratford frankly that he would have been willing to accept the
plan a month earlier, but it was now too late. Reshid agreed to communicate Stratford's views to the Council of Ministers and even offered
to let Stratford address the Council personally, or to resign if Stratford
believed Reshid to blame for the refusal. But Stratford was still convinced that Reshid was Britain's best friend, and he recognized that his
personal appearance before the meeting "would only have the effect
of . . . rivetting their resistance." This judgment was doubtless accurate,
since too energetic sponsorship by Stratford would have increased the
sense of foreign pressure. So this overture fell through.[128]

Meanwhile, the Porte was contemplating a major military enterprise.
Since the middle of the summer, there had been reports of Russian
naval activities on the Black Sea, and the Turks, with Stratford's approval, had responded by sending out detachments of their own ships
from time to time.[129] In October, a fairly large cruise was organized, but
the commander, despite "a month's extra pay," slipped back into the
Bosporus "without orders two days before war commenced." The Turks
were discouraged by the special hazards of the Black Sea at that season:
storms, fogs, treacherous currents, and an inadequately marked coast-
line. Nonetheless, they were determined "for the point of honour" to
maintain at least a token force in the Black Sea, and promptly sent out
a "light squadron of frigates and corvettes."[130] Meanwhile General-
Adjutant Kornilov had set out from Sevastopol, scouting for Turkish
vessels.[131] When news of the presence of a sizable Russian force arrived
at Constantinople, the Kaptan Pasha ordered a larger frigate, the
Nuzretieh—with Slade (who held the rank of admiral) aboard—to reinforce them. Slade's description of the ensuing voyage is a study in the
hardships faced by an inadequately equipped navy during winter conditions. No sooner had they put out than the officers ordered gratings
fitted over the hatchways, so that the men would stay on deck even if
they encountered danger. The weather was abysmal; on November 11
"several inches" of snow blanketed the decks. The men were wretch-
edly prepared: "none had flannels" and the food, which Slade disgustedly noted consisted of "biscuit, rice, olives and water," was quite
insufficient. By the time they finally crawled back into the Bosporus,
without any important encounters with Russian ships, Slade was
thoroughly annoyed with operations motivated by considerations of
prestige.[132]

Nonetheless, the Porte was determined to mount an even larger expedition before winter really set in, and there was talk of sending this fleet to winter at some point along the Anatolian coast.[133] The motives are not far to seek. Primary was the need to demonstrate that the Russians were not alone in using the Black Sea waters. They were encouraged in this intention by the relative success, thus far, of the land campaigns. There was a strategic argument also, in that the seaways were essential to supplying the troops on the eastern front, in an area where, even today, most foodstuffs are brought in by boat rather than by overland routes. In addition to the weather, there was, of course, the danger that the Russians would sooner or later respond to Turkish provocation by a decisive attack with their vastly superior forces. It seems likely that the Porte realized this.[134] On the other hand, the presence of the combined fleets in the Straits gave the Turks the impression that strong reinforcements were at hand,[135] while the emphatic British warning to the Russian command at Sevastopol made it seem unlikely that the Russians would venture interference. If, in fact, they did, the Western powers had pledged to come to the Porte's aid: the alliance, so long elusive, would become a reality.

Indeed, one is tempted to wonder whether the Porte deliberately provoked a catastrophe. Such an interpretation seems to be belied by the original plans for the expedition, which called for a much more massive demonstration. Perhaps the Porte was trying to force a decision, but not by a disaster. Even before the *Nuzretieh* started on its October cruise, naval officials, apparently on Slade's initiative, were discussing some sort of plan for sending the "entire fleet" to the Black Sea. Slade's original logic was that a large force that stayed together would be unlikely to tempt the Russians to attack, while a small force might find itself in a dangerous position.[136] The matter was laid before the *Meclis-i umumî,* along with other business concerning the war, at a meeting on the evening of November 2. The sending of the fleet, minus its three-deckers, was approved. The squadron would "cruise along the Asiatic shore, . . . round by the Crimea and the European coast." If the force met with Russian vessels, fighting was envisioned. Finally, the council asked that the British and French fleets enter the Black Sea, to make good their promise of protecting Ottoman territory.[137]

This plan was anathema to Stratford and de la Cour. Both diplomats sent strongly worded protests to the Porte against the dispatch of the Ottoman fleet.[138] Stratford was particularly adamant against the inclusion of two-deckers. Unlike Slade, he believed that an impressive force would incite the Russians to attack, whereas a modest detachment of "light vessels" would not.[139] He accordingly made use of the obvious

weapon at his disposal. Though the decision to call up the fleets had
been made in October, they were not yet all at Constantinople. Stratford now put it to Reshid very bluntly: he would not bring up the remainder of the fleet until Reshid promised not to send line-of-battle
ships to the Black Sea.[140] This worked, in that the Porte dropped the
larger ships from the expedition,[141] but de la Cour now argued that the
ambassadors must bring up the fleets or face the Porte's righteous
wrath. Starting on November 9, the remaining ships were rapidly
transferred to the Bosporus.[142]

Meanwhile, another effort was made to reinforce the Ottoman expedition to the Black Sea. The Porte had requested that British and
French ships enter those waters at the same time. Stratford was not
averse to this idea,[143] and he proposed to Dundas that a detachment
cruise along the European shore as far as the mouth of the Danube.
They would put in at Varna, where, it was hoped, they would pick up
the British consuls from Bucharest and Jassy, who had been instructed
to quit their posts because of the military situation.[144] Theoretically,
the French would join in this operation. The plan foundered on the
opposition of Hamelin, the French admiral. Hamelin at first objected
that de la Cour's replacement was about to arrive, and that such an
important step should be cleared with the new ambassador. Later,
when Baraguay d'Hilliers backed de la Cour and Stratford, further
ramifications of Hamelin's objections appeared. Hamelin was extremely worried about the feasibility of navigating the Black Sea in
winter weather. He was certain that it was most advisable to send
steamers—which would be relatively independent of winds and currents—but he argued that France had few of these compared with
Britain. Stratford, though obviously fuming at Hamelin's reluctance,
did not feel empowered to send British ships into the Black Sea alone,
although he grumbled that he would be obliged to dispatch an expedition to Varna anytime he had definite word that the consuls had arrived
at the coast.[145]

Meanwhile, the Porte was committed to the plan of sending Turkish
ships into the Black Sea. In retrospect, it would seem to have been
wiser to reconsider that decision once the size of the force and its projected support had been cut. But there still existed the hope that the
Russians had been discouraged by the French and British naval presence and by the knowledge that a Russian attack on Turkish soil would
bring Western intervention. And Stratford's argument that a few ships
might slip by without calling forth Russian hostility had a certain
plausibility; one could at least say that this had been true up to now.

But probably the determining factor was simply the prevalent Ottoman overconfidence joined with the fact that the expedition had been organized and it was easier to go ahead than to call it off—in the spirit expressed by the Kaptan Pasha to Slade: "Inshallah! ... our frigates will be safe."[146]

In fact, it is possible that the Turkish expedition might have been permitted to range the Anatolian coast at will, had not Russian thinking on the strategy of the war changed. The original Russian position had been to try to avoid engagements, in accordance with the assurances offered by Nicholas to Franz Joseph and Frederick William when they met at Warsaw at the end of September,[147] and in the hope that, if serious fighting could be prevented during the remainder of the campaigning season, negotiations during the winter might resolve the quarrel. But the failure of the Olmütz-Warsaw overtures was discouraging, and the first Turkish victories, made possible, in part, by Russia's failure to prosecute the war vigorously, made it a point of honor to make a better showing.[148] Meanwhile, the rationale was changing. On November 1, Nesselrode wrote Brunnov: "if Prince Gortschakof is lucky enough to thrash him [Omer Pasha] well, the sympathies of John Bull for the Turks will necessarily calm down." By the beginning of December, Nesselrode was hoping that there would be an opportunity to smash the Turks decisively and to "dictate an honorable peace."[149] In other words, the plan now was to knock the Turks out of the war by a decisive blow before the British and French could come in.

The Turkish expedition, under the command of Osman Pasha, set sail in mid-November, and after a difficult time with contrary winds, reached the port of Sinope, the only good, large harbor on the Anatolian coast. The day after their arrival, a Russian fleet was spotted. Osman Pasha considered returning to the Bosporus, but did not dare, since he would face more troubles with the weather and there was the chance of a Russian attack on the high seas, where the performance of his forces would certainly be worse than at anchor in the protected bay. Then four steam frigates appeared, on their way back to the Bosporus from a mission to supply ammunition to the Circassians. Osman lost a good opportunity to go back to Constantinople under their escort. His decision to stay at Sinope, his expedition reinforced by one of the steam frigates, is curious and gives some substance to Slade's charge that the Turks wanted to provoke an incident. It must also be borne in mind, however, as Slade points out, that Osman feared acting without orders,[150] an anxiety that must have been particularly acute, given the ignominious showing of prior cruises in the Black Sea. The steam frigates gave the alarm at Constantinople, but did not arrive soon enough to permit sending reinforcements.[151] Meanwhile, the Russians continued to hover around. Their hesitation is explained by confusion among the Russian commanders as to the purpose of their mission. Nakhimov, the commander, originally had been sent out to reinforce the troops in the Caucasus. His small squadron had been increased by two ships, sent by Kornilov after the latter had had a skirmish with a Turkish boat on November 5.[152] Nakhimov's original orders told him "to repel attack, but not to attack himself."[153] In giving this command, Menshikov was trying to limit Russian involvement at a time of year when extended operations might be dangerous.[154] He changed the orders in November, however, telling Nakhimov to attack; Nakhimov received his new instructions on November 1 / 13.[155] Menshikov also sent further reinforcements when he realized that Nakhimov was facing a sizable Turkish force at Sinope.[156] Nakhimov still hesitated, for he was nervous about Turkish shore batteries. But the odds seemed overwhelmingly in his favor; he now had six big vessels and two frigates (716 guns), while the Turks had seven frigates and four light ships (472 guns). Nakhimov did not notice any steamships among the Turkish forces (although presumably there was one). He could also count on the fact that the position of the Turkish ships (at anchor) and the difficulties of maneuvering inside the bay, would reduce their fire by permitting them to use only the weapons on one side of the ships—or 236 guns.[157]

On the thirtieth of November, Nakhimov's forces steamed into the bay. One Turkish ship, the *Taif*, had been ordered to leave the harbor before the fighting commenced; after a running battle with Russian ships, it escaped, and after standing by long enough to see how things were going, it sped to Constantinople with the news. For those within the bay, the engagement turned into a massacre. The redoubted shore batteries turned out to be ineffective: they were not in good repair (one actually included three "old Genoese guns"[158]) and were not well manned, since the pasha had told everyone to evacuate the city.[159] Although Nakhimov had ordered his men to concentrate their fire on the Turkish vessels and to avoid firing on shore, where there might be danger of damaging Europeans' persons or property, the Moslem quarter was set on fire and was severely damaged.[160] The only European resident, the Austrian consul, had retired, however. In the bay itself, the outcome was never in any real doubt; as the noted British naval historian Bartlett remarks, the extraordinary thing is that it took as long as two hours for ships of the line to demolish the greatly inferior Turkish force. The loss of life was enormous: estimates at the time reached the figure of four thousand.[161] The problem was compounded by the fact that many sailors simply swam ashore and disappeared into the countryside in order to avoid continued "service."[162]

Hardly had the news of the disaster at Sinope reached Constantinople when word came of an important Russian advance on the eastern front, giving them control of Başgedikler, on the road to Kars (November 19 / December 1). The two victories were a conclusive demonstration of Russian military superiority. The European powers now had the choice of supporting the Porte militarily or of acquiescing in her defeat, with all its important and unforeseeable consequences.[163]

In considering the stages by which the war had escalated, it must be admitted that Ottoman policy played an important role. At the beginning of the war, the Porte faced a peculiar combination of circumstances, which could only serve to encourage the warlike disposition so evident during September. The French and British governments agreed to support the Ottoman Empire with the presence of their fleets and warned the Russians that they would intervene if there were a naval attack on Turkish territory. Meanwhile, the Russians determined to stand on the defensive on the Danube, in the hopes that further negotiations might resolve the disagreement. In the vacuum left by this Russian decision, the Turks were able to push forward and "win" a couple of minor engagements on the left bank of the Danube. These insignificant successes impelled the Turks to refuse further negotiations and to proceed with the planning for a major naval expedition, which would force a decision in the Black Sea and would perhaps bring Britain and France into the war. Both the ambassadors' qualms about sending a large force and French hesitations, which went back to Drouyn's instructions, about any kind of supporting action, undermined the expedition to the point where it was incapable of serious resistance. When the Russians, seeking to demolish the Turkish war effort with a single, decisive blow, attacked in force at Sinope, the result was catastrophe. The Turks, without entirely foreseeing the consequences, had very neatly sprung the trap that the British and French governments had set for themselves. The dispatch of an inadequate force had tempted the Russians to reprisals. The Turkish navy had been crippled and the town of Sinope severely damaged. Without ever having actually made a clear decision, the British and French governments were now virtually obligated to enter the war. The British cabinet, in particular, felt its responsibility: they were enraged by the violation of the conditions that they believed, erroneously, the Russians had accepted early in October: the Russians would not send their fleet out of Sevastopol or attack Ottoman territory; if they did, the British would intervene. In a more general sense, the British were humiliated by the fact that the Russians had been able to cripple the Ottoman navy while the combined fleets were standing by. And the ease with which the Russians had defeated the Turks confirmed fears that the dissolution of the Ottoman Empire—and the loss of Britain's prominence in the strategic eastern Mediterranean—might be at hand.

Chapter VI

The Reaction to Sinope

"ON DECEMBER 2," Temperley tells us (quoting, in part, from Slade), "the news of Sinope reached Constantinople. The Turkish ministers received it 'in a cheerful cushioned apartment, with a panoramic view of the Bay of Sinope before them.' They listened, apparently unconcerned, 'to the woful tale . . . as if listening to an account and looking at a picture of a disaster in Chinese waters.'" But, as Slade noted, this indifference was assumed.[1] The blow to the Ottoman navy was severe. There was fear that the battle might be the signal for a general attack on the Turkish coast, with landings at Trebizond or Batum.[2] Prior to the incident, it had been possible for many of the ministers to delude themselves with a falsely optimistic picture of the effectiveness of the Ottoman forces, an estimate that was nurtured by Omer Pasha's reports from the front. These impressions had been confirmed by too ready a disposition to magnify the insignificant successes at Calafat, Oltenița, and Saint Nicholas. The Porte had rejected Buol's and Clarendon's overtures for further negotiations and had resolved to prosecute the war. Now this policy had to be reevaluated. The Russians were in a position to chase the Ottoman navy off the Black Sea. And this, in turn, affected the land campaigns, for, as we have seen, the ability to supply troops by sea, and to mount combined actions, was very important. Particularly critical was the situation of the Ottoman army on the eastern frontier: once in the best position to push the Russians back, it was now virtually cut off. The battle of Sinope aroused a strong desire for revenge among many Turks. It also proved to many that revenge, unless conducted in concert with the British and French navies, was a suicidal program. It made some leaders even more aggressive, but it also strengthened those who wanted negotiations and briefly put Stratford and Baraguay d'Hilliers in a stronger position that had been enjoyed by any ambassador for some months.

As soon as news of the disaster reached the capital, the Porte asked that French and British ships join with Turkish vessels in an immediate entry into the Black Sea. This request precipitated a debate between the two ambassadors and the two admirals as to the possible objectives and scope of the mission. The British admiral Dundas advocated decisive action. He wanted to enter the Black Sea; to scour it for the Russian squadron; to bring back the Russian ships to the Bosporus if they were still about; and, in any case, to make the presence of the combined fleets so obvious in all parts of the Black Sea, especially the eastern end, that the Russians would be thoroughly discouraged. These plans went far beyond the instructions sent to the French representatives by Drouyn de Lhuys, and although Baraguay agreed on the principle that something must be done right away to boost Ottoman morale, he preferred a simple reconnaissance mission. Stratford apparently hesitated to endorse the Dundas plan wholeheartedly.[3] In any case, upon de la Cour's replacement by Baraguay d'Hilliers, he had to deal with a far weightier colleague. Indeed, Baraguay's appointment had been motivated partially by Napoleon's sense that de la Cour had been too subservient to Stratford.[4] The new French ambassador was much tougher material, a general who had a reputation as a "brise-raison et mauvais coucheur," and there were confident predictions that he would quarrel with Stratford.[5] In fact, Stratford's first reactions were not unfavorable: he called Baraguay "a thorough African soldier ... not without a fund of dry quaint fun set off with the graces of a hearty laugh and loud tones." But he could not resist the sarcastic remark that "I should never be surprized to find that, like the man in Rabelais, he had turned in with his spurs on."[6]

In any event, Baraguay's plan was now adopted, and the Porte was notified that two British steamers and two French would set out for Sinope in company with Turkish vessels, in order to assist in the care and evacuation of the wounded. But this did not satisfy the Ottoman desire for revenge, and on December 3, Reshid notified Stratford and Baraguay that the Porte planned to send the Ottoman fleet on a further expedition to the Black Sea, which he asked that the French and British fleets join.[7] This decision showed more spirit than sense (indeed, Temperley considers it proof of incapacity); and after further consultation, Stratford and Baraguay proposed that the Turkish fleet stay in port while the British and French squadrons assume the hazards of a winter cruise in the Black Sea.[8]

Meanwhile, with no knowledge of the turn of events in the East, the diplomats in Europe had been working on a refurbished plan for a negotiated settlement. Buol's attempt in November to urge a solution unilaterally on the Porte had failed; but he had continued the conferences with the representatives of the powers at Vienna. On December 5, a protocol was signed by Austria, Prussia, France, and Britain, in which they affirmed their concern for the maintenance of the territorial status quo in the Near East and proposed their good offices to Russia and the Porte.[9] Parallel efforts were underway at Constantinople, but at first seemed fruitless. Although Baraguay heard an encouraging report on December 4, it was apparently a false rumor, for on December 5, Stratford wrote that the Porte seemed to be completely disillusioned with negotiations; even Reshid was now in a thoroughly warlike frame of mind.[10] But Reshid suffered a curious change of heart. According to Stratford's own report, he had "a private conversation with Reshid Pasha" and won him around to his own pacific views. He and Reshid worked out a plan that was communicated first to Baraguay, then, on December 12, to all four great-power representatives in a meeting at Bruck's residence. A draft was later drawn up according to the sense of the meeting and was revised in a second diplomatic gathering on December 13. The final text was officially communicated to Reshid under the date of December 15.[11] Certain conditions for negotiations were laid down: Moldavia and Walachia were to be evacuated as quickly as possible by the Russians, while the Porte would communicate its firman of 1853 confirming the privileges of the Christian millets and would pledge further efforts to better the situation of all Ottoman subjects. Existing treaties—and specifically the Straits Convention of July 13, 1841—were to be reaffirmed. If these provisions were met, the Porte would appoint a delegate who would go to some neutral city to arrange an armistice and a final settlement.[12] Barely had this draft been agreed upon than the text drawn up by the Vienna conference reached Constantinople; the representatives decided to continue with their own formula, however, on the grounds that it was similar in all essentials to the Vienna text.[13]

The December 15 note was presented to the *Meclis-i umumî* in two extended meetings on December 17 and 18. The debate was heated, and a split seems to have materialized within the ranks. Some, including the ulema and Mehmet Ali Pasha, continued to believe that the continuation of the war was necessary, as the only way to obviate the Russian danger. But others, including some of the reformers like Ali Pasha and Fuad Efendi, favored the peace plan. They pointed to the difficulties that the Porte faced in prosecuting the war, such as internal unrest and fiscal embarrassment, and argued that the terms proposed offered an honorable exit. With the stipulation that there would be *"an arrangement with the Powers that would guarantee the future,"* the plan was unanimously accepted.[14] But obviously some members, notably Mehmet Ali, were disgusted with this outcome:[15] their agreement was a tactical move before they took up the battle in another form.

Why did the Porte suffer this change of heart? Certainly one disquieting factor was the news from Persia. A report from Tavernier, the French resident at Bagdad, dated November 30 indicated that a special

mission from Nicholas had persuaded the shah to cooperate militarily
with the Russians. The shah had ordered the mobilization of seventy-
five thousand men, and the Ottoman embassy and the British legation
were said to be planning to leave. Although it was doubtful that the
Persians could act in the near future, Tavernier reported considerable
anxiety at Bagdad.[16] His view of the seriousness of the situation was
confirmed to the British by Rawlinson, their consul at Bagdad.[17] Early
in December, the Porte received more details about the special mission
from the Ottoman minister in Teheran. The Russian emissary, Dol-
goruky, was said to have offered support for the Persian war effort in
the form of settlement of the outstanding Persian debt to Russia of
twenty-three million piastres plus aid against the British through Russian occupation of Afghanistan. On the other hand, if the Persian government refused, the Russians threatened to invade Azerbaijan and the
area around the Caspian Sea. Thus caught between two fires, the shah
yielded to Russian pressure,[18] at least for the moment. By the end of
the month, largely as a result of British threats,[19] the shah seemed to
have reversed himself—although the situation remained critical, and
Ottoman feelers for an alliance were brushed aside.[20]

The British had actually broken relations with Persia in November
1853; though the immediate cause of this action was an insult to the
servants of the British chargé, Thomson, the long-range objective was
to keep the Persians out of the war. London ordered Bombay to mount
an expedition against the island of Khārk in the Persian Gulf. The
instruction was quickly countermanded,[21] but contingency orders remained in effect. They envisaged even a landing at Būshehr and a
march on Shīrāz, or alternatively, assistance to the Turks at Basra or
Bagdad. In all of this, the British were worried, as were the Turks,
about the stability of the Ottoman Asiatic provinces; but the British
had a further concern. Implicit in their thinking was the assumption
that Persia could never challenge Russian mastery of the Caspian Sea;
it followed that Persia must be more or less written off to Russian
domination. This, in turn, made British influence in the Ottoman Empire and in Afghanistan crucial to the "northern tier" of buffer states
that protected India.[22] Since Afghanistan was in a highly fluid condition, considerable weight attached to the traditional British policy of
maintaining the Ottoman Empire.

All these factors may have contributed to making both the British
and the Turks want peace at the end of 1853; but these worries continued throughout the month of December, and they therefore do not
explain the turn towards negotiations that took place between December 5 and 12. To understand this, we must go back to Stratford and

his tantalizing "private conversation with Reshid Pasha." Bernadotte Schmitt asserts that Stratford had refused the cooperation of the combined fleets in the Black Sea unless Reshid were willing to agree to negotiations. Although Stratford did not explicitly admit this in his report to London, Schmitt seems to have been right in his interpretation of the document.[23] As we have seen, on December 11, Stratford and Baraguay d'Hilliers had suggested that the combined squadrons enter the Black Sea, while the Ottoman fleet stayed in port. On December 12, the day of the first conference about the new draft, they reversed themselves. They continued to oppose an Ottoman expedition, but they now argued that French and British intentions were sufficiently demonstrated by the presence of the two squadrons in the Bosporus; ships would not be sent into the Black Sea unless the Russians attempted to land troops.[24] The new decision was certainly welcome to Hamelin, the French admiral. On December 13, he wrote an eloquent summary to Baraguay of his objections to a winter cruise in the Black Sea,[25] but it does not seem likely that representations from Hamelin caused the shift. The long-standing dispute between the diplomatic representatives and Hamelin that had plagued de la Cour in November was not something Baraguay was prepared to put up with. After a peppery exchange of letters with Paris, Hamelin was firmly instructed to subordinate his judgment of navigational possibilities to Baraguay's perception of political necessities.[26] In any event, Baraguay testified that he had been prepared to join Stratford in ordering a joint expedition to Varna and Sinope, as a demonstration designed to intimidate the Russians, when Stratford changed his mind.[27] Apparently Stratford had talked to Reshid about negotiations, found him recalcitrant, and then decided to cancel the sending of the combined fleets until Reshid produced a formal pledge to further discussions from the Porte.

French and British support in the Black Sea was crucial to the Turkish war effort. Slade, who was close to Mehmet Ali Pasha and to influential figures in the Ottoman navy, penned an appeal to Stratford on December 15 that outlines some obvious considerations that must have influenced the Porte's reaction to Stratford's refusal. Both Russia and the Ottoman Empire depended on the sea route to supply and reinforce their armies in the east. Furthermore, unless the combined fleets were actually in the Black Sea, their presence did little good. The prevailing winter winds in the Black Sea are from the northeast. The Russian fleet could slip out of Sevastopol and do great damage while the Western squadrons were held down on the lee shore around the Straits. The only solution, according to Slade, was the solution Stratford had just rejected: a strong detachment of ships should enter the Black Sea.

Based at Sinope, they could exercise a commanding influence.[28] Presumably, the lack of this crucial allied support forced the Porte to agree to negotiations after December 12. Not until December 19, after the *Meclis-i umumî* had formally accepted the peace plan (December 18), did Stratford return to the idea of a Franco-British cruise in the Black Sea; he now suggested exactly what Slade had wished, that a combined force establish itself at Sinope.[29] The coincidence of dates seems to verify Schmitt's contention and to prove that Stratford took advantage of the Porte's weakness after Sinope to force the Ottoman ministers to negotiate as the price of effective Franco-British naval support, without which their war effort was doomed.

But Stratford was playing a dangerous game. Mehmet Ali and the hard core of the war party did not want to negotiate; they still took comfort from the Turkish successes on land and felt that it was grossly unfair to call off the fight at the end of the first round, before the Ottoman armies had had a chance to win territory from Russia.[30] Other, more personal factors confirmed Mehmet Ali's discontent. In the aftermath of the disaster at Sinope, the Kaptan Pasha—Mehmet Pasha, who had been one of Mehmet Ali's followers—was dismissed. He was replaced by Riza Pasha—broadly speaking, a partisan of Reshid's. Another supporter of Reshid's, Halil Pasha, was also added to the ministry. It looked as though the power of Mehmet Ali's group was being systematically reduced.[31]

Apparently, Mehmet Ali Pasha and the Sheikh ul Islam now worked on the grievances of the students in the *medreses* in Constantinople to produce further disturbances. The resulting outbreaks were very much like the troubles in September, only far more serious. On December 21,[32] the students started a strike against classes. Announcing, "In such times it is not possible to read a lesson," they abandoned their schoolwork and hung their reading desks off the minaret of the Bayezit mosque in sign of protest. Demonstrations followed. The ministers were alarmed. Reshid immediately resigned and took refuge at his son's home in Beşiktaş. Most of the others prudently stayed at their country homes, well away from the riots in Stambul.[33] Rumors flew: the students were going to burn Constantinople; they were going to start a massacre of Christians.[34]

Stratford afterwards made light of the incident, as well he might, for it was an embarrassing one for British policy. In a letter to his wife, he tossed off the disturbances with the reflection: "two advantages were secured. The fire-engine was exercised, and I shewed my gallantry by inviting all the pretty women of my acquaintance to take refuge in the palace." But when the diplomats and their families gathered at the

British palace, the mood was grim. Stratford, after consulting his colleagues, fired off a note to Reshid Pasha, in which he urged firmness and underlined the Porte's solemn accountability if harm touched the Christians.[35] There was talk of sending French and British steamers to the scene, and some were prepared.

Part of Stratford's anxiety stemmed from the fact that he could not find Reshid. Not until the morning of December 22 did he locate him. He promptly went off to confer with his protégé, but found the atmosphere discouraging. While he was talking with Reshid, word arrived from the President of the Council (*Meclis-i Vâlâ*) that the students were still rampaging and that there was some danger of the unrest spreading to the lower classes and even to the troops. To make matters worse, Reshid claimed that the Sultan was unwilling to act.

Stratford, naturally, did not hesitate a minute. He went right on to see the Sultan and insisted on firm measures.[36] The Sultan agreed on a vigorous counteroffensive. A naval force was sent from its anchorage up the Bosporus to a position off Constantinople. ("A whole squadron of steamers, French and English, came smoking down from Baycos," as Stratford put it with satisfaction.)[37] The Sultan convoked Mustafa Nâilî Pasha, Mehmet Ali Pasha, and the Sheikh ul Islam and announced that he intended to hold a council meeting at the Porte in Stambul.[38] Mehmet Ali realized that the plot had failed. Accordingly, he sent a company of soldiers into the heart of the disturbed area, around the Suleimaniye mosque. They rounded up a group of *softas* and held them at Bayezit. Mehmet Ali appeared and addressed them. He stressed the impossibility of revolution and urged that they return to calm.[39] Eventually, the police rounded up about 160 student leaders.[40] They were brought before the council meeting and given the option of service in the army or exile in Crete. They chose Crete. Reshid, who had handed in his resignation, refused to come to the meeting, but his resignation was not accepted.[41] Minor disturbances continued for some days, and further arrests were made.[42] The Porte felt it necessary to order an investigation of the schools.[43] But to all intents and purposes, the resistance was broken.

The December riots marked another stage in the erosion of what popular support Reshid may have enjoyed and was another step in the process of converting Mustafa Nâilî's government into a ministry of British puppets. The episode also shows the difficulties inherent in Britain's peace policy. Stratford had acted forcefully and shrewdly in order to exploit the Porte's weakness after Sinope, in the interests of negotiations that might lead to a diplomatic solution of the quarrel before it escalated into a general European war. But his energetic action was

opposed by a substantial group of Turks, and it simply ignited disturbances that could only be repressed by a show of foreign military force.
Quite apart from the ideological implications of such action, which
would be troubling for a self-styled liberal power, there was an obvious
limit to how long such a policy could be effectively carried out. But
almost before the problem was posed, it was resolved by new information from London and Paris.

In both capitals, the news of the disaster at Sinope caused important
reactions, both in the government and in the public at large. Speaking
in very general terms, in France, the public took the battle as a matter
of course, while the Emperor was upset; in Britain, the reverse was true.
Considerable study of French public opinion has not entirely eluci-
dated its direction, and the problem, which was compounded by government control of the press, is worse for the earlier part of the reign.
Lynn Case, in his fundamental study of French public opinion on foreign affairs, argues that feeling in this instance was divided. Simpson
tells us that the French public reacted to news of Sinope "calmly,"
while Jomini discovers a certain "satisfaction" that the Turks had been
repaid for the tendency to push matters to extremes. Most of the government apparently shared these sentiments; the battle was seen as a
normal act of war. Napoleon III, however, was determined to make an
issue out of the incident, partly from the calculation that this was an
opportunity for "cementing his alliance with England,"[44] partly from
the belief that a Bonapartist regime could not slough off military humiliation.[45] Accordingly, Napoleon proposed that the combined fleets
enter the Black Sea and force Russian warships or troopships to stay at
anchor. Drouyn de Lhuys declared that, if Britain would not cooperate, France would go in alone. It seems doubtful that the French government intended to make good this threat, but the British cabinet
could not afford to take a chance,[46] nor, in Clarendon's view, could
they overlook the possibility that France might back out of the alliance
with Britain entirely.[47]

At first, the British ministers were not unduly excited about the action at Sinope. There was a general tendency to feel, as in Paris, that
the Turks had brought their defeat upon themselves. They did expect
that the squadrons would now enter the Black Sea, "to protect Constantinople," but they did not see the need for any special measures
against the Russian war effort. But at this point, their own views were
overwhelmed by a violent outburst of public opinion, which really
made it impossible for them to refuse to act with the French. Public
excitement was fanned by Palmerston's resignation.[48] Although Palmerston's action was almost certainly motivated as much by disagree-

ment with Lord John Russell over projected suffrage reform as it was by the Eastern Question,[49] popular legend quickly added another chapter to the doughty lord's championing of the unfortunate Turk.[50] The agitation actually grew worse in January, after Palmerston's return to office; it turned against Prince Albert, who was believed (on the precedent of Pam's 1851 resignation) to have worked against the minister and, by a flight of fancy, to be in league with the tsar. As rumors flew that both Victoria and Albert had been immured in the Tower on a charge of high treason, the Queen actually considered abdication.[51] Ultimately, of course, the excitement blew over. The significance of the public reaction lies in the fact that it forced the Cabinet to concur in Napoleon's plan for energetic anti-Russian action in the Black Sea and, in a longer view, tied the ministers' hands with respect to further overtures for peace. Malmesbury, the former foreign secretary, was probably not exaggerating when he concluded: "Public indignation has been so universally aroused by the manner in which the Russians behaved at Sinope that war has become inevitable...."[52] There has been a tendency among historians to see this public agitation as unwarranted and harmful hysteria. Anderson, for example, declares: "This violent reaction to the 'massacre of Sinope' was quite unjustified. The battle was a perfectly legitimate operation of war."[53] The last sentence is true; but from the moment that the British government had warned against Russian attacks in the Black Sea, the public had every right to consider the operation an affront to Britain, if not an atrocity. Whether the Cabinet had been justified in issuing a warning that they were ill prepared to back up is another question. It seems almost certain that they were not justified in doing so, but more blame should attach to the Cabinet's policy in October than to the public's views in December.

As a result of Napoleon III's proposal and the British public's agitation, the order was dispatched to the ambassadors to send the fleets into the Black Sea. Baraguay informed Drouyn on the 26th that the command had been passed on to the squadrons. At the same time, he noted that the council was considering the details of the peace proposals.[54] The Sultan had promised Stratford in the middle of the riots that he would continue to work for peace along the lines adopted on December 18.[55] A manifesto "read in the mosques" during the height of the trouble (December 23) had reaffirmed the government's commitment.[56] It would not be stretching the facts to say that continuing the negotiations was part of the price for Franco-British naval support in intimidating the rioters. One may wonder how long negotiations thus brought about could have gone on. But, in fact, the question is academic. Once the fleets had been ordered into the Black Sea, full British and French participation in the war was almost unavoidable. As it was to turn out, the Porte's acceptance of the new bases for negotiation on December 31 was negated by events.[57]

What is noteworthy about the December 31st meeting is the deep bitterness expressed by the ulema. Despite full explanations of the absolute necessity for European aid and the consequent inevitability of negotiations as the precondition for that aid, the discussion was lengthy and coarse. Many of the *hocas* refused to believe that the Ottoman forces had suffered more than a temporary setback. Many precedents were brought up, demonstrating that seemingly desperate situations could be turned around. It would be shameful to call off the fight before the Ottoman armies had had a chance to prove themselves. As a minimum demand, this group wanted the Russians to pay an indemnity covering Ottoman expenses in the brief war; but their real hope was for territorial conquests. When several of the ministers intervened to explain the seriousness of the situation, they were met with accusations. One of the most learned of the ulema, Hace-i Şehriyârî Hâfiz Efendi, insisted that the only solution lay in "effort and persistence." Disgustedly, he declared that he had sat through thirty years of discussions of what ought to be done, and in all that time, he had seen nothing worthwhile accomplished. "Perhaps angels from the sky will come to do the things you now admit you didn't do," he sneered.[58]

Goaded by such remarks, the advocates of negotiation became increasingly outspoken. Continuing the war to the kind of conclusion the religious leaders expected would mean invading Russia and going as far as Moscow, or even Saint Petersburg, in the opinion of Fuad Efendi. Such expectations were totally out of touch with reality, argued Ali Pasha; even Napoleon, with all his armies, had not been able to carry out a successful invasion of Russia. And if, by some extraordinary feat, the Ottomans were able to conquer Russian territory, the great powers would surely force them to return it in the peace treaty. As the debate continued to circle around the same points, several of the ministers resorted to sarcasm: Rifat declared in no uncertain terms that the *hocas* did not know what they were talking about, and suggested that their words would be more appropriate in the mosque during Ramazan.

Ultimately, agreement to continue negotiations was won. Undoubtedly, the prompt reaction of the British and French to the threat of revolution was in everybody's mind. One of the ministers, Molla Efendi, provided a face-saving argument: the outcome of further fighting was uncertain and should not be forecast too optimistically. "The possibility of gain is not gain," he declared. "The possibility of injury, is real injury." It would go against Koranic law to pass up the hope of a just international settlement now for some hypothetical future advantage. And, as Rifat pointed out, the willingness to negotiate did not preclude further campaigning. Even if a peace treaty were signed, it would be possible for the Porte to build up its forces and to repudiate the agreement when the time was suitable.[59]

Meanwhile, this discomfiture contributed to a delay in moving the squadrons out of the Bosporus. Temperley lays the delay to bad weather, always an important consideration at that time of year.[60] But there was another factor, of some importance. The Porte wanted to take advantage of the expedition of the combined fleets to send troops to the eastern frontier. Reinforcements were needed,[61] and this was obviously the only safe way of getting them there. It was also important to Ottoman pride, as can be seen from the article in the *Takvim-i Vekâyi*, to portray the cruise as a joint operation rather than as a rescue action.[62] But the troops were at Constantinople under the orders of the Serasker Pasha, Mehmet Ali; and in the tense situation during the last days of December, he was reluctant to release them and diminish his power still further. It began to look as though the combined fleets might sail before the soldiers could be embarked. This problem the Kaptan Pasha solved very neatly by refusing to make pilots available for the French and British vessels until the Turks were ready to move also.[63] Not until January 3 did the three squadrons start sailing eastward.[64]

With the entrance of the combined fleets into the Black Sea, war between Britain and France and Russia became almost unavoidable. Had their instructions been evenhanded, as Aberdeen had wished,[65] there might have been a slim chance that the war could yet have been localized; but in view of the fact that the British and French orders were directed against Russian naval action—calling for protection of Turkish "shipping" and coasts[65]—widening of the conflict was certain. The month after the battle of Sinope had afforded one of the last opportunities for restraining the Porte, since the battle had dramatically demonstrated how desperately the Ottoman military effort depended upon foreign aid. Stratford apparently recognized this, and, after authorizing a modest relief expedition to assist the victims at Sinope, he used his influence over the fleet movements to force the Porte to accept negotiations. The fate of Stratford's scheme is a good example of the problems involved when a big power tries to coerce a small power. In the first place, a substantial group of Turks resisted, going so far as to riot for several days in the old quarter of Constantinople. It was clear that Stratford's game would only work with those Ottoman leaders who were ready to play it; and it might be necessary to maintain them in power by force, ultimately not a rewarding prospect. Secondly, Stratford's attempt to be tough was almost immediately overruled by orders from home. The decision to send the fleets forward had been arrived at through the touchiness of the head of state in France and the runaway enthusiasm of public opinion in Britain. Ten or fifteen years of propaganda for the Turkish reform movement and an even longer period of intermittent Russophobia had left their mark. But the real Ottoman Empire, whatever its merits, was certainly very different from the stereotype built up in the public mind out of the dreams and visions of politicians and publicists such as Palmerston, Stratford de Redcliffe, and David Urquhart.

Chapter VII

The War Becomes General

WITH the entry of the combined fleets into the Black Sea, the Russo-Turkish war was on the way to being transformed into a European war. Since the fleets' instructions favored the Ottomans, it seemed probable that the fighting would go forward and that further negotiations would be purely a matter of form. The fears of Mehmet Ali and his friends that the Western powers would somehow force the Porte to stop were no longer valid. It was even becoming clear that France and Britain would help the Porte, and thus the aim of Reshid's policy was accomplished. But the likelihood of an increasingly close, even supervisory, relationship between the Porte and her allies, particularly Britain, remained. The price to the Porte, in terms of a sacrifice of pride, was high. Yet even before the Western powers declared war, there were signs that close cooperation with the Porte would lead those governments to support policies that could only with difficulty be reconciled with their ideological pretensions. In this sense, the Porte used Britain and France as well as being used by them.

The combined fleets' initial cruise in the Black Sea was not a long one. The naval staffs had little desire to extend the adventure under winter conditions. Less than three weeks after their departure from the Bosporus,[1] the admirals informed the ambassadors that they wished to return. This brought forth strenuous objections from Stratford and Baraguay, who were concerned because news of the return had had a disastrous impact on Constantinople. They immediately wrote, suggesting that the fleets stay at Sinope and warning that the commanders would reenter the Bosporus on their own responsibility. Nonetheless, the fleets returned,[2] but shortly departed again to convoy some Turkish troopships, frigates, and corvettes carrying reinforcements to Trebizond. The fleets' activities were welcomed by the Turks; at Trebizond, a Moslem believer told Slade that "the Prophet ... had certainly granted a dispensation for Palmerston" so he might go to Paradise.[3]

Meanwhile, the reaction of the Russian government was hostile. Nesselrode made it clear that the mere fact of entry into Black Sea waters would not be taken as a casus belli;[4] the question was whether the squadrons would interpose equally between Turks and Russians, sending ships of either power back to port.[5] When, however, the British and French governments "refused to forbid the Turks free passage between Turkish ports,"[6] while admitting that they would "prevent any movement of men or supplies from one Russian port to another," the anti-Russian import of the instructions was obvious, and the tsar determined to break relations. On February 4, Brunnov and Kisselev announced their intention of leaving London and Paris; some two weeks later, Seymour and Castelbajac quit Saint Petersburg.[7] Nicholas made a point of taking a formal farewell of Castelbajac, and the tsarina favored his wife with the gift of "a magnificent Turkish shawl." As a deliberate affront to Britain, however, Nicholas did not even see the Seymours before their departure.[8] It was the opposition of the British—whom he had believed closer to Russia—that annoyed Nicholas most.

Although Britain and France did not declare war for another month, that step would have been hard to avoid after the diplomatic break with Russia, and indeed, the diplomatic break was itself almost inevitable once the combined squadrons had entered the Black Sea with instructions to turn back Russian shipping, but not Turkish. Bruck optimistically suggested that the Russians might retreat before the new pressure from the combined fleets,[9] but the presence of those fleets in the Black Sea was far more likely, at this stage, to enrage Nicholas than to intimidate him. Although the next two and one-half months were filled with negotiations, there was little or no realistic hope of averting a general war. Those discussions can be summarized very briefly in terms of what they foreshadowed for the course of the war, particularly as it would affect the Ottoman Empire.

The Porte's acceptance of the new bases for negotiations, contained in the note to the great-power representatives of December 31, was duly forwarded to the ambassadorial conference at Vienna. The representatives there certified that the text coincided with their own proposals and agreed to transmit it to Saint Petersburg by the Protocol of January 13.[10] According to information Seymour gathered at Saint Petersburg, the tsar's first impulse was not even to reply.[11] He thought better of this, however, and sent back a response that was considered by the conference on February 2. Nicholas refused the note proposed and put forth his own terms for a settlement, which included reaffirmation of all previous treaties between Russia and the Ottoman Empire and refusal to evacuate the Danubian Principalities until such a pledge had been given.[12] These propositions were judged to be so far from the conference's original plan as not even to merit referral to Constantinople.[13] A final message from the tsar reached Vienna early in March and crossed with the ultimatum from Britain and France; it was briefly considered and rejected by the conference, mainly as a matter of form.[14]

With the breakdown of four-power negotiations and the imminence of war, two efforts were made to change the emerging alignments by bilateral agreements. On January 29, 1854, Napoleon III wrote a letter to Nicholas I, in which he advocated simultaneous withdrawal from Moldavia and Walachia and from the Black Sea and an end to the war through direct negotiations between Russia and the Porte.[15] Although Napoleon had originally hoped to associate the British government with his gesture, the Cabinet's objections persuaded him that he would have to act alone.[16] Russian historians have sometimes seen the letter as a pure play for publicity; and perhaps this attitude is the key to Nicholas's haughty refusal.[17] Probably there was more to the French emperor's move than that, however. Simpson has pointed to public opinion, which apparently did not support the war, as an important factor.[18] Kinglake argued that Napoleon's basic motive throughout the crisis had been "conspicuousness," and his policy could best be capped by a spectacular eleventh-hour solution.[19] Indeed, if we look at French diplomacy in the preceding months, a pattern of pairing aggression with conciliation emerges. Napoleon sent the fleet to Salamis in the spring of 1853, but agreed to a settlement of the Holy Places Question. The fleet was advanced to Besika Bay, but the French took a leading part in working out the Vienna Note. The French pushed the fleet's move to the Bosporus, but hung back on instructions to Hamelin to enter the Black Sea, while in November 1853, Napoleon had taken no steps to raise additional troops. Napoleon finally forced the naval entry into the Black Sea, but as late as mid-January 1854 he maintained "that from the commencement of the question he had made up his mind not to send a soldier to the East,"[20] and he sent the January 29 letter. Perhaps Napoleon was following the policy many Britons later believed their government should have adopted—namely, a policy of showing firmness, while offering the tsar suitable ways of extricating himself. But what is important in the present context of Ottoman policy is the fact that Napoleon was less convinced than was the British Cabinet of the needfulness of resorting to war and was more concerned with casting around and keeping an eye open for new combinations. These observations, fully borne out by French policy during the war and in the immediate postwar years, imply that France was less committed to the Ottoman Empire and less committed to any specific program for the area. This, in turn, enhanced the British predominance at Constantinople, which they had been building for some years.

Simultaneously with Napoleon III's overture, an attempt was made at bilateral Russo-Austrian negotiations; this effort, though also a failure in terms of its stated objectives, was to have even more important consequences for the Ottoman Empire. During the winter, Nicholas had become increasingly convinced that Russia's best hope lay in raising the Balkan Christians. The entry of the French and British squadrons into the Black Sea seemed to confirm the wisdom of a strike to the west rather than a march through the eastern Balkans. But this plan obviously touched on Austrian sensibilities, since any attempt to raise the Slavs of the Ottoman provinces might have repercussions within the Hapsburg monarchy. Accordingly, Nicholas recognized the need for a special mission that would communicate his plans to Franz Joseph and would endeavor to win his commitment, along with that of Prussia, to a policy of benevolent neutrality. Nicholas chose Orlov, who accepted rather against his better judgment, for he considered the chances of success slim.[21]

Orlov's mission bore out his predictions. His first days were devoted to ritual social contacts and passed pleasantly enough: on the first day, "a dinner almost *en famille*" with Franz Joseph; on the second day, a "ball at the archduchess's, lots of pretty women." But when, on the fourth day, he finally got down to business in an audience with Franz Joseph, he did not find the monarch inclined to consider his projects seriously.[22] Orlov had been empowered to demand that Austria, Prussia, and, if possible, the German Confederation sign a declaration of neutrality. In return, Nicholas promised that Russia would send military aid if this neutrality should be threatened by Britain or France (an obvious allusion to Franz Joseph's expressed fears that Napoleon would make good his threats of stirring up trouble for the Hapsburgs in Italy). Nicholas also agreed to consult Austria and Prussia before making any changes in the Ottoman Empire and specifically suggested that, if the Porte's rule should collapse, Austria and Russia should share protectorates over Serbia, Moldavia, Walachia, and Bulgaria.[23] Franz Joseph quickly made it clear that he wished for the maintenance of the Ottoman Empire and would only cooperate with the tsar if the latter promised to make no changes in the border Ottoman provinces.[24] This, of course, was unacceptable to Nicholas, and so the mission failed.[25] As a matter of fact, it worsened the Russian position, rather than otherwise. Moved by the evidence of Russian ambition, the Austrian government decided to increase its forces on the Serb border—first by thirty thousand, later by twenty-five thousand, additional troops.[26] And a meeting of Franz Joseph's closest advisers on January

31 expressed strong sentiment in favor of an Austrian occupation of Serbia to coincide with a Russian crossing of the Danube. Indeed, the chief military figures, Generals Grünne and Hess, favored an immediate entry into Serbia, in order to anticipate Russian moves.[27] And in February, General Hess leaked the possibility of Austrian occupation to the Russian ambassador, Meyendorff.[28] All of this had a highly discouraging effect on Russian plans for a Christian revolution and for operations in the western Balkans—or even, for that matter, in the eastern Balkans.[29] Reinforcing Paskevich's preference for a campaign along the Black Sea coast, these considerations contributed to the eventual decision to attack at Silistria.[30] But more important from the point of view of the Porte, in delaying the danger of a Christian uprising in the north Balkans—based in Serbia and aided by Russian arms—the Austrian action had done much to insure the survival of the Ottoman Empire.

The most important developments in foreign policy, however, in the early months of 1854 involved the increasing cooperation between the British and French governments and the Porte. We can trace the emergence of the wartime alliance in three areas: first, intrigues at the Porte; second, arrangements for military, including naval, cooperation; third, the Western powers' confrontation with, and assumption of responsibility for, Ottoman internal problems. In the decisions that were taken in these three fields, we can see the shape of the wartime alliance emerging and can get some idea of the results of Ottoman policy during the months before the war.

One of the dominant themes in that policy had been the rivalry between Mehmet Ali Pasha and Reshid Pasha. Mehmet Ali's appeals to Islamic teachings and to past Ottoman glories had the benefit of tradition; and his trump card was the ability to stir up the populace, particularly the students, and to reach the troops through his control of the ministry of war and his association with Omer Pasha. Although his two attempts at a coup in 1853 had not been successful, he was an extremely powerful figure, and he owed his failure primarily to the naval intervention of Britain and France. Naturally, Reshid was not eager to continue sharing office with him; he had strong political motives for revenge. In addition, there was competition for a closer relationship with the Sultan; both men were intriguing to marry their sons into the Sultan's family.[31] And finally, there was the unfinished business of the scandal over the customs at Constantinople. At the start of the 1853 crisis, Reshid had been in disgrace because of transactions in which Mehmet Ali had apparently also been implicated; Mehmet Ali had managed, however, to use his high position (he was then grand vizier) to turn the blame on Reshid. Now there was every temptation for Reshid to repay Mehmet Ali in his own coin.

Reshid's strongest card was his close relationship with Stratford and the fact that—if the British government were to move into a wartime alliance with the Porte, with all the delicate attendant problems that would need solution—the British ambassador would not be likely to accept an Ottoman government with which he found it difficult to work. Accordingly, Reshid began to try to influence Stratford. His campaign evidently emphasized the themes of disunity in the Ottoman Council of Ministers and the detrimental effect this would have on the government's efficiency. He also brought out Mehmet Ali's ties with extremists and "fanatics." Stratford's reports show the influence of such hints: admitting that some of Mehmet Ali's colleagues would like to get rid of him, Stratford came forward with the judgment that "at present he acts with too much independence and obstinacy for a Minister who has more resolution than discernment, and more self-confidence than knowledge." Stratford also warmed to the themes of Mehmet Ali's divisiveness and fanaticism and explained that he was trying to overcome by personal appeals the Sultan's opposition to his dismissal. Needless to say, these representations were successful. Mehmet Ali was dismissed from his post as Serasker Pasha and the Kaptan Pasha, Riza, replaced him; the vali of Adrianople (and former ambassador to Britain)[32] became Kaptan Pasha.[33]

The Sultan sweetened the pill by a masterly solution of the marriages problem. Shortly after Mehmet Ali's dismissal, it was known that the Sultan's eldest daughter, after great pressure from Reshid, would be betrothed to Reshid's son, Ali Ghalib. But another daughter would marry Mehmet Ali's son, and still another, the son of Fethi Ahmet Pasha.[34] The Sultan's power to limit Mehmet Ali's disgrace was not complete, however. Mehmet Ali's banker and agent in the affair of the Constantinople customs, Cezayirli Oğlu Miğirdiç, was arrested, and his financial records were impounded. Malicious gossip, which was probably not without foundation, suggested that, in seizing Miğirdiç's books, Reshid was protecting himself quite as much as gathering evidence against Mehmet Ali. Indeed, Mehmet Ali told Reshid bluntly: "Reshid Pasha, you accuse us of corruption. Your own honesty and integrity are in question." But for the moment, it was Reshid who was in a position of power. Mehmet Ali was forced to repay large sums of money to the government and was given token banishment to Kastamonu, in the interior of Anatolia.[35] Mehmet Ali's removal, though it limited the power of the old Turkish hard-liners, did not lead, however, to perfect

harmony within the Porte or between the Porte and the Western ambassadors. There were too many problems and too many rivalries for
the elimination of any one individual to be able to accomplish that.
Probably Stratford did serve his own convenience, in that he found it
easier to deal with Reshid and wished his favorite to be as strong as
possible; but, given the fundamental Ottoman distrust of Western interference, which was shared by many besides Mehmet Ali, this policy
soon reached a point of diminishing returns.[36] In fact, it is impossible
not to conclude (what Stratford, in his arrogance, evidently did not
suspect) that Reshid had neatly used him for his own plans.

Stratford had asserted that it would be impossible to reach agreements with the Porte for prosecuting the war until the ministerial situation had been solved.[37] In February and March, plans were being
actively debated in London and Paris for military expeditions to supplement the naval aid already made available. The widespread scorn
for the Ottoman army led to fears that, as soon as the campaigning season started, the Russians would take the offensive and sweep over the
Danube and across the Balkan range. This assessment, which turned
out to be far too pessimistic, actually worked in the Porte's favor, for
there was a sense of urgency to get the troops to the Levant soon
enough "to save Constantinople."[38] In mid-February, official notice
was sent to the Porte that British and French troops were about to be
dispatched;[39] the news arrived early in March.[40] Military experts were
sent out to study the terrain and to advise on future plans. The British
Sir John Burgoyne left Britain at the end of January; the French Bosquet and Canrobert followed in March.[41] Important conferences were
held in Paris between British and French authorities to explore preliminary plans of campaign. Immediately, a difference appeared between the two powers. The British favored the scheme outlined by
Burgoyne when he stopped in Paris; this called for a landing at Gal-
lipoli and a cautious advance into the interior. Bosquet and Canrobert
preferred a landing at Varna, to forestall a Russian drive before it could
really get started. Meanwhile, Napoleon—though momentarily convinced by Burgoyne's arguments—dreamed of some dramatic coup that
would crumple Russian resistance; the attack on Sevastopol was already taking shape in his mind, to the disquiet of the British.[42] These
disagreements were to continue and would worsen during the war. But
what was immediately significant for the Porte was that the Western
powers were rushing material aid to the Levant.

Before Western troops arrived and before the Russians crossed the
Danube, the Porte needed help because of disturbances in another area.
In the northwestern Balkans the Turks resisted effectively. A Russian

attempt to advance in the Calafat area was met by the Ottoman army in the battle at Cetate on December 31. The action, though strenuous, was again indecisive; once more, both sides were able to claim victory.[43] As a result, the Turks remained contained within a small area around Calafat,[44] but congratulated themselves that the Russians were not able to move into Serbia.[45]

Meanwhile, the Porte issued a solemn confirmation of Serbian privileges, which was sent to Prince Alexander in January.[46] The seemingly generous gesture was loaded with implications, as was fully realized in Belgrade. Despite pressure from Constantinople to support the Sultan as overlord, the Serbian government had maintained neutrality and had advanced the argument that Serbia had legal ties with both the Porte and Russia. Hence, in a quarrel between its two protectors, Serbia was bound to remain neutral.[47] The confirmation of privileges, like the concurrent charter to Moldavia and Walachia,[48] was designed to eliminate Russian involvement in the constitutional structure of the Balkans, on the argument that the war suspended all existing treaties.[49] The Porte would appear as the only suzerain and the duty of the populace in all three principalities to aid the Ottomans would be clear.

Actually, these legal arguments were rather abstruse, and it seems unlikely that the Porte expected practical results. More apposite was the calculation that, if the government in Belgrade responded with even the mildest expression of thanks, the Serbians would be embroiled with the Russians. In fact, the Serbian government was careful to be as ungracious as possible in its reply, which came only after careful consultation with the Russian and Austrian authorities; and a commentary in Serbian, added when the document was read, did much to nullify its import.[50] Prince Alexander was not very impressed by the Porte's concessions, for his real aim in the crisis was far higher, involving at least an affirmation of the heritability of his office.[51]

Meanwhile, revolutionary and pro-Russian sentiment mounted among the populace, and as Ottoman troops faced Serbian militia on the border and Russian agents were active,[52] there was grave danger of an incident, which might have thrown the whole area into warfare. Only the certainty that Austrian troops would immediately march in and doubts as to Russian capacity to win the war prevented fighting in Serbia, which could have linked with unrest in Montenegro and risings in Thessaly and Epirus to create a problem of major proportions for the Porte.[53]

In Montenegro, as in Serbia, there was great local unrest. No less a person than Nesselrode deigned to involve himself in financial aid to the Principality;[54] and both the Russian and the Austrian governments

maintained active military missions.[55] Indeed, the Austrians were re-
puted to have five thousand infantrymen ready to invade at the first
sign of serious trouble.[56] In February 1854, General Mamula, the
military commandant of Dalmatia, had exacted a promise from Prince
Danilo that he would refrain from military action. This promise did
not eliminate border incidents (nor did it satisfy Mamula's own desire
to annex Montenegro to Austria); but it accomplished a reasonable
approximation of Vienna's wish to damp down the Montenegrin
issue.[57]

With the Ottoman army entrenched in Bulgaria and the Russian
forces in Moldavia and Walachia, the major remaining trouble spots
were Thessaly and Epirus, bordering on Greece. Greek pressure on
this area had been mounting for many months: for more than a year,
active preparations had been underway for a campaign in which a local
uprising would be sparked and secretly supported from the Kingdom of
Greece.[58] Particularly tense relations between the kingdom and the
Ottoman Empire had prevailed throughout 1853, and they were not
improving as the year ended. In mid-November 1853, a report reached
the Porte that the Greek army was constructing massive fortresses
around Athens, which would be equipped with big guns; the King and
Queen had made a special point of visiting the construction sites.[59] In
December, protests from the Ottoman ambassador, Neşet Bey, about
a border incident were met by the Greek foreign minister Paicos, with
the sort of response that exasperated the Turks and helped to persuade them of Greek bad faith. Paicos first minimized the incident,
then wrote a second letter, later in the same day (supposedly on the
basis of later information), in which he discussed the incident at greater
length, but emphasized the tranquillizing role played by the Greek
army and the determination of the government to prevent any trouble
on the frontiers.[60] In January, revolts broke out, first in Epirus and
then in Thessaly, which were clearly aided by men, money, and supplies from Greece. What might at first have been dismissed as the
natural intensification due to war of endemic unrest took on in a few
weeks the proportions of a serious challenge to Ottoman rule. For a
time, there seemed a possibility that the troubles would spread to neighboring Slavic areas and to Albania.[61] It is possible, as Jomini believed,
that the Russians missed a good opportunity by failing to join with the
rebels. But the Russians apparently were not very impressed with these
events. Quite apart from the ubiquitous worry about Austrian reactions,[62] Epirus and Thessaly were relatively remote, and Nesselrode believed that the uprisings would quickly simmer down into guerilla fighting in the mountains, which might indeed be an embarrassment to the

Turks, and might even lead to the detachment of some troops from the Danube front, but would not bring important results.[63] In this he was supported by Gorchakov's halfhearted and Meyendorff's negative evaluations.[64]

The Porte could not take such a cavalier attitude; and the situation remained a prime worry as late as June. The British and French were also extremely concerned,[65] not only because of the tangible danger to the main Ottoman war effort, to which they were now committed, but also because this posed, for the British particularly, some difficult philosophical questions. Doubt as to whether Britain, as a Christian power, should put herself in the position of aiding a regime whose policy towards its Christian subjects had not always been blameless had plagued Aberdeen from the start and had contributed to his strong desire to find a diplomatic solution. Clarendon, on practical grounds, had feared that, while Britain was defending the Ottoman Empire from an external foe, it would collapse from internal weakness.[66] The practical resolution of this moral dilemma, forced by the revolts in Thessaly and Epirus, was an important stage in the forging of the Anglo-Turkish alliance.

The causes of the uprisings were many. The Tanzimat had been introduced in Yanina relatively late, in the mid-1840s.[67] We have seen that the implementation of the reforms often worsened, rather than bettered, the condition of the Christians in the short run; there is no reason to suppose that the situation in Epirus was any exception. Coming on the heels of the transition period, the war increased problems by raising the hopes of the unruly bashi-bazouks, who wished to recover their "dominancy" over the Christians.[68] Specific appointments compounded the situation in some instances: for example, Haci Hussein Pasha, made commander of the Ottoman frontier guard in 1852, had been accused of disloyalty to the Porte.[69] And the process of recruiting for the army was bound to lead to incidents.[70] A striking example, related by the British consul Longworth at Monastir, will suffice. A certain "Hakie Pasha" (Hakki Pasha?), though crippled, had been sent to Monastir to recruit five thousand Albanians. His appeals were so energetic that far more candidates than necessary turned up at Monastir. He took the number commissioned and turned the others away, without any compensation for their trouble in coming to Monastir. Naturally, these individuals, hundreds in number, recouped their loss on the way home. Meanwhile, he was not successful in controlling the men he had retained under his command: practices such as the issuance of twenty billets for his personal guard of two hundred inevitably created disorders.[71] The Christians, the principal victims of administrative disorganization, became more and more ripe for revolt. Their discontents were fanned by Greek Orthodox priests.[72] But, in the circumstances of the mid-nineteenth century, the creation in 1832 of a free Greece with a large irredentist problem had inevitably laid up trouble for the Ottoman government, even assuming the very best intentions and the wisest statesmanship.

An example of Greek propaganda is the "Proclamation to all Greeks and Philhellenists, Believers in Christ," which was published in an Athenian newspaper under the date of January 6, 1854, and circulated in Epirus.[73] The proclamation charged:

> The cruel bondage under which we, the population of Grecian Epirus, have laboured for upwards of four centuries, is not unknown to the Sovereigns and people of Christendom. Tyrannical fury has spared neither life nor property, nor left us any kind of liberty. God created us men in His own image and similitude; whereas we are treated as beasts. The temples of our ancestral faith have been a thousand times impiously polluted and despoiled; the graves of our fathers opened, and their bones frequently cast into the fire; the honour of our wives and children continually outraged; so that our breath alone remains to us, and that but to augment our sufferings. Our voice and language only avail us to appeal and protest against such impious acts of the infidels; latterly, since the differences on the Russo-Turkish question, the oppressions towards us Christians have been multiplied. Cumulated oppressions, insults, and dishonour, sacrifice of life without end, spoliation upon spoliation, and all the direful woes of Hades itself, are written in our book of life.
>
> For these and other like reasons, which words cannot describe, we have resolved to peril all for the common weal, and either bury ourselves under the ruins of our country, or live for the future as men breathing in freedom the sweet air of liberty; wherefore we consider it our first duty to proclaim this our resolve to the whole world, and to invoke the aid and succour of all retainers of the Gospel and liberty without exception.

The proclamation continued with further exhortations to rise and concluded with an interesting appeal to the Turks to join them. The men of Epirus, to believe the proclamation, had no desire for revenge. On the contrary, they promised the Moslems: "Your faith shall be unmolested and inviolate, your lives and honour secure, your property safe."[74]

After a series of incidents, starting with an apparently spontaneous rising in the Radoviš area[75] on January 22, a band of frontier police under the leadership of the son of a prominent Greek nationalist, Karaïskakis,[76] crossed the frontier and attacked the region around Arta. Colonel Pierrako, as the son was called, picked up volunteers from the Greek Orthodox villages of Epirus. In addition, volunteers came from Greece; army officers resigned, and headed for the border; and even a group of prisoners, liberated by a mob, was sent to the frontier. By early in February, the Porte saw the situation as a general attack from Greece all along the border into the southern section of Epirus. Information reaching the Porte from Nauplia in mid-February suggested that the invaders were mounting a careful campaign to allay the fears of the inhabitants and to win them over to the cause, while their own presence would be excused, if this became a diplomatic necessity, as purely accidental.[77] Incursions now were occurring along the entire border area, including Thessaly as well as Epirus: Longworth reported bands operating as far east as Lárisa.[78]

The fighting remained sporadic, and there was a minimum of organization and planning, in accordance with the Greek klephtic tradition.[79] Still, it is possible to construct a rough outline of the campaign from the reports reaching the Porte and from the observations and rumors recounted by French and British consuls and agents. In February and March, the disturbances centered on Epirus. The rebels forced the Turks back on Arta and, under the leadership of Demitrachi, laid siege to the citadel.[80] This raised fears in the mind of Sir Henry Ward, British governor of the Ionian Islands, for the security of the entire adjacent coast and ultimately for the British-ruled islands themselves. His anxieties were fed by the knowledge that the troubled years 1848-49 had seen the birth of a pro-Greek independence movement in the islands; in terms of Ionian politics, British interests coincided with Turkish. Ward now ordered Captain Peel to defend Préveza with British gunboats, in order to prevent the extension of the revolt to this coastal city. Peel, instructed to hold Préveza against all attack, replied in the laconic tradition: "I have the honor to acknowledge the receipt of your Excellency's Dispatch of last night's date, and to state, in answer thereto, that I engage to hold Prevesa against all assailants until the pleasure of Her Majesty's Government is known."[81] Peel was seriously worried, however, about the propriety of intervening to protect the Porte against domestic dissidence; he had contented himself with sending one gunboat, the *Shearwater,* while appealing to higher authority.[82] Ward's official case was based on the presence of a Russian squadron at Trieste and the resultant possibility that the disturbances "originated in foreign intrigues."[83] When the matter reached Clarendon, he came down on the side of Ward, arguing that the Russian squadron, by its mere presence, must have encouraged the revolt at least indirectly. It was therefore appropriate for Peel to cruise along the coast and to bring the weight of his presence to bear.[84]

Meanwhile, the local authorities had sent to Monastir to demand reinforcements. The military commander there, Abdi Pasha, was asked to send three battalions of redif to Yanina and two to Lárisa in Thessaly. At the same time, Omer Pasha had ordered practically the entire force at Monastir to Şumla on the Danube to meet the Russian offensive expected in the spring. And it was impossible, in the troubled state of affairs, to leave Monastir completely unprotected. Abdi Pasha's worries were compounded by the realization that the Turkish forces in Epirus desperately needed a high-level commander; yet he hesitated to go without authorization.[85] And he was obviously embarrassed by the probing of the British consul, who charged him with evasion.[86]

During the delays occasioned by Abdi Pasha's agonies as to how to divide up his troops and by the further time necessary for moving them to the scene of action, the situation continued to deteriorate. The Turks were bottled up in Arta and in other towns and villages; one group had struggled through to Arta with a loss of seventy men, but was not able to raise the seige.[87] And in Thessaly, the disturbances around Lárisa, which at first had amounted to mere cattle stealing, began to take on serious proportions.[88] Only gradually did a somewhat more hopeful note appear. Captain Peel's presence at Préveza saved the situation there. A band of two thousand Albanians reinforced Arta and ended the siege. And encouraging news came that a half battalion of redif were moving southwards from Yanina.[89] But the movement of troops created its own problems: the Albanians' destructive advance across the plains of Arta ignited further disturbances.[90] And the rebels, dislodged from Arta, simply moved northwards. By the 22nd, there were rumors that Colonel Pierrako and General Grivas were two hours' march from Yanina.[91] In Thessaly, a parallel move was driving towards the important interior center of Trikkala.[92] Gradually, the troubles spread up the coast to the regions around Filiátes and Margariti; most of the ablebodied men had gone to the relief of Arta, and the small Turkish community remaining at Filiátes was quickly surrounded and cut off from the interior. Despite appeals, Ward refrained from coming to their relief, but did sell them gunpowder. Meanwhile, Grivas, with the principal group of rebels, was concentrating on Yanina; on the 28th of February, he was "only nine miles off." Yanina itself was held by a garrison of perhaps a thousand Turks, comprising regular soldiers and artillery men. If the six thousand Christians of the city joined with the insurgents, this important city, the provincial seat of Epirus, would fall, and it seemed likely that the rebels would move to establish a provisional government.[93] Meanwhile, in Greece, the king was preparing to put himself at the head of the Greek forces.[94]

During March, the beginning of a three-cornered Turkish counteroffensive began to take shape. From Constantinople, it was fairly easy to get at the region around Volo, on the eastern side of the peninsula. On March 1, a preliminary group of one thousand foot soldiers was rushed to Volo by Turkish steam frigate.[95] And a British, a French, and an Austrian ship put into port at Volo in rapid succession in the first days of March.[96] Shortly afterwards, Blunt, the British consul at Salonica, was instructed by Stratford to cruise along the coast from Salonica to Volo in the *Spitfire*.[97]

Meanwhile, the Turks were beginning to move against the rebels in Epirus. Between February 28 and March 4, the tiny band of Turks at Yanina held off Grivas singlehandedly: on March 4, Abdi Pasha arrived from Monastir with reinforcements, a cavalry regiment. The Porte had sent Fuad Efendi to Préveza to take charge of the military and domestic effort as Special Commissioner. But Fuad was, for the moment, almost powerless. He was able to establish himself at Préveza and could certainly move to Arta; but he had very few troops at his disposal, and until reinforcements had been received, it would be impossible for him to beat his way through the rebel bands in the interior and to effect a junction with the forces of Abdi Pasha operating out of Yanina.[98]

As reports on conditions in Epirus and Thessaly poured into Constantinople, the Porte realized that speedy action on several fronts was essential. It was necessary, somehow, to get additional troops to the spot. It was necessary, since all the evidence pointed to the complicity of the Greek government, to make strong representations in Athens and to somehow turn off the rebellion at its source. And it was vital to pin down British and French support on a question that could be very embarrassing to them. As the Porte acted in all these areas, we see the local British and French representatives, like the consuls in the field, moving with some caution, in order not to compromise their home governments.

As early as February 19, Reshid asked the cooperation of the British and French navies in transporting troops to the scene of the insurrection at Volo and Préveza.[99] The ambassadors duly consulted the admirals; but both Dundas and Hamelin refused. Stratford insisted; he pointed out that the Turkish squadron, which had been unavailable on a Black Sea cruise at the time the matter first came up, had returned in the meantime.[100] The limitations of Turkish naval power, especially in the wake of the Sinope disaster, were obvious. As serious news continued to come in, Stratford decided that speed was vital. He and Reshid accordingly planned that the Porte would send a fleet with four battalions to Volo and Préveza, accompanied by an escort of one

British steamer and one French. Other troops would go overland to Yanina.[101] But when Baraguay again appealed to Hamelin, the answer was again, no. Baraguay was disturbed, for he felt it was important for France and Britain to act together at all times. He went so far as to send to Athens to ask reinforcement from French ships there, but to no avail. It was left to Dundas to go alone.[102]

Meanwhile, the reports of Neşet Bey, Ottoman representative at Athens, had continued to complain of the Greek government's lying explanations and aid to the rebels.[103] The British and French ambassadors, Wyse and Forth-Rouen, were also alarmed, and on February 24 the two went to the palace to deliver a homily. Since the king and queen had plotted the revolt from the beginning,[104] this turned out to be a thoroughly frustrating exercise. The king was polite but indicated that any more effort on his part to swim against the tide of public opinion might cost him his throne. Then the queen appeared (to call the king to lunch), and the real sentiments of the royal couple began to show. The queen appealed to Forth-Rouen on the basis that Napoleon III, "the man elected by eight million hearts," would understand their predicament. When Forth-Rouen demurred, her language became even wilder: she actually threatened to join the guerillas. Forth-Rouen found her seductive but exasperating. Meanwhile, Wyse, in earnest conversation with the king on the other side of the room, was encountering similar attitudes in the German-born monarch, who now maintained that he could only "sympathize with my people." Later, a last attempt made by Forth-Rouen found the king and queen almost incoherent; he concluded: "I no longer heard anything, I say, but the words: God! Providence! Holy cause! Give our blood! Europe duped, delivered over to the Antichrist."[105] In this atmosphere, needless to say, the answer returned on February 25 to the earlier Ottoman protest was not satisfactory. A further note from the Greek government on March 7 actually demanded satisfaction from the Porte, on the grounds that Ottoman forces had deliberately chased a group of Christian villagers— who had innocently fled onto Ottoman territory—back into Greece and had then engaged Greek soldiers on Greek soil.[106] In fact, both sides were ready for war. The Greek government took the view that the present situation of undeclared hostilities could not go on.[107] Paicos appealed to the Austrian government with the proposal that Austria, Russia, and Greece divide the southern Balkans: Austria would take Macedonia, Russia would have Thrace, and Greece would receive Thessaly and Epirus.[108] The Porte, making an excuse of the many demonstrations that had taken place in Athens in favor of the rebels, wanted to break diplomatic relations immediately. Stratford counseled against this plan, and managed to persuade the Porte to send a last demand for explanations.[109] Neşet presented the document on March 19. The Cabinet met that evening and decided not to meet the Porte's requests. A meeting of the Chambers, called for the next morning, endorsed the decision. Neşet prepared to depart, and relations between Constantinople and Athens were broken.[110]

The insurrection placed all the British and French representatives in the Near East in a delicate position. They could not let the Porte, as a prospective ally, founder on a revolutionary movement; and all became persuaded of the danger. But they could not be too zealous in aiding in the suppression of Christians until they had some guidance from home. Thus we see Ward, from Corfu, sending a gunboat and munitions but refusing outright aid, and Peel distinguishing sharply between help against outside attack and help against internal dissidence; we see the ambassadors supporting Ottoman protests against Greek involvement but trying to prevent a rupture; and we see the admirals refusing naval assistance to Turkish troops or limiting it to convoy duty. One might expect that, in London and Paris, where the sense of danger might be less acute, the hesitations about helping the Porte might have been greater. Quite the contrary is the case. Both the British and the French governments made it clear from the early stages of the crisis that they intended to support the Ottoman Empire wholeheartedly. The French were particularly vocal. According to Cowley, early in February, Drouyn de Lhuys instructed Forth-Rouen to warn the Greek government in no uncertain terms of France's attitude.[111] On the 18th, Drouyn wrote Baraguay of the need to assist the Porte and suggested that a group of French and British warships be sent to cruise off the Gulf of Arta and the Albanian coast. Baraguay's report of Hamelin's unwillingness to participate in naval action called forth Drouyn's marginal strictures.[112] In fact, a French frigate was sent directly to Athens, with instructions to work with the British "for preventing the encouragement by the Greek Government of any attack on Turkey,"[113] while Napoleon III sent off a severely worded letter to the King of Greece.[114] The British, though less vocal, were equally categoric. Clarendon had a conversation with Tricoupi, the Greek minister at London, in which he pressed the diplomat concerning Greek complicity in the revolt and finally explained Britain's position in unmistakable language: "I distinctly warned M. Tricoupi that his Government had now to choose between the goodwill of England and France and the blockade of Athens, as the two Governments, while engaged in defending the Ottoman territory from Russian aggression, would certainly not tolerate that the Greek subjects of the Sultan should be excited to rebel against his authority, in consequence of measures sanctioned by the Greek Government."[115] This was not an idle threat; the British and French eventually sent warships to occupy Piraeus and maintained that force until 1857,[116] long after Fuad had snuffed out the revolt in June 1854 with the help of troops sent to Volo and Préveza.

The high-handed proceedings by the French and British governments called forth a series of official rationalizations. France's policy was less ambiguous and contained fewer internal contradictions. As the French agent Bourée, put it: "we are practicing Politics not Philanthropy."[117] As Catholics, Frenchmen subscribed to the idea that Rome was head of the universal church, and they were less susceptible than many Englishmen to appeals to a vague Christianity that turned out to be composed mainly of schismatic Greek Orthodox. And when they looked at conditions in the Balkan peninsula in a political context, it was clear to them that the Porte's rule was the best solution. For example, Bourée's travels through European Turkey in the summer and autumn of 1853 left him with few illusions about the effectiveness of Ottoman rule; but he was profoundly unimpressed by the calibre of the native Christian leaders he met, such as Prince Alexander of Serbia and Prince Danilo of Montenegro. He concluded that liberation of the Balkan peoples and redrawing of the boundaries in accordance with the principle of nationalities, however desirable it might be on moral grounds, would simply create a power vacuum that would lead to an enormous extension of Russian influence. The best course for French policy was to maintain connections with local potentates, while awaiting the moment when they would be strong enough to stand alone.[118] A similar hard-boiled attitude towards Ottoman politics probably lay behind French toughness towards the Porte on a number of occasions: in 1852, in such incidents as the sending of the *Charlemagne* and the bombardment of Tripoli, and again in the spring of 1854, when, on learning that the Porte intended to make the Greek insurrections the excuse for expelling all subjects of Greek origin from the Empire, Baraguay threatened to break relations.[119]

The British had a much more difficult time with their consciences because they tended to put their entire policy with regard to the Ottoman Empire into a framework of morality and uplift. Britain's special relationship with the Porte in the 1840s had been justified to British public opinion on the grounds that the Turks, through British tutelage, were becoming more civilized—indeed, more anglicized—every day. When, then, the rebellious Greeks of Epirus and Thessaly made the point that something was amiss in the best of all possible worlds, the

British were forced to reexamine their position. The aid to the Porte in suppressing the rebels was made the subject of searching inquiries in both the House of Commons and the House of Lords, and it is clear from the debates that many individuals—including Earl Grey, Earl Ellenborough, and Monckton Milnes—had doubts about British policy.

The most comprehensive statement in favor of the Porte was made by Lord Shaftesbury in the Upper House on March 10, 1854.[120] Shaftesbury's speech is particularly interesting, because it shows how support for the Turks fitted in with the prejudices common in the Evangelical movement. Shaftesbury's language revealed a bitter Protestant prejudice against both Catholics and Orthodox—of the sort that had influenced Lord John Russell's recent sponsorship of the Ecclesiastical Titles Bill[121] and the violent criticisms of Newman and the Tractarians. He argued that the Christians were as much the victims of the Greek Orthodox priesthood as they were of the Ottoman administration. This point, often made, was underlined by the peculiar conditions of British missionary work in the Ottoman Empire. The Porte forbade attempts to convert Moslems. The Protestant missionary field was therefore limited to other Christians, a fact that ensured that virtually every convert would come equipped with tales of the evil conduct of the Catholic or Orthodox priesthood and their nefarious efforts to prevent those who had seen the light from publicly acknowledging their change of faith. The best hope for the Balkans, according to Shaftesbury, did not lie in improved facilities for the benighted Catholic and Orthodox rites; better would be the mass adoption of Protestantism through a vigorous missionary effort. And from this perspective, it was not hard to choose between the political alternatives that faced the peninsula: Turkish rule was much more favorable to the spread of Protestantism than Russian rule would be. Shaftesbury pointed out that Nicholas did not even allow the circulation of the Bible in the vernacular in his dominions! Should Nicholas conquer Ottoman territory, the same dark night of the soul would descend. The Turks, on the other hand, were not hostile to Protestantism. Shaftesbury cited instances in which the Porte had intervened to save Protestant converts from persecution by other Christians. And a prime exhibit in his case was the Porte's grant of millet status to the Protestant religion in 1850.[122] Shaftesbury omitted to mention that converts from Islam were put to death by Ottoman law, a point made by Earl Grey in his rebuttal.[123] But his telling statement of the manifest destiny of Protestantism and its seeming affinity with the Turkish outlook could be duplicated at many levels of society. One might cite the individual who informed a public meeting in Newcastle: "The Turk was not infidel. He was Unitarian. As to the Russian Greeks or Greek Christians, he said nothing against their creed, but they were a besotted, dancing, fiddling race. He spoke from personal observation."[124] At a secularized and more sophisticated level, an essentially similar argument was used by the consuls on the spot: the Christians would be better off under a reforming Ottoman regime than in the chaos and misgovernment that would attend their attempt to take over their own destinies.[125] Seen from this perspective, it was Britain's obvious duty to force the unwisely discontented Christians of Epirus and Thessaly to be happy.

As British policy was under debate in Parliament, the government was moving in conjunction with France to formalize relations with the Ottoman Empire and to make the final break with Russia. On February 27, Britain and France sent their ultimatum, asking Russian evacuation of the Danubian Principalities by April 30.[126] On March 12, a treaty of alliance was signed between Britain, France, and the Ottoman Empire. The Western powers promised military, including naval, aid, and the terms of that aid were stipulated in some detail. The purpose, stated in the preamble, was the maintenance of the territorial integrity of the Ottoman Empire.[127] Finally, on March 28, the Western powers declared war on Russia.[128] The Russo-Turkish struggle had become a general European war.

The events of the first months of 1854 are in some ways anticlimatic. With the move of the combined fleets into the Black Sea, it had become almost inevitable that Britain and France would move into the war in support of the Ottoman Empire. But these last months do shed important light on the nature of the alliance that had emerged and on the perspectives for the future. One of the Porte's major worries throughout the crisis leading to war had been very largely dispelled: there was no longer much likelihood of a Christian uprising that would substantially aid the Russians. This was made evident early in 1854, with the Austrian government's sharp opposition to any Russian plans for a change in the status quo—an opposition that had already made some Austrian leaders advocate the preventive occupation of Serbia and that was to lead to the occupation of Moldavia and Walachia by Austrian troops and to the removal of the campaign from the Balkans. Furthermore, it became evident early in 1854 that, in the area that did revolt— namely Thessaly and Epirus—the British and French were prepared to assist the Porte in reasserting Ottoman authority. Whether British and French rationalizations of this course would have held up in the face of a large-scale uprising encompassing a large part of the Balkans is open to question; but a problem of this magnitude had been precluded by Austria's stand.

The first months of 1854 also saw the formalization of the alliance between the Western powers and the Porte that had been emerging for some time. The dismissal of Mehmet Ali Pasha, the debates on specific plans for the sending of British and French troops, and the aid in suppressing the insurrections in Thessaly and Epirus all provided background for the signing of the treaty. In these events (as throughout the year before the war), the Ottoman ministers had been the manipulators as well as the manipulated, in a way that their allies did not wish fully to recognize. From the breakdown of negotiations with Russia in the summer of 1853, the Turks had pushed consistently for war, and they had got it. Reshid had wished to inveigle Britain and France into a military alliance designed to defeat the Russians in the field and thus to win a breathing space for the Ottoman Empire, and he had done it. He had hoped, in the process, to assure his own position as the mediator between the Porte and the West—or, more specifically, with Stratford. The British and French declarations of war found him in power and seemingly in the ascendancy after Mehmet Ali's dismissal— though no position was safe for long in the roller coaster of Ottoman politics. And the British and French endorsement of the Porte's policy was sufficiently unconditional that they were ready to aid the Porte in putting down Christian revolts despite the many statements that the British in particular had made about sponsoring a better life for Christians.

But if the British and French had lent their strength to Ottoman objectives, it was in part because they too had stakes in the quarrel. For Napoleon III, the consolidation of the alliance with Britain outweighed the observation that he was "starting his reign with 1812."[129] He would split Austria from Russia and would effectively check the growth of Russian influence in the Levant, though at a higher price than he had wished to pay. And he had forced out into the open the confusion about policy that affected all the great-power foreign offices after 1848; all this might ultimately create new options for France. Yet these goals might have been served short of war; and Napoleon, from his January 29 letter to the final calling of the peace conference at Paris, was more ready than the British to consider diplomatic solutions.

For the British, Russia's demands had raised the spectre of an Ottoman Empire that would develop along the lines of greater power to the millets. This would increase the pressures towards separatism and would give the Russians ample opportunity to support the eventual creation of new small Balkan states that might then become Russian satellites. In contrast to this, the British supported the continuation of the Porte's regime and the modernization effort associated with it. This entailed increasing centralization and uniformity imposed from above by the Westernized bureaucracy. Religious differences would eventually fade into a purely private matter as Ottoman citizenship became the accepted self-image of the Porte's subjects. Much idealism of a Liberal and Protestant nature surrounded these projects; and popular affection for the Porte, based on a false conception of Ottoman eagerness to anglicize, built up into a public pressure for military aid that was a far from negligible factor in the government's decision. But quite apart from that, the Porte, under the Tanzimat, was giving the British important economic, political, and strategic influence in a wide area. When British statesmen spoke of preserving the integrity of the Ottoman Empire, they were being hypocritical—as Mehmet Ali Pasha and other anti-western Turks recognized. What they really meant was that they opposed Russian threats to the Ottoman Empire's territorial integrity because this would diminish the area over which they themselves wielded influence.

Chapter VIII

Conclusion

IN THE first chapter of this work, three lines of explanation for the outbreak of the Crimean War were described. Some have seen the war as the outcome of mistakes and misunderstandings. Some have related the war to the European revolutions of 1848 and have emphasized the great-power rivalries that developed from that period. Others have considered the war as primarily the result of the evolution of the Eastern Question.

If a choice must be made between these three interpretations, the present work supports the third. A dangerous situation had developed in Constantinople in the late 1840s because, in a period of great-power disinvolvement, Britain had come to exercise a virtual protectorate without being obliged to make corresponding sacrifices. When, after 1848, the Near East became once more a theatre for great-power competition, the British found that they would have to commit more resources to an increasingly active support of Ottoman policy if they did not want the Ottomans to turn elsewhere. The British reaction to the crisis over Moldavia and Walachia, where revolutions broke out in 1848, and to the crisis over the Russian invasion of Hungary in 1849, left much to be desired from the Porte's point of view. It is true that, in the end, during the negotiations over the repatriation of the Hungarian refugees, the British did send their fleet to the eastern Mediterranean, in conjunction with the French; but they consistently evaded Ottoman attempts to interest them in some kind of long-term alliance that would set up a special relationship, like the British relationship with Portugal. Meanwhile, the Russians seemed to be gaining enormously in the Balkans, through temporary occupations of Moldavia, Walachia, and Hungary and through widespread propaganda elsewhere.

In fact, it was the French who reacted with most alertness to the Russian challenge. Napoleon III picked up grass-roots missionary sentiment in favor of official French sponsorship of the claims of the Roman Catholic Church in the Ottoman Empire, and he used this issue as an indirect slap at the tsar, the traditional patron of the Greek Orthodox, whose position the Catholics assailed. As the quarrel over the Holy Places merged in the larger issue of the rights of the Greek

Orthodox millet in other parts of the Ottoman Empire—notably in Montenegro and Bosnia, where the introduction of the Tanzimat reforms seemed to hurt the Christians, at least in the short run—Nicholas I decided to come to grips with Balkan instability, which he now saw as one of the major unsolved problems of his reign. He accordingly sent Prince Menshikov to Constantinople to demand a *sened* that would confirm the privileges of the Greek Orthodox millet and would authorize the Russian government to intervene on its behalf. It is clear that Nicholas was willing to go to war over the issue, although he hoped to avoid European intervention. Though the Ottoman government, headed by the traditionalist grand vizier Mehmet Ali Pasha, was willing to consider an accommodation, Menshikov's high-handed insistence on complete submission (based on his knowledge of the tsar's readiness to fight if need be), ended by arousing a wave of xenophobia. Mehmet Ali, a devout Moslem, had never been a supporter of strengthened Christian rights, and after his dismissal—at Menshikov's instigation—in favor of Reshid Pasha, he became an uncompromising advocate of war.

Stratford de Redcliffe, the powerful British ambassador, exercised a mediatory role in this stage of the crisis. He suggested that the Sultan issue firmans confirming the rights of all the millets and communicate them formally to all the great powers; his proposal found favor because it combined lip service to the idea (so popular in Europe) of a better life for Christians, with avoidance of any new provisions for changing the actual status of the Christians. Stratford's plan, which was taken up by the Council of Ministers and later formed the basis of the so-called Turkish Ultimatum, did not find favor with the Russians, while the Vienna Note, which was produced by the ambassadorial conference at Vienna as a formula for agreement, proved unacceptable at Constantinople, unless significantly amended. Though some historians have blamed Lord Stratford for the Ottoman refusal, the Porte was coming to see war as the only honorable course, and it had ample reasons for rejection of the note: misplaced, but real, confidence in Ottoman resources; suspicion of Austrian notives; and a distortedly favorable analysis of British policy conveyed by the Ottoman representative in London, Musurus Bey. Once the Vienna Note plan was aborted, it proved impossible to halt the drift into war; the Porte declared war on Russia on October 4, 1853, and after increasing pressure on both sides for some dramatic stroke before winter set in, the Russians annihilated a Turkish fleet at Sinope on November 30. Although Stratford tried faithfully to win Ottoman acceptance of the various peace plans put forward in Europe and by the great-power representatives in Constantinople, he found himself caught in an inescapable dilemma. If he insisted that the Ottoman ministers negotiate, he risked igniting revolution. (Indeed, for a few days in mid-December, Stratford was obliged to keep Reshid Pasha in power by military force, an embarrassing position for the emissary of a liberal power.) But if Stratford allowed the Porte to prosecute the war as the Ottoman ministry wished, the result would be catastrophic defeat and pressure for intervention at home in Britain—where the public had been fed for many years on the legend of the reforming Turks, "not infidel," but "Unitarian,"[1] a view unsuccessfully challenged early in 1854 by Christian revolts in Thessaly and Epirus.

The French, despite Napoleon's last-minute efforts to conjure up a compromise, did not shy away from a military test. And so the war became general. Only the Austrians, desperate to hold their increasingly ramshackle empire together, managed—somewhat ungracefully—to stand aside.

If we study the immediate origins of the war in search of an instigator, we are forced to recognize that we are really dealing with two different wars. There was, first of all, a Russo-Turkish war, on the model of the wars of 1828-29 and 1877-78. But, superimposed on this local war, there was also a European war, starting some five months later.

It is easy enough to determine the origins of the Russo-Turkish war. Nicholas I planned it. Documentary evidence shows that he was certainly ready to make war on the Ottoman Empire in the spring of 1853. Although presumably he would have accepted a sufficiently favorable resolution of the question of the status of the Greek Orthodox millet, war was probably the alternative he preferred, as being the course most likely to cut through the complexities of the problem and to bring a lasting solution within his own lifetime. But the war Nicholas planned was a localized war that could be rapidly and efficiently prosecuted and could be terminated before the other European powers became involved, other than diplomatically. He recognized that it might be impossible to gauge the consequences of the application of force to the shaky structure of the Ottoman Empire; he might well provoke its total collapse. In view of his relatively good relations with other European powers during the preceding decade or so, however, he believed that an equitable partition could be worked out.

Like Nicholas I, the Ottomans contemplated war. But their enthusiasm for war did not coincide with Nicholas's. Nicholas, ready to fight in the spring and early summer of 1853, cooled off when he realized that Russia was likely to face a European coalition. The Turks, on the other hand, were ready to settle until mid-May, but became increasingly bellicose in the summer and autumn because of the humiliations meted out to them by all the great powers and because of Russian un- willingness to compromise until too late. For a couple of days between May 11 and May 13, it looked as though Mehmet Ali Pasha, Rifat Pasha, and Menshikov might arrive at a solution of the problem through a note that would confirm the privileges of the Greek Ortho- dox millet without carrying the binding legal force of a treaty. When, on May 13, Menshikov forced the dismissal of Mehmet Ali and Rifat and their replacement with Mustafa Nâilî Pasha and Reshid Pasha, he made a cardinal mistake, however: his insulting treatment of the Porte played into the hands of the most belligerent members of the Ottoman Council of Ministers. A large and vocal group became increasingly convinced, through faith in the justice of their cause and in Allah, that war was the only honorable course. They remained convinced, despite the earnest, if somewhat clumsy, efforts of Austria, Britain, France, and Prussia to mediate through the Vienna Note plan.

If things had gone according to pattern, the war between Russia and the Ottoman Empire that broke out on October 4, 1853, should have run its course as a symbolic bloodletting, after which the four neutral great powers would have been able to step in and impose, or at least ratify, a negotiated solution. The fact that things went otherwise im- plies that these other European powers, although they did not plan war, nonetheless had reasons for wanting it.

Napoleon III (whom Kinglake accused of starting the war[2]) wanted war originally to strengthen his own dynasty. A successful tourney in the Middle East could give his government the cachet of military glory, so important to a Bonapartist regime. Furthermore, a war that divided Russia from Austria would inevitably lead the way to new diplomatic combinations and would enhance the position of France, long held down by the so-called Holy Alliance. Preserving the Ottoman Empire was definitely of secondary importance to the French, for they believed it could not be done—not, that is, as a long-term proposition. But the fact that the Middle East was in a state of flux gave it an enduring fascination for Napoleon: it might be exploitable in the future as a laboratory for his cherished "principle of nationalities."

The British had grown accustomed to exercising what amounted to an informal protectorate at Constantinople. Although a highly quali- fied observer like Stratford de Redcliffe had already come to doubt the feasibility of this position as a long-term policy, it was supported by influential members of the government, most notably Lord Palmerston, and aroused significant popular enthusiasm. Britain's power at Con- stantinople rested on an association with the Tanzimat reformers and their policies of centralization, secularization, and economic accessibility. All these factors were challenged, more or less directly, by Russia's demands in the spring of 1853. The British had strong reasons for moving to counter these demands and to maintain their position: their motives included Britain's prestige as a great power and her credibility as a friend; the strategic balance in southwestern Asia, where—with Persia essentially written off and Afghanistan in turmoil—Britain's influence in the Ottoman Empire was essential to her dominance of both the eastern Mediterranean and the approaches to India; and finally, her economic stake in the Ottoman Empire, particularly the large market for British exports and the availability of grain from Moldavia and Walachia. All these considerations made the British vulnerable to the virtuoso performance of Reshid Pasha, who deserves recognition for the extraordinary skill with which, step by step, he implicated the British in the military defense of objectives that they had intended to safeguard by diplomatic means alone.

In the end, Reshid was helped not only by the sloppiness of some of the details of British policy towards the Ottoman Empire—which were arrived at by compromise in a coalition Cabinet—but still more by the mind-set of ordinary Englishmen, who had been taught for years that Russia was evil and Turkey was good, and that Roman Catholics and Greek Orthodox were superstitious while Moslems and Protestants were progressive. British policy rested on a series of fundamental misconceptions about the nature of the Ottoman Empire; the character of its leaders' feelings for foreigners, particularly Englishmen; and the desirability, let alone the feasibility, of rapid Westernization under foreign sponsorshop. As these misconceptions were gradually exposed, the British grew increasingly disillusioned with the Ottoman Empire and with the whole policy of the Crimean Alliance: although their interests in the area were real, a different and less ambitious policy could ultimately serve them just as well. Thirty years later, the British tacitly accepted the idea of partition of the Ottoman Empire and, in taking Cyprus and Egypt for themselves, safeguarded the essence of their position. These developments, in seeming to demonstrate that the Crimean War had not been necessary, helped to entrench the "bluffs and blunders" theory so dear to British historians.

For the French, on the other hand, the war was, on the whole, a success. Certainly Napoleon's prestige rose enormously as a result of the leading role played by France. This prestige was enhanced during the first months of the fighting, when the French army seemed so much better organized and so much more effective than any of the other forces in the field. The choice of Paris as the site for the peace conference in 1856 seemed to crystallize French dominance. In fact, Napoleon had achieved one of his objectives: the war sowed dissension between Austria and Russia. Although Prussia and Russia remained staunch allies, the old Holy Alliance, which had preserved the conservative orientation of European diplomacy since 1815, had been dealt a blow from which it would not recover until after 1870, when the success of the Italian and German unification movements had changed the rules of the game.

In another sense, however, Napoleon's triumph was illusory—ultimately more apparent than real. As Winfried Baumgart has recently pointed out, he missed the opportunity to put through important territorial changes, which would have upset the Vienna settlement and would have implemented his "principle of nationalities."[3] His hesitancy to push the war to its logical conclusion by opening new theatres of conflict after the fall of Sevastopol was probably sound; but the fact remains that he would never be so powerful again as he was in the early 50s. He let the opportunity slip and lost control of the forward movement in European politics; the big revisions would be masterminded by Bismarck and Cavour. How did Napoleon judge the stakes of the game? Would things have been better for France and for Bonapartism if he had gambled from strength in the 1850s rather than from weakness in the 1860s? Or would the final debacle simply have come sooner? Scholarly evaluation, to the extent that it is possible at all, founders on the mystery of Napoleon's estimates and intentions. It is not surprising—in view of the lack of trustworthy, firsthand sources concerning Napoleon's thinking—that French policy still awaits modern, in-depth analysis.

For the Ottomans, the war was a successful phase in the long Turkish retreat from Europe that dominated the eighteenth and nineteenth centuries. Thanks to British and French aid, the Porte emerged on the winning side, in contrast to the results of the wars of 1828–29 and 1877–78. The Russians were beaten to a standstill, and the Porte gained a breathing space of some twenty years. Yet when it came to making peace, the Porte's allies consulted their own interests, rather than those of the Ottoman Empire. When Ottoman claims conflicted with Western concerns, as in the question of autonomy for Moldavia and Walachia, the Porte was forced to yield. Only when there was a coincidence of aims, as in the neutralization of the Black Sea, did the Porte come away from the bargaining table with gains; and even then, the arrangement—both in form and in durability—was dependent on British good will. The Porte's only unequivocal gain by the treaty was the retrocession by Russia of the eastern Anatolian fortress of Kars;

and everyone had recognized even before the war that Kars, although locally and symbolically important, was peripheral to the Ottoman state.

Greater ultimate significance attaches to the effects of the war on Ottoman society. The important Islâhat Fermani (known in the West as the Hatt-i Humayun, or Imperial Rescript, of 1856), which was issued by the Sultan and was noted by the signatories in the peace treaty, was the most radical statement yet by the Tanzimat reformers of the secular character of Ottoman citizenship and of the purely private nature of individual religious beliefs. It incorporated the objectives of Ottoman Westernizers, and it provided the springboard for a further stage of reform, culminating in the constitution of 1876. More indirectly, the war had furthered Westernization through the example set by the thousands of European troops who spent a long or a brief time in Constantinople and by the dramatic borrowing by the Ottoman treasury from foreign banking houses, a process that started with the need to finance the war effort and climaxed with Ottoman bankruptcy in 1876.

This last event is a sign that short-term advance in Western influence did not necessarily bring long-term Western-style "progress." Ottoman fiscal problems and the backlash generated by the attempts to modernize in the 1860s fostered new opposition movements such as the Yeni Osmanlılar (Young Ottomans) and contributed ultimately to acceptance of the despotic rule of Abdul-Hamid II. The relative international security of the Empire after the Crimean War undercut one of the reformers' standing arguments for change, the need to curry favor with the West. Meanwhile, in Europe, closer exposure to Ottoman ways brought disillusionment. Many, particularly in Britain, gradually revised their optimistic notions of Ottoman society. When the next major international crisis came in the 1870s, the Ottoman Empire was both weaker and more isolated than it had been twenty years before. Despite the reformers' best efforts and despite periodic successes like the Crimean War, the century-long trend was downhill. Although Turkish historians have seen the war as a successful operation, Westerners have been more impressed with the overall failure: the inability of the Tanzimat reformers to rejuvenate Ottoman society and Britain's final abandonment of the informal protectorate have allowed later historians to discount the importance of Ottoman problems in causing the war in the first place.

It is appropriate to say a word about the Italian role in the Crimean War, since the Kingdom of Sardinia eventually joined the Crimean alliance. Although Italian instability had obvious implications for nditions in the Hapsburg Empire and in the Ottoman Balkans, the diplomacy of the war was marginal in the calculations of Italian statesmen. Sardinian participation did not come from prescience on Cavour's part; it did, however, turn out to be a lucky move, since Cavour was thus enabled to win friends and influence people, particularly Lord Clarendon, at the peace congress. When Italy was, in fact, unified some five years thereafter, the Crimean episode could serve as part of the legend. It acquired an importance in retrospect that it certainly did not deserve by any objective standard.[4]

The most significant aspect of the war for Sardinia was not what happened to Italy; it was what happened to Austria. Ironically, Austria—though never technically a participant—was the real loser in the war. While the Russians suffered a temporary setback, the Austrians endured a permanent defeat. Austria's action in forcing the Russians to evacuate Moldavia and Walachia, which were then occupied by Austrian troops, shifted the whole scene of the war away from the tinderbox of the Balkans to the relatively peripheral Crimean peninsula. It was a step from which both the Austrians and the Ottomans benefited; but the Austrians ultimately paid the price. The resulting strain on Hapsburg resources, particularly finances, left a lasting mark. Furthermore, the Austrians incurred the enmity of the Russians without gaining the friendship of Britain and France. About all that recent defenders of Buol's policy have been able to claim is that anything else he might have done would probably have been worse.[5] The fact remains that, without the Crimean War, neither Italian unification nor German unification could have taken place when and as it did. It is no wonder that historians studying the Crimean War from an Austrian or a German point of view have emphasized the importance of rivalries growing out of Central European instability.

As for the Russians, they were forced to accept the status of victim in the peace treaty; but their defeat was only partial. It was a blow to the tsarist system of government, rather than to the Russian state, as such. Russian resources remained essentially untapped; Russian territory had barely been touched. If the tsar and his advisers judged it impossible to continue the war, it was because an inefficient and antiquated system of government could not mobilize the enormous reserves of Russian strength.[6] In this context of governmental failure, Tarle was right to emphasize the theme of faulty communications within the tsarist government as a factor in causing the war. And it is tempting, and not unreasonable, to see Russia as the victim of British aspirations for hegemony in the world struggle for power, especially economic power, or even to pick out individual Englishmen, like Stratford

Canning, as bogeymen. Still the Russians were not permanently downed; after all, of the three great multinational empires involved in the Crimean War, only Russia survives today.

It should be apparent from this analysis that interpretations of the origins of the Crimean War have been crucially influenced by perceptions of its results. For the British and the Russians, both of whom came to see the war as tangential to their real strength and essential interests, it was natural to portray the conflict as the outcome of personal accidents and governmental deficiencies. Tarle's picture of bureaucrats afraid to tell the truth to the tsar is logically complementary to Kingsley Martin's study of the overly individualistic, conflict-ridden Aberdeen coalition Cabinet. For Austrians and Germans, the fact that the Crimean War afforded the springboard for radical change has underscored the importance of revolutionary movements going back to 1848 and of diplomatic rivalries growing out of them. For historians of the Eastern Question, the centerpiece of the struggle has been the problem posed by the Sick Man of Europe, or, to view the situation from the other side, the impediments to modernization through consensus that were exacerbated by the self-serving policies of meddling foreign powers.

But whether one sees events in the Near East as the Eastern Question or the Western Question, it remains important that the Crimean War represented a high point of great-power involvement. The next "Eastern crisis" in 1876–78 brought frenzied international activity, but only the Russians, among the great powers, went to war. Later problems, such as the Bulgarian crisis of the 1880s, the Bosnian Crisis of 1908, or the Balkan Wars of 1912–13, were fought out locally by local combatants. Although the new, small Balkan states served, in some instances, as great-power surrogates, the great powers themselves stayed aloof. When the Austrians kept the Crimean War out of the Balkans, not only did they cushion its impact on the Ottoman Empire, but, in adding to their own almost unbearable responsibilities for the Balkan ethnic mess, they fell heir to many of the Ottomans' problems. Recent accounts have praised Buol for winning sixty years of peace for Europe. Certainly it was no mean accomplishment; it was, indeed, an accomplishment that has not been equalled in our time. But the war that Buol postponed was fought later, under worse conditions. The death toll was high at Sevastopol, but it did not compare with the carnage achieved by improved firepower in the trenches at the Somme. And the Ottoman Empire, as the Sick Man of Europe, was perceived by Europe as occupying an inferior, quasi-colonial status. Although the Ottomans had considerable room for maneuver, and they had learned to use their position with consummate skill, ultimately it was possible for other, stronger powers to reach an agreement over their heads, as was done at the peace congress in 1856. When Austria became the Sick Man of Europe, this freedom was restricted. The Austrians, after all, were Europeans; they had to be treated as equals. The conflicts arising out of the breakup of the Hapsburg Empire were not susceptible to mediation from above; they were fought out to the end. What will happen, in a nuclear age, if the Russian "Empire" ever breaks up, remains to be seen.[7]

Notes
Bibliography
Index

Notes

Preface

1. Brison D. Gooch, "A Century of Historiography on the Origins of the Crimean War," p. 46.

Chapter 1

1. Disraeli, quoted in Kingsley Martin, *The Triumph of Lord Palmerston*, p. 30; Morier, quoted in J. A. R. Marriott, *The Eastern Question*, p. 249; M. S. Anderson, *The Eastern Question, 1774–1923*, p. 132.

2. Gooch, "A Century of Historiography"; J. B. Conacher, *The Aberdeen Coalition, 1852–1855;* Paul W. Schroeder, *Austria, Great Britain, and the Crimean War;* Bernhard Unckel, *Österreich und der Krimkrieg;* Winfried Baumgart, *Der Friede von Paris, 1856;* John S. Curtiss, "Nicholas I, Austria, and the Eastern Question" and "Russian Diplomacy in the Mid-Nineteenth Century"; Brison D. Gooch, *The New Bonapartist Generals in the Crimean War.*

3. See Alan Dowty, *The Limits of American Isolation: The United States and the Crimean War;* Garry J. Alder, "India and the Crimean War."

4. Anderson, *Eastern Question*, p. 71.

5. Philip E. Mosely, *Russian Diplomacy and the Opening of the Eastern Question in 1838 and 1839*, pp. 9–22.

6. Donald Southgate, *"The Most English Minister . . . ," The Policies and Politics of Palmerston*, pp. 61–66; Palmerston, quoted in Sir Charles Webster, *The Foreign Policy of Palmerston, 1830–1841*, 1:282–83.

7. Vernon John Puryear, *International Economics and Diplomacy in the Near East*, pp. 15–16; H. W. V. Temperley, *England and the Near East*, pp. 76–77 (hereafter cited as Temperley, *Crimea*).

8. Puryear, *International Economics*, pp. 108–9, 124–27; Anderson, *Eastern Question*, p. 93.

9. [Frank Edgar] Bailey, *British Policy and the Turkish Reform Movement: A Study in Anglo-Turkish Relations, 1826–53*, pp. 189–90; Puryear, *International Economics*, pp. 102–3.

10. Bailey, *British Policy*, p. 188.

11. For a telling description of this process, see D. C. M. Platt, *The Cinderella Service: British Consuls since 1825*, pp. 125–79.

12. See Bernard Lewis, *The Emergence of Modern Turkey*, pp. 122–25, and George G. Arnakis [and Wayne S. Vucinich], *The Near East in Modern Times*, 1:200–1.

13. Stanford J. Shaw, "The Ottoman View of the Balkans," p. 73.

14. Walter Ralls, "The Papal Aggression of 1850: A Study in Victorian Anti-Catholicism," pp. 244–47.

15. PRO: Cowley to Palmerston, March 26, 1848 (FO 78/728); PRO: Stratford Canning to Palmerston, July 1, 1848 (FO 78/733); Stanley Lane-Poole, *The Life of The Right Honourable Stratford Canning*, 2:177–86.

16. Temperley, *Crimea*, pp. 258–59; PRO: Stratford Canning to Palmerston, November 20, 1848 (FO 78/736).

17. Radu R. Florescu, *The Struggle against Russia in the Roumanian Principalities, 1821–1854*, p. 208.

18. Southgate, *"The Most English Minister,"* p. 237.

19. PRO: Stratford Canning to Palmerston, January 4, 1849 (FO 78/772), May 3, 1849 (FO 78/775).

20. H. C. F. Bell, *Lord Palmerston*, 2:13.

21. Charles Sproxton, *Palmerston and the Hungarian Revolution*, pp. 11–38; AE: Palmerston quoted in Drouyn de Lhuys to de Tocqueville, August 22, 1849 (Angleterre 674). All references to the AE are to the Correspondance Politique.

22. Palmerston to Lord John Russell, September 29, 1849, in G. P. Gooch, ed., *The Later Correspondence of Lord John Russell, 1840–1878*, 2:9; Temperley, *Crimea*, p. 263.

23. PRO: Stratford Canning to Palmerston, September 17, 1849 (FO 78/779).

24. The most illuminating contemporary evidence on this question is to be found in Augustus Phillimore, *The Life of Admiral of the Fleet Sir William Parker*, 3:528–648. For a résumé of the historiographical debate, see Temperley, *Crimea*, appendix IV, pp. 499–506. See also Brian Connell, ed., *Regina v. Palmerston: The Correspondence between Queen Victoria and Her Foreign and Prime Minister, 1837–1865*, pp. 111–12.

25. Vernon John Puryear, *England, Russia, and the Straits Question, 1844–56*, pp. 173–76. (Hereafter cited as Puryear, *Straits Question*.)

26. PRO: Stratford Canning to Palmerston, November 24, 1849 ("Most Confidential") (FO 78/782); November 30, 1849 ("Most Confidential") (FO 78/782); and December 29, 1849 ("Private and Confidential") (FO 78/783).

27. PRO: Stratford Canning to Palmerston, November 30, 1849 ("Private") (FO 78/782); Temperley, *Crimea*, p. 315.

28. Temperley, *Crimea*, pp. 280–86.

29. [Aleksandr, baron Jomini,] *Diplomatic Study on the Crimean War (1852 to 1856)*, 1:137; Edmond Bapst, *Les Origines de la guerre de Crimée*, p. 165; L[ouis] Thouvenel, *Nicolas Ier et Napoléon III*, p. 4; Temperley, *Crimea*, p. 286.

30. AE: de la Hitte to Aupick, January 16, 1850 (Turquie 303), May 25, 1850 (Turquie 303), Aupick to de la Hitte, January 30, 1850 (Turquie 303), de la Hitte to Aupick, March 7, 1850 (Turquie 303).

31. AE: Aupick to de la Hitte, January 30, 1850 (Turquie 303), December 14, 1850 (Turquie 304), [Brenier] to Aupick, January 28, 1851 (Turquie 305).

32. AE: Aupick to Brenier [Baroche], April 15, 1851, and Lavalette to Baroche, May 20, 1851 (Turquie 305), Baroche to Lavalette, June 17, 1851 (Turquie 306).

33. Cf. Eichmann, *Die Reformen des osmanischen Reiches*, pp. 83–85.

34. Bekir Sıtkı Baykal, "Makamat-ı mübareke meselesi ve Babıâli," *Belleten*, 23 (1959), p. 249 and n. 15. (Hereafter cited as Baykal, *Belleten*.)

35. AE: Lavalette to Drouyn de Lhuys, August 3, 1852 (Turquie 309); Temperley, *Crimea*, pp. 292–95.

36. Temperley, *Crimea*, pp. 294–95.

37. This point was made by John S. Curtiss in a conversation with me.

38. Nicholas I, "Note at the Time of the Menshikov Mission, 1853," in A. M. Zaionchkovsky, *Vostochnaya Voyna 1853–1856, Prilozheniya*, 1:357–58. (Hereafter cited as Zaionchkovsky.)

39. Count Karl Robert Nesselrode, "Summary of the Year 1852," in Zaionchkovsky, 1:312–32, and "Memorandum," December 20, 1852, in ibid., 1:354–57.

40. Nicholas I, "Note at the Time of the Menshikov Mission, 1853," in ibid., 1:357–58.

41. Nicholas I, "Note," January 7, 1853, in ibid., 1:582–83.

42. Admiral Kornilov, "List of Transport Available from the Black Sea Fleet," February 1853, in ibid., 1:583–84, and "Discussion on the Assumption of Equipping a Descent with Landing of Troops for Action in Turkey" [end of 1852 or early 1853], in ibid., 1:585–94.

43. Theodor Schiemann, *Geschichte Russlands unter Kaiser Nikolaus I*, 4:278–79.

44. H. E. Howard, "Brunnow's Reports on Aberdeen, 1853," p. 315.

45. Nesselrode, "Summary of the Year 1852," in Zaionchkovsky, 1:318; Charles W. Hallberg, *Franz Joseph and Napoleon III, 1852–1864*, pp. 43–44.

46. Gavin Burns Henderson, *Crimean War Diplomacy*, pp. 5–6.

47. Seymour, quoted in Temperley, *Crimea*, p. 272. Temperley notes that the tsar really said, "the bear is dying," but the metaphor was bowdlerized for the Blue Book.

48. Puryear, *Straits Question*, p. 212. For texts of Seymour's reports, see J. von Jasmund, *Aktenstücke zur orientalische Frage*, 1:24–54 (hereafter cited as Jasmund).

49. Temperley, who summarizes Nicholas's plan (*Crimea*, p. 276), has neatly compared this partition scheme with ideas already discussed with Paskevich, which were less favorable to Britain (ibid., p. 461).

50. Seymour to Russell, February 9, 1853, quoted in Temperley, *Crimea*, p. 275.

51. Temperley, *Crimea*, p. 273.

52. Schiemann, *Geschichte Russlands*, 4:275.

53. Nesselrode to Brunnow, January 14, 1853, quoted in I. de Testa [*et al.*], *Recueil des traités de la Porte ottomane avec les puissances étrangères*, 3:259–62 (hereafter cited as Testa); PRO: Clarendon to Stratford de Redcliffe, April 5 and 18, May 7 and 26, 1853 ("Private") (FO 352/86).

54. Cf. Puryear, *Straits Question*, pp. 222–23.

55. Cf. Evgeniy Viktorovich Tarle, *Krymskaya Voyna*, vols. 8 and 9 in *Sochineniya*, vol. 8, *passim*.

56. Steven Stanojević, *Narodna Enciklopedija Srpsko-Hrvatsko-Slovenacka* (Zagreb, [1925]-29) 4:942–43. I am indebted for this information to Professor David MacKenzie of the University of North Carolina at Greensboro.

57. Temperley, *Crimea*, pp. 208–13.

58. Ibid., pp. 212–13.

59. Ibid., pp. 214–15.

60. Ibid.

61. Eg[or Petrovich] Kovalevsky, *Der Krieg Russlands mit der Türkei*, pp. 60–61.

62. Temperley, *Crimea*, pp. 216–18.

63. Unckel, *Österreich und der Krimkrieg*, pp. 58, 62.

64. HHSA: Pamphlet received from the Porte concerning Montenegro, annexed to Klezl to Buol, January 13, 1853, #4A (PA XII/46). All citations from HHSA are from the Politisches Archiv.

65. Eichmann, *Die Reformen des osmanischen Reiches*, p. 14.

66. Unckel, *Österreich und der Krimkrieg*, p. 60.

67. Cf. AE: Bourée to Drouyn de Lhuys, August 5, 1853 (Turquie 318A).

68. Temperley, *Crimea*, pp. 221–22.

69. HHSA: Pamphlet annexed to Klezl to Buol, January 13, 1853, #4A (PA XII/46).

70. Unckel, *Österreich und der Krimkrieg*, pp. 70–71.

71. HHSA: Klezl to Buol, January 6, 1853, #2C (PA XII/46).

72. PRO: Fonblanque to Rose, January 2, 1853 (FO 195/407).

73. AE: Leiningen to Fuad Efendi, February 3, 1853, annexed to Lavalette to Drouyn de Lhuys, February 5, 1853 (Turquie 311).

74. Unckel, *Österreich und der Krimkreig,* pp. 67–70.

75. HHSA: Klezl to Buol, February 7, 1853, #11 (PA XII/46), February 17, 1853, #13A (PA XII/46), February 17, 1853, Reserviert #13B (PA XII/46), and *passim.*

76. Unckel (*Österreich und der Krimkrieg,* pp. 76–77) tells us that the Porte shifted its position on February 14, one day after information about the Menshikov mission reached Constantinople on February 13. Klezl, on the other hand, tells us that Fuad had already adopted a more conciliatory tone when Steindl delivered the final Austrian note on February 12. Later that same day, Steindl was invited to confer with Fuad early the following morning, February 13 (HHSA: Klezl to Buol, February 17, 1853, #13A [PA XII/46]). Not until the afternoon of February 13 did Ozerov receive instructions to work with Leiningen; at the same time he evidently received word of the Menshikov mission, for he communicated this news to the Austrians along with his new instructions. (HHSA: Klezl to Buol, February 17, 1853, Reservient #13B [PA XII/46]). But Ozerov had already, upon his own initiative, impressed on Fuad how seriously Russia viewed the negotiations (HHSA: Ozerov to Nesselrode, January 31/ February 12, 1853, #14, annexed to Buol to Bruck, March 7, 1853, Reserviert #2 [PA XII/48]).

77. HHSA: Klezl to Buol, March 7, 1853, Reserviert #18C (PA XII/46).

78. Unckel, *Österreich und der Krimkrieg,* p. 78–79.

79. Nesselrode, "Summary of the Year 1852," in Zaionchkovsky, 1:332.

80. This thesis has recently been persuasively presented by Unckel in *Österreich und der Krimkrieg.*

Chapter II

1. Peter von Meyendorff to Alexander von Meyendorff, February 1/13, 1853, in Otto Hoetzsch, ed., *Peter von Meyendorff, ein russischer Diplomat an den Höfen von Berlin und Wien: Politischer und Privater Briefwechsel, 1826–1863,* 3:10–11. (Hereafter cited as *Meyendorff.*) The Julian calendar, still used in Russia and Greece and in other Orthodox countries in the nineteenth century, was then about two weeks behind the Gregorian calendar used in the rest of Europe. When documents are dated by the Julian calendar, the date according to the Gregorian calendar is provided second.

2. Tarle, *Krymskaya Voyna,* 8:156–58.

3. Nesselrode to Menshikov, January 28, 1853, in Zaionchkovsky, 1:371–73, 374–76.

4. Nesselrode to Menshikov, January 28, 1853, "Secret Instructions," in ibid., 1:376–77.

5. Emperor Nicholas to the Sultan, January 24, 1853, in ibid., 1:386–87; "Project of a Separate and Secret Act," in ibid., 1:385–86; "Project of a Convention between Russia and the Porte," in ibid., 1:382, 383, 384–85.

6. A. J. P. Taylor, *The Struggle for Mastery in Europe, 1848–1918,* p. 52; this interpretation of Kutchuk-Kainardji had already been presented to the Ottoman Commission (See Baykal, *Belleten,* p. 249 and n. 15).

7. Temperley, *Crimea,* pp. 308, 309.

8. İbnülemin Mahmut Kemal İnal, *Osmanlı Devrinde Son Sadriâzamlar,* 1:156. (Hereafter cited as İnal.)

9. [Modest Ivanovich] Bogdanovich, *Vostochnaya Voyna 1853–1856 godov,* 1:38. (Hereafter cited as Bogdanovich.)

10. Nesselrode to Nicholas I, January 1853, in Zaionchkovsky, 1:370; Clarendon to Reeve [March 27, 1853], in John Knox Laughton, *Memoirs of the Life and Correspondence of Henry Reeve,* 1:297.

11. Baykal, *Belleten,* p. 253.

12. Stratford, quoted in Allan Cunningham, "Stratford Canning and the Tanzimat," pp. 257–58.

13. For an excellent analysis of Sadık Rifat's views and their relation to the Tanzimat, see Şerif Mardin, *The Genesis of Young Ottoman Thought,* pp. 175–95; a useful biographical sketch is Ali Fuat, "Rical-i Tanzimattan Sadık Rifat Paşa." |

14. HHSA: Klezl to Buol, March 7, 1853, Reserviert #18C (PA XII/46).

15. J. C. Hurewitz, "The Beginnings of Military Modernization in the Middle East: A Comparative Analysis," p. 151.

16. Temperley, *Crimea,* p. 161.

17. Baykal, *Belleten,* p. 254; Temperley, *Crimea,* p. 530.

18. HHSA: Klezl to Buol, March 10, 1853, #19C (PA XII/46). On this whole incident, see Felix Bamberg, *Geshichte der orientalischen Angelegenheit,* pp. 54–56, and Bekir Sıtkı Baykal, "Die Frage der Heiligen Stätten im gelobten Lande und die Hohe Pforte," pp. 413–14.

19. *Note verbale* presented March 4/16, 1853, in Zaionchkovsky, 1:387–91. Quotations are taken from p. 391.

20. *Note verbale* presented March 10/22, 1853, in ibid., 1:391–92; Note accompanying the draft convention annexed to Menshikov to Nesselrode, March 12/24, 1853, in ibid., 1:393–94; Menshikov to Nesselrode, March 12/24, 1853, in ibid., 1:392–93.

21. Thouvenel, *Nicolas Ier et Napoléon III,* p. 92.

22. Edouard Driault and Michel Lhéritier, *Histoire diplomatique de la Grèce de 1821 à nos jours,* 2:375.

23. HHSA: Klezl to Buol, April 21, 1853, Reserviert #31C (PA XII/46).

24. Friedrich Wilhelm Fernau, *Patriarchen am Goldenen Horn: Gegenwart und Tradition des orthodoxen Orients,* p. 40.

25. PRO: Rifat Pasha to Metaxas, 29 Cemaziyelevvel 1269/March 10, 1853; official note, Porte to Greek Ministry, 29 Cemaziyelevvel 1269/March 10, 1853, annexed to Stratford de Redcliffe to Clarendon, April 26, 1853 (FO 78/931). Where documents are dated according to the Moslem calendar, the equivalent date according to Western European usage is given afterwards. Moslem months are spelled as in modern Turkish.

26. Tarle, *Krymskaya Voyna,* 8:175–76, recounts that Menshikov was so little interested in the Graeco-Turkish boundary question that he had neglected to bring a map with him to Turkey. He was obliged to send for one from the nearest Austrian military command, ten days' journey each way by special courier.

27. Hans Rall, "Griechenland zwischen Russland und dem übrigen Europa: Die 'Grosse Idee' der Griechen zwischen 1847 und 1859," pp. 174–75.

28. See Driault, *Grèce,* 2:374–75. Eugenia Voyiatzis Nomikos, "The International Position of Greece during the Crimean War," concludes this was simply a courteous gesture (p. 46).

29. PRO: Paicos to British, French, and Russian representatives in Athens, March 19/31, 1853, annexed to Stratford de Redcliffe to Clarendon, April 26, 1853 (FO 78/931).

30. PRO: Longworth to Stratford de Redcliffe, April 21, 1853 (FO 195/392).

31. PRO: Stratford de Redcliffe to Clarendon, April 26, 1853 (FO 78/931).

32. Nomikos, "International Position of Greece," pp. 70–71.

33. Nil A. Popov, *Rossiya i Serbiya,* 2:343.

34. Ibid., pp. 344–47; PRO: Fonblanque to Rose, March 25, 1853 (FO 195/407), February 11, 1853 (FO 195/407).

35. Stratford de Redcliffe to Clarendon, April 20, 1853, quoted in Great Britain, *Sessional Papers,* 1854, "Correspondence Respecting the Rights and Privileges of the Latin and Greek Churches in Turkey," Part I, 71:156; AE: De la Cour to Drouyn de Lhuys, April 23, 1853 (Turquie 312).

36. İnal, 1:63; Tarle, *Krymskaya Voyna,* 8:153.

37. HHSA: Klezl to Buol, April 4, 1853, #26A and #26B (PA XII/46).

38. HHSA: Klezl to Buol, March 28, 1853, #24; April 4, 1853, #26A; April 11, 1853, #28A (PA XII/46).

39. Temperley, *Crimea,* p. 310. For the bitter quarrel that had erupted between Stratford and Colonel Rose in 1851, see PRO: annexes to Stratford Canning to Palmerston, October 1, 1851 ("Private"), Stratford Canning to Palmerston, October 18, 1851 ("Private"), and October 25, 1851 ("Private and Confidential") (FO 78/859).

40. [Jean Gilbert Victor Fialin,] duc de Persigny, *Mémoires,* pp. 226–34.

41. F. A. Simpson, *Louis Napoleon and the Recovery of France, 1848–1856,* p. 224 (see also Henderson, *Crimean War Diplomacy,* pp. 6–8); Nassau William Senior, *Conversations with M. Thiers, M. Guizot, and Other Distinguished Persons during the Second Empire,* 1:142; Driault and Lhéritier, *Grèce,* 1:375.

English anxiety concerning French invasion was based on the development of steam navigation during the 1840s, which was thought to render a surprise attack across the Channel, independent of winds and tides, really feasible for the first time (C. J. Bartlett, *Great Britain and Sea Power, 1815–1853,* pp. 155–57).

42. HHSA: Klezl to Buol, March 28, 1853, #24 (PA XII/46); AE: Benedetti to Drouyn de Lhuys, March 14, 1853 (Turquie 312).

Though the grand vizier, in his conversation with Rose, had played down Russia's hostile aims, he did not have solid information about the objectives of the Menshikov mission until March 16, after he had changed his mind about the fleet. It seems, therefore, that his reevaluation of Ottoman defenses must have been of greater importance in motivating his retraction.

43. Laughton, *Henry Reeve,* 1:311, n. 2.

44. PRO: Slade to Stratford de Redcliffe, May 12, 1853 (FO 78/932).

45. Ibid.

46. Kornilov to Prince Constantine (for transmission to Nicholas I), March 19, 1853, in Zaionchkovsky, 1:595–96.

47. L. Gorev, *Voyna 1853–1856 gg. i oborona Sevastopolya,* p. 61. Menshikov's communication is summarized in a letter by Nicholas I, March 22 and 23, 1853, in Zaionchkovsky, 1:597.

48. Nicholas I, March 22 and 23, 1853, in Zaionchkovsky 1:597–98; Paskevich to Nicholas I, March 24, 1853, in ibid., 1:599–600; Nicholas I, April 8, 1853, in ibid., 1:601–3; Paskevich to Nicholas I, March 24, 1853, in ibid., 1:600–1.

49. Baykal, *Belleten,* p. 255. Baykal reaches this conclusion on the basis of protocols of Rifat's conversations with Menshikov.

50. At least this was the advantage accruing to the Russians as the Porte perceived it. See Protocol summarizing the discussions of the *Meclis-i umumî* held to consider Menshikov's second ultimatum, in Ali Fuat Türkgeldi, *Mesail-i Mühimme-i Siyasiyye,* 1:284–85. (Hereafter cited as Türkgeldi.)

51. Bogdanovich, 1:44–46; Menshikov to Nesselrode, March 29/April 10, 1853, in Zaionchkovsky, 1:400; Protocols in Türkgeldi, 1:274–91.

52. AE: Drouyn de Lhuys to de la Cour, March 22, 1853 (Turquie 312), March 28, 1853 (Turquie 312).

53. Alexander W. Kinglake, *Invasion of the Crimea*, 1:94; Taylor, *Struggle for Mastery*, p. 53. The text of Stratford's instructions is given in H. W. V. Temperley and Lilian M. Penson, *Foundations of British Foreign Policy*, pp. 139–44.

54. Cf. Cunningham, "Stratford Canning," pp. 262–63; PRO: Stratford Canning to Palmerston, November 5, November 11, and November 19, 1850 (FO 78/824).

55. Enver Ziya Karal, *Islâhat Fermani devri, 1856–1861*, in *Osmanlı Tarihi*, 6:29.

56. Cunningham, "Stratford Canning," pp. 250, 260; Davison, *Reform*, p. 34.

57. Cf. Cunningham, "Stratford Canning," p. 254.

58. Menshikov to Nesselrode, March 29/April 10, 1853, in Zaionchkovsky, 1:399; Menshikov to Nesselrode, April 14/26, 1853, in ibid., 1:405; Jasmund, 1:69–70; Memorandum sent to the Sultan by the Foreign Minister, Rifat Pasha, summarizing the negotiations with Prince Menshikov concerning the problem of the Holy Places, in Türkgeldi, 1:257–64; Decisions . . . concerning the Holy Places, in Türkgeldi, 1:264–66.

59. Menshikov to Nesselrode, March 12/24, 1853, in Zaionchkovsky, 1:393; Bogdanovich, 1:46; Argyropoulos to Menshikov, March 17/29, 1853, in Zaionchkovsky, 1:397–98.

60. Menshikov to Nesselrode, March 29/April 10, 1853, in ibid., 1:400–401; Nesselrode to Menshikov, April 11, 1853, in ibid., 1:404–5; Menshikov to Nesselrode, March 29/April 10, 1853, in ibid., 1:401; Nesselrode to Menshikov, April 11, 1853, in ibid., 1:405.

61. HHSA: Klezl to Buol, March 31, 1853, #25A (PA XII/46); April 14, 1853, Reserviert #29B (PA XII/46); April 18, 1853, Reserviert #30C (PA XII/46).

62. Temperley, *Crimea*, p. 316; Kinglake, *Invasion of the Crimea*, 1:96; Stratford de Redcliffe to Clarendon, April 11, 1853, in Great Britain, *Sessional Papers*, 1854, "Correspondence . . . ," Part I, 71:135–36.

63. Lane-Poole, *Stratford Canning*, 2:255–56, 259.

64. Menshikov to Nesselrode (private letter), April 14/26, 1853, in Zaionchkovsky, 1:406.

65. Menshikov to Rifat Pasha, April 23/May 5, 1853, in Zaionchkovsky, 1:407–8.

66. [Eugène,] vicomte de Guichen, *La Guerre de Crimée (1854–1856) et l'attitude des puissances européennes*, p. 36.

67. PRO: Etienne Pisani to Stratford de Redcliffe, May 11, 1853 (FO 78/932); Menshikov's interview with Namık Pasha is dated May 7 by Temperley (*Crimea*, p. 323).

68. Kinglake, *Invasion of the Crimea*, 1:114–17.

69. Protocol summarizing the discussions of the *Meclis-i umumî* held to consider Menshikov's second ultimatum, in Türkgeldi, 1:277–79.

70. HHSA: Klezl to Buol, May 5, 1853, #35A, and May 9, 1853, #36D (PA XII/46).

71. For an excellent article on Moslem-Christian relations in this period, see Roderic H. Davison, "Turkish Attitudes concerning Christian-Muslim Equality in the Nineteenth Century."

72. Lane-Poole, *Stratford Canning*, 1:264; Menshikov to Nesselrode, May 4/16, 1853, in Zaionchkovsky, 1:421.

73. Abdurrahman Sheref, *Tarih Musahabeleri*, p. 82. (Hereafter cited as Abdurrahman.)

74. This may be inferred from Menshikov to Nesselrode, May 4/16, 1853, in Zaionchkovsky, 1:421, and from the Porte's later actions.

75. Protocol summarizing the discussions of the *Meclis-i umumî* held to consider Menshikov's second ultimatum, in Türkgeldi, 1:278.

76. This quotation was translated by me from the text of the note of 2 Şaban 1269/May 10, 1853, as given in AE: Porte to Menshikov, 2 Şaban 1269/May 10, 1853 (Turquie 312). A different, less conciliatory, wording appears in Zaionchkovsky, 1:418.

77. Here again, the text preserved in the Quai d'Orsay is fuller and more explicit than that given in Zaionchkovsky.

78. [Jomini,] *Diplomatic Study,* 1:428–29.

79. "Un acte émanant de la volonté souveraine du Sultan, un engagement libre, mais solennel." The text of this note, which was presumably written in French originally, is the same in AE: Menshikov to Rifat Pasha, April 29/May 11, 1853 (Turquie 313), and in Zaionchkovsky, 1:418–19.

80. HHSA: Klezl to Buol, May 9, 1853, #36A (PA XII/46); [Menshikov to Nesselrode,] May 4/16, 1853, in Zaionchkovsky, 1:423.

81. Protocol summarizing the discussions of the *Meclis-i umumî* held to consider Menshikov's second ultimatum, in Türkgeldi, 1:281–82; Introduction, Türkgeldi, 1:19–20; Thouvenel, *Nicholas Ier et Napoléon III,* pp. 150–51.

82. Thouvenel, *Nicholas Ier et Napoléon III,* pp. 150–52.

83. Menshikov, quoted in H. W. V. Temperley, "Stratford de Redcliffe and the Origins of the Crimean War," pt. 1, p. 615, n. 1. Temperley argues that Mehmet Ali was not ready to negotiate a note with Menshikov; his basis is Mehmet Ali's statement to the British Embassy's dragoman, Pisani, on May 4 to the effect that he had "refused" to meet Russian terms. But this disclosure does not affect the case, since it predates even Menshikov's call for a *sened* on May 5.

84. For a summary of their relationship, see Lane-Poole, *Stratford Canning,* 1:104–7.

85. Memorandum by Nesselrode, December 13, 1852, in Zaionchkovsky, 1:353. Reshid had actually suggested that the tsar demand special rights concerning the Greek Orthodox millet on the basis of the Treaty of Kutchuk-Kainardji. It seems unlikely that this overture was decisive in Russian policymaking. The Russian government had already elaborated plans for the mission, and Kutchuk-Kainardji had already been adduced in support of the protectorate (Baykal, *Belleten,* p. 249 and n. 15). But the proposal did serve notice to the Russians that Reshid might be willing to bargain with them. The Russians continued to distrust Reshid, however (see the discussion that follows, in text), and indeed, it seems most likely that his motive was a desire to get back into power at a time when his stock with the British was very low.

86. Thouvenel, *Nicholas Ier et Napoléon III,* pp. 145–54; see also the testimony of Rifat's son, Rauf Bey, in Türkgeldi, 1:20, n. 10.

87. Tarle, *Krymskaya Voyna,* 8:191.

88. Temperley, "Stratford de Redcliffe and the Origins of the Crimean War," pt. 1, p. 613.

89. See Nesselrode's comments in Zaionchkovsky, 1:353. For the Sultan's views, see Abdurrahman, p. 82.

90. Menshikov to Reshid Pasha, April 28/May 10, 1853, in Zaionchkovsky, 1:417.

91. [Menshikov to Nesselrode,] May 4/16, 1853, in ibid., 1:423.

92. Edouard Driault, *La Question d'orient,* p. 172.

93. [Menshikov to Nesselrode,] May 4/16, 1853, in Zaionchkovsky, 1:423.

94. Baykal, *Geschichte,* p. 415.

95. Temperley, "Stratford de Redcliffe and the Origins of the Crimean War," pt. 1, p. 611, n. 1.

96. İbrahim Alâettin Gövsa, *Türk Meşhurları Ansiklopedisi,* "Büyük Mustafa Reşit Paşa," pp. 322–23. (Hereafter cited as *Türk Meşhurlari Ansiklopedisi.*)

97. İnal, 1:59–60; "Damat Mehmet Ali Paşa," in *Türk Meşhurları Ansiklopedisi,* p. 245.

98. Niyazi Berkes, *The Development of Secularism in Turkey,* p. 177. For a contrasting, but not necessarily conflicting, emphasis on self-interest as the basis of bureaucratic rivalries, see Mardin, *The Genesis of Young Ottoman Thought,* pp. 110, 120–22.

99. İnal, 1:74–75.

100. Mardin, *The Genesis of Young Ottoman Thought,* pp. 191–93.

101. İnal, 1:75.

102. *Takvim-i Vekâyi* #487 (17 Şaban 1269/May 27, 1853). According to [Menshikov to Nesselrode,] May 4/16, 1853 (Zaionchkovsky, 1:424), the exchange between Fethi Ahmet and Namık had already occurred and was merely confirmed at this time.

103. Menshikov to Nesselrode, May 4/16, 1853, in Zaionchkovsky, 1:427.

104. Ali Fuat, *Mecmuası,* pp. 6–7.

105. Tarle, *Krymskaya Voyna,* 8:181; [Menshikov to Nesselrode,] May 4/16, 1853, in Zaionchkovsky, 1:424–25.

The council, along with the rest of the May negotiations, is summarized in Türkgeldi, 1:274–91. This account, written at the end of May, emphasized the Porte's unyielding opposition to a *sened;* in view of hints contained in other versions, it seems likely that the Porte's consistency was exaggerated in the immediacy of the confrontation with the Russians at the end of May.

106. [Menshikov to Nesselrode,] May 4/16, 1853, in Zaionchkovsky, 1:424–25. The passage quoted appears on p. 425.

107. Ibid.

108. Davison, "Turkish Attitudes," *passim.*

109. Menshikov to Nesselrode, May 9/21, 1853, in Zaionchkovsky, 1:429.

110. Only twenty-five years before, on the occasion of the last war with Russia, Fuad Efendi's father, İzzet Molla Keçecizâde, had nearly been executed because he advised against war on "rational grounds" (Mardin, *The Genesis of Young Ottoman Thought,* p. 108, n. 5; pp. 172–73).

111. Stratford de Redcliffe to Clarendon, May 14, 1853, in Great Britain, *Sessional Papers,* 1854, "Correspondence . . . ," Part I, pp. 214–15; Tarle, *Krymskaya Voyna,* 8:181. Reshid's account does not seem to be an accurate description of the sense of the Council (cf. [Menshikov to Nesselrode,] May 4/16, 1853, in Zaionchkovsky, 1:424–25).

112. Stratford de Redcliffe, May 15, 1853, in Great Britain, *Sessional Papers,* 1854, "Correspondence . . . ," Part I, p. 195. His draft is annexed as Enclosure #1, p. 196.

113. AE: De la Cour to Drouyn de Lhuys, May 15, 1853 (Turquie 313).

114. Protocol summarizing the discussions of the *Meclis-i umumî* held to consider Menshikov's second ultimatum, in Türkgeldi, 1:287.

115. The texts of Reshid's note and Menshikov's reply are given in Great Britain, *Sessional Papers,* 1854, "Correspondence . . . ," Part I, pp. 208–9.

116. [Menshikov to Nesselrode,] May 4/16, 1853 in Zaionchkovsky, 1:424–25. In another letter to the chancellor on May 4/16 (ibid., 1:427), Menshikov stated revealingly: "Reshid seems to me to be in good faith with regard to us, insofar as a Turk is capable of it."

117. This council was an enlarged form of the *Meclis-i Vâlâ-yı Ahkâm-ı Adliye.* For its founding and functions, see Mardin, *The Genesis of Young Ottoman Thought,* pp. 152–54, and Stanford J. Shaw, "The Central Legislative Councils in the Nineteenth Century Ottoman Reform Movement before 1876."

118. Menshikov to Nesselrode, May 9/21, 1853, in Zaionchkovsky, 1:428.

119. Abdurrahman, pp. 83–84.

120. Menshikov to Nesselrode, May 9/21, 1853, #45, in Zaionchkovsky, 1:428.

121. Menshikov to Nesselrode, May 9/21, 1853, #46, in ibid., 1:429–30. See also Guido Quazza, "La politica orientale sarda nei dispacci del Tecco (1850–1856)," pp. 667–70. An account of this meeting is given in the Protocol summarizing the discussions of the *Meclis-i umumî* held to consider Menshikov's second ultimatum, in Türkgeldi, 1:283–87.

122. Menshikov to Nesselrode, May 9/21, 1853, #45, in Zaionchkovsky, 1:428–29.
123. Türkgeldi, 1:289.
124. Stratford de Redcliffe to Clarendon, May 19, 1853, in Great Britain, *Sessional Papers*, 1854, in "Correspondence ...," Part I, p. 205; Menshikov to Nesselrode, May 9/21, 1853, in Zaionchkovsky, 1:428–29. Temperley telescopes the two meetings into one, which he places on May 17 (*Crimea*, pp. 326–27) or on either May 17 or 18 ("Stratford de Redcliffe and the Origins of the Crimean War," pt. 1, p. 611), but this is clearly contradicted by the documents cited above.
125. HHSA: Klezl to Buol, May 19, 1853, #40B (PA XII/46).
126. Temperley, *Crimea*, p. 328. Apparently Menshikov also hoped that someone at the Porte would think better of the refusal; see Argyropoulos's evidence, cited in Temperley, "Stratford de Redcliffe and the Origins of the Crimean War," pt. 1, p. 612.
127. Sir Adolphus Slade, *Turkey and the Crimean War*, pp. 90–91.
128. Draft note proposed by Menshikov to the Porte, May 8/20, 1853 in Zaionchkovsky, 1:434–36; passage quoted appears on p. 435.
129. Stratford de Redcliffe to Clarendon, May 20, 1853, in Great Britain, *Sessional Papers*, 1854, "Correspondence ...," Part I, p. 219.
130. [Menshikov to Nesselrode,] n.d., #146, in Zaionchkovsky, 1:434; Tarle, *Krymskaya Voyna*, 8:201; [Jomini,] *Diplomatic Study*, 1:183. Stratford de Redcliffe later obtained statements from Alison and Reshid to the effect that Reshid had not wished to accept the proposals (annexes to Stratford de Redcliffe to Clarendon, June 24, 1853, in Great Britain, *Sessional Papers*, 1854, "Correspondence ...," Part I, pp. 336–38). Temperley accepts this version ("Stratford de Redcliffe and the Origins of the Crimean War," pt. 1, p. 612), but Reshid's comments, as quoted by Temperley, are more than a little ambiguous: according to Stratford, Reshid "had examined the Prince's paper [of the 20th] with every wish to find a hope of accommodation but could discover nothing of the kind."
131. Cf. Temperley, "Stratford de Redcliffe and the Origins of the Crimean War," pt. 1, pp. 612–13, and *Crimea*, pp. 328–29.
132. Stratford de Redcliffe to Clarendon, May 20, 1853, in Great Britain, *Sessional Papers*, 1854, "Correspondence ...," Part I, p. 219. For the text of the note, see Zaionchkovsky, 1:430–31.
133. Cf. Zaionchkovsky, 1:430–31.
134. Temperley, *Crimea*, p. 329.
135. Slade, *Turkey and the Crimean War*, p. 91.

Chapter III

1. The text of Nesselrode's note of May 19/31, 1853, has been published by Jasmund (1:95–97), Testa (4:257–58), and Zaionchkovsky (1:441–42).
2. Puryear, *Straits Question*, p. 267.
3. R. W. Seton-Watson, *A History of the Roumanians*, p. 232, says the mission took place in May, but evidently it was postponed. Schroeder (*Crimean War*, pp. 44–45) describes the mission as occurring in July and says that the Russians discounted Gyulai's warnings, in the belief that his instructions reflected Buol's views, not a consensus.
4. Nicholas I, May 16/17, 1853, communicated to Gorchakov May 28, 1853, in Zaionchkovsky, 1:603–4.
5. Tarle, *Krymskaya Voyna*, 8:232; Meyendorff to Franz Joseph, annexed to Meyendorff to Nesselrode, May 26/June 7, 1853, in Zaionchkovsky, 2:43–44; [Jomini,] *Diplomatic Study*, 1:202–3.

6. Meyendorff to Nesselrode, June 18/30, 1853, in Zaionchkovsky, 2:45–47; Tarle, *Krymskaya Voyna*, 8:232.

7. J. B. Kelly, *Britain and the Persian Gulf, 1795–1880*, p. 456.

8. Tarle, *Krymskaya Voyna*, 8:260.

9. PRO: Wyse to Stratford de Redcliffe, May 30, 1853, annexed to Stratford de Redcliffe to Clarendon, July 4, 1853 (FO 78/934).

10. Raoul Bossy, "Les Roumains et l'idée fédéraliste au XIXe siècle," pp. 170–74.

11. L. S. Stavrianos, *Balkan Federation*, pp. 73–74.

12. See Charles and Barbara Jelavich, "The Danubian Principalities and Bulgaria under Russian Protectorship."

13. Gorchakov to War Ministry, November 4, 1853, in Zaionchkovsky, 1:148–49; Marian Kukiel, *Czartoryski and European Unity, 1770–1861*, pp. 281–83; Marcel Handelsman, "La Guerre de Crimée, la question polonaise, et les origines du problème bulgare," pp. 275–79.

14. Dowty, *Limits of American Isolation*, p. 63.

15. Stratford de Redcliffe to Clarendon, May 27, 1853, in Great Britain, *Sessional Papers*, 1854, "Correspondence . . . ," Part I, p. 263; Clarendon to Stratford de Redcliffe, May 31, 1853, in Testa, 4:258–59.

16. Martin, *Triumph of Lord Palmerston*, p. 116; Clarendon, quoted in ibid., p. 106; DB: Musurus to Reshid Pasha, June 7, 1853 (Siyasiyye: Rusya 610).

17. AE: De la Cour to Drouyn de Lhuys, June 16, 1853 (Turquie 313); Stratford de Redcliffe to his wife, May 29, 1853, quoted in Lane-Poole, *Stratford Canning*, 2:274; DB: Veli Pasha to Reshid Pasha, 2 Ramazan 1269/June 9, 1853 (Siyasiyye: Rusya 1161).

18. Enver Ziya Karal, *Nizam-ı cedit ve Tanzimat devirleri 1789–1856*, in *Osmanlı Tarihi*, vol. 5, pt. 2, p. 231.

19. Puryear, *Straits Question*, p. 285.

20. Stratford de Redcliffe to Clarendon, June 3, 1853, and June 7, 1853, in Great Britain, *Sessional Papers*, 1854, "Correspondence . . . ," Part I, pp. 275, 292; DB: Musurus to Reshid Pasha, June 17, 1853 (Siyasiyye: Rusya 610); PRO: Stratford de Redcliffe to Clarendon, June 16, 1853 (FO 78/933).

21. Nesselrode to Meyendorff, July 31, 1853, in Karl Robert, comte de Nesselrode, *Lettres et papiers du chancelier comte de Nesselrode, 1760–1856*, 10:266. (Hereafter cited as Nesselrode.)

22. PRO: Stratford de Redcliffe to Clarendon, July 9, 1853 (FO 78/934).

23. AE: De la Cour to Drouyn de Lhuys, July 10, 1853 (Turquie 313).

24. Tarle, *Krymskaya Voyna*, 8:290.

25. Cowley to Clarendon, July 11, 1853, in Great Britain, *Sessional Papers*, 1854, "Correspondence . . . ," Part I, p. 357. Though Bourqueney denied authorship, he evidently was the originator of the plan (see Meyendorff to Nesselrode, July 1/13, 1853, in *Meyendorff*, 3:42).

26. Seymour to Clarendon, June 27, 1853, in Great Britain, *Sessional Papers*, 1854, "Correspondence . . . ," Part I, p. 324.

27. Seymour to Clarendon, June 28, 1853, in ibid., p. 330; Cowley to Clarendon, July 6, 1853, in ibid., p. 331; Clarendon to Cowley, July 8, 1853, in ibid., p. 342.

28. Temperley, *Crimea*, pp. 343–45.

29. Nesselrode to Meyendorff, July 9, 1853, in Nesselrode, 10:253.

30. Stratford de Redcliffe to Clarendon, August 20, 1853, in Great Britain, *Sessional Papers*, 1854, "Correspondence . . . ," Part II, p. 81.

31. Lane-Poole, *Stratford Canning*, 2:280–81; HHSA: Bruck to Buol, July 18, 1853, #13 (PA XII/47).

32. HHSA: Bruck to Buol, July 9, 1853, #9B (PA XII/47).

33. Protocol of the debate in the *Meclis-i umumi* concerning the Russian invasion of the Principalities and the response to be made, 5 Şevval 1269/12 July 1853, in Türkgeldi, 1:301–8.

34. HHSA: Bruck to Buol, July 14, 1853, #12 G (PA XII/47).

35. HHSA: Bruck to Buol, July 18, 1853, #13 (PA XII/47).

36. AE: De la Cour to Drouyn de Lhuys, July 15, 1853 (Turquie 314), July 19, 1853 (Turquie 314).

37. HHSA: Bruck to Buol, July 18, 1853, #13 (PA XII/47).

38. AE: Protocol of the conference of July 17, 1853, annexed to de la Cour to Drouyn de Lhuys, July 20, 1853 (Turquie 314).

39. HHSA: Bruck to Buol, July 18, 1853, #13 (PA XII/47).

40. For text, see Jasmund, 1:141–45.

41. AE: Protocol of the conference of July 17, 1853, annexed to de la Cour to Drouyn de Lhuys, July 20, 1853 (Turquie 314).

42. HHSA: Bruck to Buol, July 18, 1853, #13 (PA XII/47).

43. Ibid.

44. HHSA: Bruck to Buol, July 20, 1853, #14 (PA XII/47).

45. AE: De la Cour to Drouyn de Lhuys, July 19, 1853 (Turquie 314).

46. HHSA: Bruck to Buol, July 20, 1853 (telegram) (PA XII/47).

47. AE: De la Cour to Drouyn de Lhuys, July 20, 1853 (Turquie 314), July 25, 1853 (Turquie 314).

48. HHSA: Bruck to Buol, July 20, 1853, #14 (PA XII/47).

49. It is reported by de la Cour on July 19 (AE: Turquie 314) and by Bruck in a postscript to his dispatch of July 20 (HHSA: #14 [PA XII/47]); both representatives indicate that word had just arrived.

50. Nesselrode's order contained in a letter to Khaltchinski, consul-general at Jassy, June 3, 1853, was sent home by de la Cour (AE: Turquie 314, annexed to #56) and by Bruck (HHSA: annexed to #18A of July 25, 1853 [PA XII/47]).

51. Seymour to Clarendon, August 12, 1853, in Great Britain, *Sessional Papers, 1854,* "Correspondence . . . ," Part II, pp. 49–50.

52. Apostol Stan, "L'Organisation de la lutte de libération des peuples balkaniques dans les principautés roumaines pendant la phase danubienne de la guerre de Crimée (1853–1854)," p. 835.

53. AE: De la Cour to Drouyn de Lhuys, July 23 and 25, 1853 (Turquie 314).

54. The text of the note has been published on Jasmund, 1:148–49.

55. For text of the memorandum, see ibid., p. 149.

56. HHSA: Bruck to Buol, July 22, 1853, #16 (PA XII/47); AE: De la Cour to Drouyn de Lhuys, July 25, 1853 (Turquie 314).

57. Westmorland to Clarendon, July 29, 1853, in Great Britain, *Sessional Papers, 1854,* "Correspondence . . . ," Part II, p. 4.

58. Westmorland to Clarendon, July 24, 1853, in ibid., p. 1.

59. For a biographical treatment favorable to Bruck, see Richard Charmatz, *Minister Freiherr von Bruck, Der Vorkämpfer Mitteleuropas.*

60. Tarle, *Krymskaya Voyna,* 8:231.

61. For an excellent analysis of this conflict, see Paul W. Schroeder, "Bruck versus Buol: The Dispute over Austrian Eastern Policy, 1853–1855."

62. Temperley, "Stratford de Redcliffe and the Origins of the Crimean War," pt. 2.

63. For text of the Vienna Note, see Zaionchkovsky, 1:52–53, and Jasmund, 1:149.

64. Westmorland to Clarendon, October 25, 1853, in Great Britain, *Sessional Papers,*

1854, "Correspondence . . . ," Part II, p. 185; Temperley, *Crimea*, p. 345. As Temperley indicates, it is unclear whether Arif reported the Vienna Note to the Porte or not. He may have hesitated to report such bad news, or, since he was no friend of Reshid's, he may have meant to humiliate him by delaying the news. I have found no such communication in the Dişişleri Bakanliği Hazine-i Evrak; but as cataloging is, as yet, incomplete, it would be foolhardy to rule out the possibility that one exists. Even so, Temperley's point that informal consultation with Arif was not equivalent to the more formal Austrian approach to Nicholas is well taken.

65. Cf. Temperley, "Stratford de Redcliffe and the Origins of the Crimean War," pt. 2, pp. 268–69.

66. Nesselrode to Meyendorff, April 6, 1853 [evidently a mistake for August 6], in Nesselrode, 10:269; Nesselrode to Meyendorff, August 8, 1953, in ibid., 10:270.

67. Temperley, "Stratford de Redcliffe and the Origins of the Crimean War," pt. 2, pp. 268, 274.

68. See text of the Turkish Ultimatum in Jasmund, 1:141–45.

69. PRO: Clarendon to Stratford de Redcliffe, September 8, 1853 ("Private") (FO 352/36).

70. HHSA: Bruck to Buol, August 11, 1853, #22A (PA XII/47).

71. Lane-Poole, *Stratford Canning*, 2:290–91.

72. HHSA: Bruck to Buol, August 11, 1853, #22A (PA XII/47).

73. The text of this communication (Nesselrode to Meyendorff, July 25/August 6, 1853) has been published in Zaionchkovsky, 2:54, and in Testa, 4:316.

74. HHSA: Bruck to Buol, August 15, 1853, #23A (PA XII/47).

75. The British attaché Alison's name for the imbroglio (Lane-Poole, *Stratford Canning*, 2:317).

76. Temperley, "Stratford de Redcliffe and the Origins of the Crimean War," pt. 2, pp. 272–74; AE: De la Cour to Drouyn de Lhuys, August 9, 1853 (Turquie 314), August 19, 1853 (Turquie 315).

77. Slade, *Turkey and the Crimean War*, pp. 101–2, 107–8.

78. AE: De la Cour to Drouyn de Lhuys, August 19, 1853 (Turquie 315).

79. HHSA: Bruck to Buol, July 20, 1853, #14 (PA XII/47).

80. AE: De la Cour to Drouyn de Lhuys, August 11, 1853 (Turquie 314); PRO: Stratford de Redcliffe to Clarendon, August 11, 1853 (FO 78/936).

81. PRO: Stratford de Redcliffe to Clarendon, August 11, 1853, postscript of August 12 (FO 78/936).

82. AE: De la Cour to Drouyn de Lhuys, August 20, 1853 (Turquie 315).

83. AE: De la Cour to Drouyn de Lhuys, August 11, 1853 (Turquie 314), August 19, 1853 (Turquie 315).

84. AE: De la Cour to Drouyn de Lhuys, August 16, 1853 (Turquie 315); HHSA: Bruck to Buol, August 18, 1853, #24A (PA XII/47); Slade, *Turkey and the Crimean War*, pp. 108–11. Slade, who disliked and disagreed with Stratford, believed that it was on this occasion that Stratford urged the Turks to refuse the Vienna Note. The story is important, for it is the only specific version of the accusation that we have. But, as Temperley remarks, it is equally possible that Stratford meant to restrain Mehmet Ali ("Stratford de Redcliffe and the Origins of the Crimean War," pt. 2, p. 267).

85. AE: De la Cour to Drouyn de Lhuys, August 18, 1853 (Turquie 315).

86. HHSA: Bruck to Buol, August 18, 1853, #24A (PA XII/47), and August 20, 1853, #25A (PA XII/47).

87. Stratford de Redcliffe to Clarendon, August 18, 1853, in Great Britain, *Sessional Papers*, 1854, "Correspondence . . . ," Part II, p. 72; Lane-Poole, *Stratford Canning,*

2:293. These accounts, which have Stratford practically snatch partial victory from the jaws of defeat, are certainly exaggerated and are an instructive example of the caution that must be exercised in using Stratford's dispatches.

88. HHSA: Bruck to Buol, August 20, 1853, #25A (PA XII/47).

89. Draft of the Vienna Note, in Zaionchkovsky, 2:52–53; Reshid Pasha to the representatives of France, Austria, England, and Prussia, accompanying the amended draft note, August 20, 1853, in ibid., 2:60–63; examination of the three amendments, in ibid., 2:55–57.

90. See HHSA: Bruck to Buol, August 11, 1853, #22B (PA XII/47).

91. See AE: De la Cour to Drouyn de Lhuys, August 31, 1853 (Turquie 315), for the beginning of a campaign that was to increase in virulence during the autumn. De la Cour suffered under a special disadvantage, inherent in the position of a French ambassador when French and British policy were similar. If the French representative attempted to outplay Stratford, he would have to be so brusque and domineering that the Porte's objections would force his recall. This had happened to both de la Cour's immediate predecessors, Lavalette and Aupick. If, on the other hand, he were too moderate, he would be overshadowed by Stratford and might then be recalled because of a subservience judged unbecoming by the new imperial regime. This was to be de la Cour's fate.

92. Conacher, *The Aberdeen Coalition*, p. 164.

93. See Simpson, *Louis Napoleon and the Recovery of France*, pp. 234–40.

94. See Aberdeen to Lord John Russell, August 30, 1853, in G. P. Gooch, ed., *Later Correspondence of Lord John Russell*, 2:152, and Martin, *Triumph of Lord Palmerston*, pp. 124–25.

95. Dmitri de Nesselrode to Nesselrode, from Constantinople, August 24/September 5, 1853, extract in Nesselrode, 10:281–83; Nesselrode to Meyendorff, April 6, 1853 [evidently in error for August 6], in Nesselrode, 10:268–69.

96. Philip Whitwell Wilson, ed., *The Greville Diary*, 2:463–64; Charles Frederick Vitzthum von Eckstaedt, *St. Petersburg and London in the Years 1852-1864*, ed. Henry Reeve, 1:65.

97. See [Jomini,] *Diplomatic Study*, 1:209, 221; Schiemann, *Geschichte Russlands*, 4:296; Puryear, *Straits Question*, pp. 289–90; Tarle, *Krymskaya Voyna*, 8:304, 309, 314; Bapst, *Origines*, p. 435, n. 1; Simpson, *Louis Napoleon and the Recovery of France*, pp. 232–38; Guichen, *La Guerre de Crimée*, p. 66; Karal, *Nizam-ı cedit*, p. 233.

98. See Lane-Poole, *Stratford Canning*, 2:295–96; E. F. Malcolm-Smith, *The Life of Stratford Canning*, pp. 258–59; and all the works of H. W. V. Temperley on the subject. For a detailed resume of Temperley's argument, see "Stratford de Redcliffe and the Origins of the Crimean War," pts. 1 and 2. See also Leland Livingston Sage, "Lord Stratford de Redcliffe and the Origins of the Crimean War."

99. Stratford de Redcliffe to Clarendon, August 20, 1853, quoted in Lane-Poole, *Stratford Canning*, 2:295; ibid., 2:295–96, 299–30.

100. Reshid Pasha to Musurus Bey, September 25, 1853/22 Zilhicce 1269, in Testa, vol. 4, pt. 2, p. 1, and in Great Britain, *Sessional Papers*, 1854, "Correspondence . . . ," Part II, p. 147.

101. J. L. Herkless, "Stratford, the Cabinet, and the Outbreak of the Crimean War," pp. 497–98.

102. See Conacher, *The Aberdeen Coalition*, p. 179; Gooch, *Century*, p. 48; Cunningham, "Stratford Canning," pp. 263–64; Schroeder, "Bruck versus Buol," pp. 197–99. An exception is Anderson, who asserts roundly in *The Eastern Question* that "the traditional accounts of the origins of the Crimean War . . . have nearly always taken Stratford too much at his own valuation and as a result exaggerated his role" (p. 127).

103. Stratford to Lady Canning, August 20/21, 1853, quoted in Lane-Poole, *Stratford Canning,* 2:298; Stratford to Clarendon, August 20, 1853, in ibid., p. 297.

104. AE: De la Cour to Drouyn de Lhuys, August 19, 1853 (Turquie 315).

105. The Koszta Affair is analyzed by Schroeder in "Bruck vs. Buol," p. 196.

106. HHSA: Bruck to Reshid Pasha, July 30, 1853, annexed to Bruck to Buol, August 8, 1853, #21C (PA XII/47); HHSA: Bruck to Reshid Pasha, August 4, 1853, #20D (PA XII/47). Bruck says his conversation with Reshid took place "*vorgestern,*" which would literally be August 2; however, since his note of July 30 was not sent until August 8, this démarche may have preceded the note.

107. Schroeder, "Bruck vs. Buol," p. 196; Nesselrode to Meyendorff, July 19, 1853, in Nesselrode, 10:258; Schroeder, "Bruck vs. Buol," p. 196.

108. HHSA: Bruck to Buol, July 20, 1853, #14 (PA XII/47).

109. HHSA: Bruck to Buol, August 1, 1853, #19B (PA XII/47); AE: De la Cour to Drouyn de Lhuys, August 5, 1853 (Turquie 314).

110. PRO: Fonblanque to Stratford de Redcliffe, June 23, 1853 ("Private") (FO 195/407); July 19, 1853 (FO 195/407); PRO: Michael Obrenovich to Serbian Senators, July 2/14, 1853, annexed to Fonblanque to Stratford de Redcliffe, July 25, 1853 (separate) (FO 195/407).

111. PRO: Fonblanque to Stratford de Redcliffe, July 19, 1853, and August 5, 1853 (FO 195/407); PRO: Fonblanque to Stratford de Redcliffe, July 19, 1853 (FO 195/407).

112. Meyendorff to Nesselrode, July 19/31, 1853, in *Meyendorff,* 3:55.

113. PRO: Cf. Fonblanque to Stratford de Redcliffe, July 13, July 16, July 22, July 24, July 26, July 28, and August 20, 1853 (FO 195/407); arrangements concerning the courier are in Fonblanque to Stratford de Redcliffe, July 24, 1853 (FO 195/407).

114. PRO: Fonblanque to Stratford de Redcliffe, August 11, 1853 (FO 195/407).

115. PRO: Fonblanque to Stratford de Redcliffe, August 16, 1853 (FO 195/407).

116. PRO: Stratford de Redcliffe to Clarendon, August 4, 1853 (FO 78/936); August 6, 1853 (FO 78/936).

117. AE: De la Cour to Drouyn de Lhuys, August 25, 1853 (Turquie 315).

118. HHSA: Bruck to Buol, August 20, 1853, #25B (PA XII/47).

119. See PRO: [Neale] to Stratford de Redcliffe, July 29, 1853, and August 2, 1853 (FO 78/936); Slade, *Turkey and the Crimean War,* p. 112.

120. PRO: [Longworth to Stratford de Redcliffe,] June 23, 1853, enclosure #1 in #146 (FO 78/934).

121. PRO: Longworth to Stratford de Redcliffe, July 26, 1853 (FO 195/392).

122. AE: De la Cour to Drouyn de Lhuys, July 15, 1853 (Turquie 314).

123. Slade, *Turkey and the Crimean War,* pp. 116–20; Alison to Lady Stratford de Redcliffe, August 20, 1853, quoted in Lane-Poole, *Stratford Canning,* 2:296.

124. Stratford to Clarendon, August 20, 1853, in ibid., 2:295; AE: De la Cour to Drouyn de Lhuys, August 19, 1853 (Turquie 315).

125. DB: Musurus to Reshid Pasha, June 4, 1853 (Siyasiyye: Rusya 610).

126. DB: Musurus to Reshid Pasha, June 7, 1853 (Siyasiyye: Rusya 610); June 17, 1853 (Siyasiyye: Rusya 610); June 27, 1853 (Siyasiyye: Rusya 609).

217. Although the letter from Reshid is yet to be found, this much of its contents can be inferred from Musurus's reply.

128. DB: Musurus to Reshid Pasha, July 2, 1853 (Siyasiyye: Rusya 609).

129. Temperley, "Stratford de Redcliffe and the Origins of the Crimean War," pt. 2, p. 274; Clarendon to Westmorland, September 7, 1853, in Great Britain, *Sessional Papers,* 1854, "Correspondence . . . ," Part II, p. 90; Clarendon to Stratford de Redcliffe, September 10, 1853, in ibid., p. 95.

130. Isidore Heller, ed., *Memoiren des Baron Bruck aus der Zeit des Krimkriegs,* p. 105.

131. Cf. Conacher, *The Aberdeen Coalition*, p. 207.

132. DB: *Times* [London], June 13, 1853, annexed to Musurus to Reshid Pasha, June 17, 1853 (Siyasiyye: Rusya 610); *Standard* [London], June 13, 1853, annexed to Musurus to Reshid Pasha, June 17, 1853 (Siyasiyye: Rusya 610); *Sun* [London], June 25, 1853, annexed to Musurus to Reshid Pasha, June 27, 1853 (Siyasiyye: Rusya 609).

133. For further discussion of this point, see chapter VII.

134. DB: Musurus to Reshid Pasha, June 7, 1853 (Siyasiyye: Rusya 610); *Sun* [London], June 13, 1853, and other clippings enclosed in Musurus to Reshid Pasha, June 17, 1853 (Siyasiyye: Rusya 610).

135. DB: *Sun* [London], June 21, 1853, and other clippings enclosed in Musurus to Reshid Pasha, June 27, 1853 (Siyasiyye: Rusya 609).

136. AE: De la Cour to Drouyn de Lhuys, August 14, 1853 (Turquie 314).

137. DB: Musurus to Reshid Pasha, July 2, 1853 (Siyasiyye: Rusya 609).

138. Aberdeen, quoted in Martin, *Triumph of Lord Palmerston*, pp. 103–4.

139. Baumgart, *Friede*, p. 10.

Chapter IV

1. This incident is covered in HHSA: Bruck to Buol, September 1, 1853, #29B (PA XII/47); AE: De la Cour to Drouyn de Lhuys, September 5, 1853 (Turquie 315); PRO: Stratford de Redcliffe to Clarendon, September 5, 1853 (FO 78/938).

2. AE: De la Cour to Drouyn de Lhuys, September 5, 1853 (Turquie 315); HHSA: Bruck to Buol, September 5, 1853, #30 (PA XII/47).

3. AE: De la Cour to Drouyn de Lhuys, September 5, 1853 (Turquie 315).

4. PRO: Stratford de Redcliffe to Clarendon, September 5, 1853 (FO 78/938).

5. AE: De la Cour to Drouyn de Lhuys, September 5, 1853 (Turquie 315).

6. Cf. Türkgeldi, 1:301–8.

7. HHSA: Bruck's report of audience with the Sultan, annexed to Bruck to Buol, August 20, 1853, #25B (PA XII/47).

8. Clarendon to Westmorland, September 7, 1853, in Great Britain, *Sessional Papers*, 1854, "Correspondence ... ," Part II, p. 90; Clarendon to Stratford de Redcliffe, September 10, 1853, in ibid., p. 95.

9. Clarendon to Lord John Russell, August 27, 1853, quoted in Gooch, ed., *Russell*, 2:151–52.

10. Martin, *Triumph of Lord Palmerston*, pp. 133–37; Russell, quoted in ibid., p. 126; DB: Musurus Bey to Reshid Pasha, August 26 and September 10, 1853 (Siyasiyye: Rusya 610).

11. Clarendon to Seymour, September 16, 1853, in Great Britain, *Sessional Papers*, 1854, "Correspondence ... ," Part II, p. 98.

12. Cowley to Clarendon, August 30, 1853, in ibid., p. 85.

13. DB: Veli Pasha to Reshid Pasha, 25 Zilkade 1269/August 30, 1853 (Siyasiyye: Rusya 1161).

14. Bapst, *Origines*, p. 442; Thouvenel, *Nicholas Ier et Napoléon III*, p. 232.

15. Alder, "India and the Crimean War," p. 21.

16. Bapst, *Origines*, pp. 439–41; see also Martin, *Triumph of Lord Palmerston*, p. 39, and Drouyn de Lhuys to Bourqueney, September 17, 1853, in Testa, 4:333–34. Schroeder argues that the "violent interpretation" merely provided the British ministers with a rationale for doing what they wanted to do anyhow (*Crimean War*, pp. 60–65).

17. Heller, ed., *Memoiren des Baron Bruck*, pp. 110–11.

18. AE: De la Cour to Drouyn de Lhuys, September 13, 1853 (Turquie 315).

19. AE: De la Cour to Drouyn de Lhuys, September 1, 1853 (Turquie 315); HHSA: Bruck to Buol, September 1, 1853, #29B (PA XII/47).

20. AE: De la Cour to Drouyn de Lhuys, September 1, 1853 (Turquie 315).

21. Kovalevsky, *Der Krieg Russlands*, p. 52, note.

22. Uriel Heyd, "The Ottoman 'Ulema and Westernization in the time of Selīm III and Maḥmūd II," in Heyd, ed., *Studies in Islamic History and Civilization*, p. 64.

23. Mardin, *The Genesis of Young Ottoman Thought*, pp. 127–30; Heyd, "The Ottoman 'Ulema," pp. 94–95.

24. Berkes, *The Development of Secularism in Turkey*, pp. 176–77.

25. Albert Hourani, "Ottoman Reform and the Politics of Notables," pp. 67–68.

26. Kamal S. Salibi, "The 1860 Upheaval in Damascus as seen by al-Sayyid Muhammad Abu'l-Su'ud al-Hasibi, Notable and *Naqib al-Ashraf* of the City," pp. 185–202.

27. AE: De la Cour to Drouyn de Lhuys, September 13, 1853 (Turquie 315).

28. Hourani, "Ottoman Reform," p. 68; Mardin, *The Genesis of Young Ottoman Thought*, p. 18, and p. 136, n. 5.

29. See chapter II.

30. HHSA: Bruck to Buol, September 12, 1853, #32A (PA XII/47).

31. AE: De la Cour to Drouyn de Lhuys, September 11, 1853 (Turquie 315).

32. PRO: Stratford de Redcliffe to Clarendon, September 15, 1853 (FO 78/938).

33. AE: De la Cour to Drouyn de Lhuys, September 11, 1853 (Turquie 315).

34. HHSA: Bruck to Buol, September 12, 1853, #32A (PA XII/47); Stratford de Redcliffe to Lady Stratford, September 13, 1853, quoted in Lane-Poole, *Stratford Canning*, 2:300; Stratford de Redcliffe to Clarendon, September 15, 1853, in Great Britain, *Sessional Papers*, 1854, "Correspondence . . . ," Part II, p. 121; Slade, *Turkey and the Crimean War*, pp. 120–25.

35. HHSA: Bruck to Buol, September 12, 1853, #32A (PA XII/47).

36. Ibid.

37. HHSA: Bruck to Buol, August 29, 1853, #28A (PA XII/47).

38. HHSA: Bruck to Buol, September 12, 1853, #32A (PA XII/47).

39. AE: De la Cour to Drouyn de Lhuys, September 11, 1853, #83 (Turquie 315).

40. AE: De la Cour to Drouyn de Lhuys, September 11, 1853, #82 (coded) (Turquie 315).

41. PRO: Stratford de Redcliffe to Clarendon, September 15, 1853 (FO 78/938).

42. AE: De la Cour to Drouyn de Lhuys, September 11, 1853, #82 (coded) (Turquie 315).

43. Temperley, "Stratford de Redcliffe and the Origins of the Crimean War," pt. 2, p. 277.

44. PRO: Stratford de Redcliffe to Clarendon, September 15, 1853 (FO 78/938); AE: De la Cour to Drouyn de Lhuys, September 11, 1853 (Turquie 315).

45. Puryear makes his case against Stratford to this effect in *France and the Levant*, p. 222, and in *Straits Question*, pp. 293–94.

46. Drouyn de Lhuys to Walewski, August 19, 1853, and September 1, 1853, in Jasmund, 1:153–54, 155–56.

47. Aberdeen to Sir James Graham, September 6, 1853, quoted in Martin, *Triumph of Lord Palmerston*, pp. 78–79. Schroeder explains this letter away, not entirely convincingly, in *Crimean War*, p. 63.

48. Drouyn de Lhuys to Walewski, September 21, 1853, in Jasmund, 1:167.

49. Kinglake (*Invasion of the Crimea*, 1:237–38) and Temperley ("Stratford de Redcliffe and the Origins of the Crimean War," pt. 2, p. 276, n. 2) give both alternatives. In

fact, the order to the French fleet had been sent September 20 (AE: Ducos to Drouyn de Lhuys, September 20, 1853 [Turquie 315]).

50. Temperley, "Stratford de Redcliffe and the Origins of the Crimean War," pt. 2, p. 276.

51. Heller, ed., *Memoiren des Baron Bruck*, pp. 114–15; and see HHSA: Bruck to Buol, September 12, 1853, #32A (PA XII/47), a complementary account, but less revealing. Bruck said in his dispatch that the Sultan had not yet taken the decision for war or peace, but this would not preclude a hint to the war leaders, which would explain the rapid resolution of the crisis.

52. HHSA: Bruck to Buol, September 15, 1853, #33A (PA XII/47).

53. Heller, ed., *Memoiren des Baron Bruck*, p. 115.

54. Parallel accounts of the meeting are given by Bruck (HHSA: Bruck to Buol, September 15, 1853 [PA XII/47]) and by de la Cour (AE: De la Cour to Drouyn de Lhuys, September 13, 1853 [Turquie 315]).

55. HHSA: Bruck to Buol, September 19, 1853, #34A (PA XII/47).

56. AE: De la Cour to Drouyn de Lhuys, September 21, 1853 (Turquie 315).

57. HHSA: De la Cour to Bruck, September 24, 1853, annexed to Bruck to Buol, September 26, 1853, #36A (PA XII/47); Bruck to Buol, September 26, 1853, #36A (PA XII/47).

58. Temperley, "Stratford de Redcliffe and the Origins of the Crimean War," pt. 2, pp. 281–82.

59. AE: De la Cour to Drouyn de Lhuys, September 21, 1853 (Turquie 315).

60. Temperley, *Crimea*, pp. 359–60.

61. HHSA: Bruck to Buol, September 26, 1853, #36A (PA XII/47); the text of the Austro-Prussian note, with the variants adopted in the Anglo-French note, is appended to that report.

62. Temperley, *Crimea*, p. 360. Temperley gives the dates of the meeting as September 26 and 27. The reports of de la Cour (AE: De la Cour to Drouyn de Lhuys, September 26, 1853 [Turquie 315]), of Bruck (HHSA: Bruck to Buol, September 26, 1853, #36A [PA XII/47]), and of Stratford (Stratford de Redcliffe to Clarendon, September 26, 1853, in Great Britain, *Sessional Papers*, 1854, "Correspondence ... ," Part II, p. 149) give September 25 and 26.

63. HHSA: Memorandum from Schlechta to Bruck, September 27, 1853, annexed to Bruck to Buol, September 29, 1853, #37A (PA XII/47); Alison to Lady Stratford, September 28, 1853, quoted in Lane-Poole, *Stratford Canning*, 2:302.

64. HHSA: Memorandum from Schlechta to Bruck, September 27, 1853, annexed to Bruck to Buol, September 29, 1853, #37A (PA XII/47).

65. See Stanford J. Shaw, "The Central Legislative Councils."

66. HHSA: Memorandum from Schlechta to Bruck, September 27, 1853, annexed to Bruck to Buol, September 29, 1853, #37A (PA XII/47); for other European accounts, see AE: De la Cour to Drouyn de Lhuys, September 26, 1853 (Turquie 315), and PRO: Stratford de Redcliffe to Clarendon, September 28, 1853 (FO 78/938).

67. This account of the meeting is based on the protocol of the meeting of the *Meclis-i umumî* that took the decision concerning the declaration of the Crimean War, in Türkgeldi, 1:315–20.

68. HHSA: Memorandum from Schlechta to Bruck, September 27, 1853, annexed to Bruck to Buol, September 29, 1853, #37A (PA XII/47).

69. HHSA: Bruck to Buol, September 22, 1853, #35D (PA XII/47); Puryear, *Straits Question*, p. 325.

70. AE: De la Cour to Drouyn de Lhuys, September 21, 1853 (Turquie 315).

71. Westmorland to Clarendon, September 28, 1853, in Great Britain, *Sessional Papers*, 1854, "Correspondence . . . ," Part II, p. 129.

72. Taylor, *Struggle for Mastery*, p. 57.

73. Cowley to Clarendon, October 4, 1853, in Great Britain, *Sessional Papers*, 1854, "Correspondence . . . ," Part II, p. 131.

74. Clarendon to Loftus, October 5, 1853, in ibid., p. 132.

75. B. E. Schmitt, "Diplomatic Preliminaries of the Crimean War," p. 38.

76. AE: De la Cour to Drouyn de Lhuys, September 29, 1853 (Turquie 315).

77. Stratford de Redcliffe to Clarendon, September 26, 1853, in Great Britain, *Sessional Papers*, 1854, "Correspondence . . . ," Part II, pp. 148–49.

78. Clarendon to Cowley, September 23, 1853, in ibid., p. 114.

79. DB: Musurus Bey to Reshid Pasha, September 7, 1853 (Siyasiyye: Rusya 609).

80. Heller (in Heller, ed., *Memoiren des Baron Bruck*, pp. 116–17) says the declaration of war was held up until word arrived from England.

81. HHSA: Memorandum from Schlechta to Bruck, September 27, 1853, annexed to Bruck to Buol, September 29, 1853, #37A (PA XII/47).

82. Lane-Poole, *Stratford Canning*, 2:311.

83. AE: De la Cour to Drouyn de Lhuys, September 23, 1853 (Turquie 315).

84. HHSA: Memorandum from Schlechta to Bruck, September 27, 1853, annexed to Bruck to Buol, September 29, 1853, #37A (PA XII/47).

85. Protocol in Türkgeldi, 1:319.

86. Karal, *Nizam-ı cedit*, p. 233.

87. AE: De la Cour to Drouyn de Lhuys, September 30, 1853 (Turquie 315).

88. PRO: Stratford de Redcliffe to Clarendon, September 28, 1853 (FO 78/938).

89. Text given in Guichen, *La Guerre de Crimée*, pp. 75–76.

Chapter V

1. For texts, see Jasmund, 1:187–92.

2. Nesselrode to Countess Chreptowitch, October 11, 1853, in Nesselrode, 10:288; see also Tarle, *Krymskaya Voyna*, 8:324–25.

3. AE: De la Cour to Drouyn de Lhuys, October 5, 1853 (telegram) (Turquie 315); Reshid Pasha to Stratford de Redcliffe, October 8, 1853, enclosure #1 in Stratford de Redcliffe to Clarendon, October 15, 1853, in Great Britain, *Sessional Papers*, 1854, "Correspondence . . . ," Part II, pp. 189–90; Reshid Pasha to Musurus Bey, 28 Zilhicce 1269/October 1, 1853, in ibid., p. 153.

4. See AE: Foreign Ministry to Veli Pasha, October 25, 1853 (Turquie 316).

5. AE: De la Cour to Drouyn de Lhuys, October 16, 1853 (telegram), October 17, 1853 (Turquie 316); PRO: Clarendon to Stratford de Redcliffe, November 8, 1853 ("Private") (FO 352/36).

6. Temperley, *Crimea*, p. 362.

7. AE: De la Cour to Drouyn de Lhuys, October 12, 1853 (Turquie 316).

8. See AE: Drouyn de Lhuys to Maritime Prefect at Toulon, September 26, 1853 (telegram) (Turquie 315).

9. AE: De la Cour to Drouyn de Lhuys, October 12, 1853 (Turquie 316).

10. Temperley, *Crimea*, pp. 362–63.

11. Puryear, *Straits Question*, pp. 292–94, 302–3.

12. AE: De la Cour to Drouyn de Lhuys, October 4, 1853 (Turquie 315).

13. AE: De la Cour to Drouyn de Lhuys, October 21, 1853 (Turquie 316).

14. AE: Reshid Pasha to de la Cour and Stratford de Redcliffe, 16 Muharrem 1270/ October 19, 1853, annexed to de la Cour to Drouyn de Lhuys, October 21, 1853 (Turquie 316).

15. AE: De la Cour to Drouyn de Lhuys, October 26, 1853 (Turquie 316).

16. PRO: Clarendon to Stratford de Redcliffe, November 8, 1853 ("Private") (FO 352/36).

17. AE: Foreign Ministry to Veli Pasha, October 25, 1853 (Turquie 316).

18. AE: De la Cour to Drouyn de Lhuys, October 26, 1853 (Turquie 316).

19. I have not been able to find such a dispatch in the DB or the BA. On the other hand, the relative paucity of Veli's official communications suggests that much of his information was sent directly to his grandfather Mustafa Nâilî Pasha, the grand vizier, and therefore is not contained in the archives.

20. Gooch, *Bonapartist Generals,* p. 37; PRO: Clarendon to Stratford de Redcliffe, November 8, 1853 ("Private"); and December 8, 1853 ("Private") (FO 352/36).

21. AE: De la Cour to Drouyn de Lhuys, October 26, 1853 (Turquie 316).

22. HHSA: Bruck to Buol, October 27, 1853, #46 (PA XII/47).

23. Martin, *Triumph of Lord Palmerston,* pp. 162–64, 167.

24. Clarendon, quoted in Taylor, *Struggle for Mastery,* p. 58; Aberdeen, quoted in Conacher, *The Aberdeen Coalition,* p. 207.

25. Aberdeen to Princess Lieven, November 15, 1853, in E. Jones Parry, ed., *The Correspondence of Lord Aberdeen and Princess Lieven, 1832-1854,* 62:653. Shortly before Munich, Chamberlain said: "How horrible, fantastic, incredible, it is that we should be digging trenches and trying on gas-masks here because of a quarrel in a far-away country between people of whom we know nothing . . ." (Keith Feiling, *The Life of Neville Chamberlain* [London, 1947], p. 372).

26. See Abderdeen to Gladstone, October 1853, quoted in Martin, *Triumph of Lord Palmerston,* p. 143; PRO: Clarendon to Stratford de Redcliffe, October 18, 1853 ("Private"), and October 25, 1853 ("Private") (FO 352/36).

27. Conacher, *The Aberdeen Coalition,* pp. 194–95.

28. [Jomini,] *Diplomatic Study,* 1:223.

29. Clarendon to Stratford de Redcliffe, October 8, 1853, in Great Britain, *Sessional Papers,* 1854, "Correspondence . . . ," Part II, pp. 142–43, and in Jasmund, 1:192.

30. Nicholas to Menshikov, October 9/21, 1853, in Zaionchkovsky, 2:120–21; Memorandum by Count Nesselrode, February 1854, in ibid., 2:235; PRO: Clarendon to Stratford de Redcliffe, November 29, 1853 ("Private") (FO 352/36).

31. Victoria to Clarendon, October 11, 1853, in *The Letters of Queen Victoria,* ed. Arthur C. Benson and Viscount Esher, 2:555.

32. PRO: Clarendon to Stratford de Redcliffe, October 25, 1853 ("Private") and October 18, 1853 ("Private") (FO 352/36).

33. Cowley to Clarendon, October 9, 1853, in Great Britain, *Sessional Papers,* 1854, "Correspondence . . . ," Part II, pp. 146–47; AE: Drouyn de Lhuys to de la Cour, October 10, 1853 (Turquie 315).

34. Michel Cadot, *La Russie dans la vie intellectuelle française, 1839-1856,* pp. 345–46.

35. John H. Gleason, *The Genesis of Russophobia in Great Britain,* p. 204.

36. AE: Drouyn de Lhuys to de la Cour, October 9 and October 10, 1853 (Turquie 315); Drouyn de Lhuys to Baraguay d'Hilliers, October 30, 1853 (Turquie 316); Clarendon to Stratford de Redcliffe, October 8, 1853, in Great Britain, *Sessional Papers,* 1854, "Correspondence . . . ," Part II, pp. 142–43, and in Jasmund, 1:192.

37. Kovalevsky, *Der Krieg Russlands,* pp. 62–63.

38. AE: De la Cour to Drouyn de Lhuys, October 4, 1853 (Turquie 315).

39. Stratford de Redcliffe to Clarendon, October 5, 1853, in Great Britain, *Sessional Papers*, 1854, "Correspondence . . . ," Part II, p. 167.

40. AE: De la Cour to Drouyn de Lhuys, October 15, 1853 (Turquie 316).

41. AE: De la Cour to Drouyn de Lhuys, October 4, 1853 (Turquie 315).

42. See Frederick Stanley Rodkey, "Ottoman Concern about Western Economic Penetration in the Levant, 1849–1856."

43. AE: De la Cour to Drouyn de Lhuys, October 15, 1853 (Turquie 316).

44. PRO: Stratford de Redcliffe to Clarendon, November 5, 1853 (FO 78/940).

45. Tarle, *Krymskaya Voyna*, 8:341.

46. PRO: Clarendon to Stratford de Redcliffe, November 8, 1853 ("Private"), and December 8, 1853 ("Private") (FO 352/36).

47. Donald C. Blaisdell, *European Financial Control in the Ottoman Empire*, pp. 27–28.

48. AE: De la Cour to Drouyn de Lhuys, October 4, 1853 (Turquie 315).

49. PRO: Stratford de Redcliffe to Clarendon, September 30, 1853 (FO 78/938).

50. AE: De la Cour to Drouyn de Lhuys, September 30, 1853 (Turquie 315).

51. AE: De la Cour to Drouyn de Lhuys, October 15, 1853 (Turquie 316); Kovalevsky, *Der Krieg Russlands*, p. 63.

52. Tarle, *Krymskaya Voyna*, 8:256; Paskevich to Nicholas I, September 11, 1853, and September 24, 1853, in Zaionchkovsky, 2:101–5, 107–11.

53. DB: Nicholas I, Manifesto, October 28, 1853 (Siyasiyye: Rusya 1512); text published in Jasmund, 1:194.

54. Proclamation, Grand Vizier to the inhabitants of Constantinople, Eyub, Scutari, Galata, 5 Muharrem 1270/October 8, 1853, in Testa, vol. 4, pt. 2, pp. 18–19; *Takvim-i Vekâyi* #494 (23 Muharrem 1270/October 27, 1853).

55. Stratford de Redcliffe to Clarendon, October 31, 1853, in Great Britain, *Sessional Papers*, 1854, "Correspondence . . . ," Part II, p. 246.

56. *Takvim-i Vekâyi* #498 (4 Rebiyülâhır 1270/January 5, 1854).

57. HHSA: Bruck to Buol, September 29, 1853, #37A (PA XII/47).

58. PRO: Stratford de Redcliffe to Clarendon, October 15, 1853 (FO 78/939).

59. Wyse to Clarendon, October 7, 1853, in Great Britain, *Sessional Papers*, 1854, "Correspondence . . . ," Part II, p. 168.

60. Driault and Lhéritier, *Grèce*, 2:382.

61. Ibid., p. 386; Nomikos, "International Position of Greece," pp. 80–81.

62. See PRO: "Passages extracted from a Greek Pamphlet entitled 'a lift towards the solution of the Eastern Question,'" annex #2 to #266 (FO 78/938).

63. Driault and Lhéritier, *Grèce*, 2:382–83, 385–86.

64. Nomikos, "International Position of Greece," pp. 94–96.

65. PRO: Stratford de Redcliffe to Clarendon, August 25, 1853 (FO 78/937); Meyendorff to Nesselrode, August 16/28, 1853, in *Meyendorff*, 3:65.

66. Guichen, *La Guerre de Crimée*, p. 83.

67. Stavrianos, *Balkan Federation*, pp. 73–74.

68. Fonblanque to Clarendon, October 16, 1853, in Great Britain, *Sessional Papers*, 1854, "Correspondence . . . ," Part II, p. 163.

69. DB: Summary of reports from the Muhafızı Pasha [commander of the Ottoman garrison] of Belgrade, 12 Safer 1270/November 10, 1853 (Siyasiyye: Rusya 661).

70. DB: Ahmet İzzet Pasha (Belgrade) to Porte, 19 Muharrem 1270/October 22, 1853 (Siyasiyye: Rusya 661); "Belgrad Muhafızı Paşa hazretlerinden," n.d. (Siyasiyye: Rusya 609).

71. Westmorland to Clarendon, November 22, 1853, in Great Britain, *Sessional Papers*, 1854, "Correspondence . . . ," Part II, p. 261.

72. Westmorland to Clarendon, December 3, 1853, in ibid., p. 277.

73. Tarle, *Krymskaya Voyna,* 8:325.

74. DB: "Belgrad Muhafızı Paşa hazretlerinden," n.d. (Siyasiyye: Rusya 609).

75. Paskevich to Nicholas I, July 2/14, 1853, in Zaionchkovsky, 2:98–101.

76. Paskevich's attempt to defend his plan is contained in Paskevich to 'Nicholas I, September 11, 1853, in ibid., 2:101–5.

77. "Annotations écrites par Sa Majesté l'Empereur," App. No. 139, in ibid., 2:321–24.

78. AE: De la Cour to Drouyn de Lhuys, October 4, 1853 (Turquie 315).

79. Ibid.

80. Karal, *Nizam-ı cedit,* p. 234; Mark Pinson, "Ottoman Bulgaria in the First Tanzimat Period—the Revolts in Nish (1841) and Vidin (1850)," p. 105.

81. AE: De la Cour to Drouyn de Lhuys, October 20, 1853 (Turquie 316).

82. Prince Ghyka to Reshid Pasha, October 14, 1853, annexed to Stratford de Redcliffe to Clarendon, November 21, 1853, and Stirbey to Reshid Pasha, October 11/23, 1853, annexed to Stratford de Redcliffe to Clarendon, November 5, 1853, in Great Britain, *Sessional Papers,* 1854, "Correspondence . . . ," Part II, pp. 252, 287.

83. Rescript, Nicholas I to Gorchakov, November 30, 1853, in Testa, vol. 4, pt. 2, p. 25. Actually the arrangements had been laid down before this (see Clarendon to Seymour, November 1853, in Great Britain, *Sessional Papers,* 1854, "Correspondence . . . ," Part II, p. 237).

84. Bogdanovich, 1:257–58.

85. Seymour to Clarendon, November 1, 1853, in Great Britain, *Sessional Papers,* 1854, "Correspondence . . . ," Part II, p. 225.

86. Kovalevsky, *Der Krieg Russlands,* p. 68.

87. PRO: Stratford de Redcliffe to Clarendon, November 4, 1853 (FO 78/939).

88. Gorchakov to War Ministry, November 4, 1853, in Zaionchkovsky, 2:148–49.

89. AE: De la Cour to Drouyn de Lhuys, October 20, 1853 (Turquie 316).

90. Ibid.

91. Letter from General-Adjutant Berg, November 17, 1853, in Zaionchkovsky, 2:292–93.

92. Seymour to Clarendon, October 9, 1853, in Great Britain, *Sessional Papers,* 1854, "Correspondence . . . ," Part II, p. 162.

93. Gorev, *Voyna 1853–1856,* p. 139.

94. This point has recently been impressively demonstrated in Khadzhi Murat Ibragimbeili, *Kavkaz v Krymskoi voine 1853–1856 gg, i mezhdunarodniye otnosheniya.*

95. Vorontsov to War Ministry, October 5, 1853, in Zaionchkovsky, 2:163–64; Tarle, *Krymskaya Voyna,* 8:353. For British reluctance to intervene, see PRO: Clarendon to Stratford de Redcliffe, October 10, 1853 ("Private") (FO 352/36).

96. Stratford de Redcliffe to Clarendon, October 21, 1853, in Great Britain, *Sessional Papers,* 1854, "Correspondence . . . ," Part II, p. 198.

97. Temperley, *Crimea,* p. 365.

98. [Jomini,] *Diplomatic Study,* 1:445.

99. PRO: Clarendon to Stratford de Redcliffe, December 8, 1853 ("Private") (FO 352/36).

100. Kovalevsky, *Der Krieg Russlands,* pp. 64–65, 70. On p. 65, Kovalevsky gives September 15/16 as the date of the occupation of the island, but this is apparently a misprint for October 16 (see Kovalevsky, p. 70). For other accounts of the battle, see *The Annual Register* (1853), p. 302; Ahmet Lûtfi, "Tarih" (1270), pp. 84–85; *Takvim-i Vekâyi* #495 (14 Safer 1270/November 17, 1853).

101. Felix Bamberg, *Geschichte der orientalischen Angelegenheit*, p. 83.

102. Tarle, *Krymskaya Voyna*, 8:270–71.

103. Kovalevsky, *Der Krieg Russlands*, p. 79.

104. Bogdanovich, 1:137–38; Tarle, *Krymskaya Voyna*, 8:278.

105. Kovalevsky, *Der Krieg Russlands*, pp. 78–79.

106. Bogdanovich, 1:138; Kovalevsky, *Der Krieg Russlands*, p. 78; Nicholas I's notes on the battle at Oltenița, in Zaionchkovsky, 2:145–47.

107. *Takvim-i Vekâyi* #495 (14 Safer 1270/November 17, 1853); see also Ahmet Lûtfi, "Tarih" (1270), pp. 85–86.

108. Heinrich Friedjung, *Der Krimkrieg und die österreichische Politik*, p. 9.

109. Bogdanovich, 1:138–39.

110. Slade, *Turkey and the Crimean War*, p. 138.

111. Unckel, *Österreich und der Krimkrieg*, pp. 103–4.

112. PRO: Clarendon to Stratford de Redcliffe, November 18, 1853 ("Private") (FO 352/36).

113. Unckel, *Österreich und der Krimkrieg*, pp. 108–9.

114. AE: De la Cour to Drouyn de Lhuys, October 5, 1853 (Turquie 315).

115. Temperley, *Crimea*, p. 356.

116. Lady Stratford to Stratford de Redcliffe, November 3, 1853, quoted in Lane-Poole, *Stratford Canning*, 2:314.

117. DB: Musurus to Reshid Pasha, October 25, 1853 (Siyasiyye: Rusya 661).

118. DB: Musurus to Reshid Pasha, November 3, 1853 (Siyasiyye: Rusya 661).

119. Lady Clarendon's Journal, October 14, [1853,] quoted in Sir Herbert Maxwell, *The Life and Letters of George William Frederick, Fourth Earl of Clarendon*, 2:26; DB: Musurus to Reshid Pasha, October 25, 1853 (Siyasiyye: Rusya 661).

120. DB: Musurus to Reshid Pasha, October 28, 1853 (Siyasiyye: Rusya 661).

121. DB: Musurus to Reshid Pasha, November 7, 1853 (Siyasiyye: Rusya 661).

122. DB: Musurus to Reshid Pasha, November 3, 1853 (Siyasiyye: Rusya 661).

123. Stratford de Redcliffe to Lady Stratford, November 19, 1853, quoted in Lane-Poole, *Stratford Canning*, 2:320; Thouvenel to Castelbajac, December 1, 1853, quoted in Thouvenel, *Nicholas Ier et Napoléon III*, pp. 273–74.

124. Stratford de Redcliffe to Clarendon, November 24, 1853, in Great Britain, *Sessional Papers*, 1854, "Correspondence . . . ," Part II, p. 290.

125. Stratford de Redcliffe to Clarendon, November 19, 1853, in ibid., p. 281.

126. Ibid.

127. AE: De la Cour to Drouyn de Lhuys, November 13, 1853, and Baraguay d'Hilliers to Drouyn de Lhuys, November 19, 1853 (Turquie 317).

128. Stratford de Redcliffe to Clarendon, November 19, 1853, in Great Britain, *Sessional Papers*, 1854, "Correspondence . . . ," Part II, p. 281; Protocol of the meeting is annexed to Stratford de Redcliffe to Clarendon #357 (PRO: FO 78/940).

129. See PRO: Stratford de Redcliffe to Clarendon, July 20 and July 25, 1853 (FO 78/935), and August 29, 1853 (FO 78/937).

130. Slade, *Turkey and the Crimean War*, pp. 127, 134, 131.

131. General-Adjutant Kornilov to Prince Menshikov, n.d., Zaionchkovsky, 2:125–28.

123. Slade, *Turkey and the Crimean War*, pp. 131, 132–34.

133. Ibid., pp. 128–29.

134. Cf. Alison to Lady Stratford, December 25, 1853, quoted in Lane-Poole, *Stratford Canning*, 2:334–35.

135. Karal, *Nizam-ı cedit*, p. 236.

136. Slade, *Turkey and the Crimean War*, p. 128.

137. Stratford de Redcliffe to Clarendon, November 5, 1853, in Great Britain, *Sessional Papers,* 1854, "Correspondence . . . ," Part II, p. 250.

138. DB: De la Cour to Schefer, November 3 and November 4, 1953, and Stratford de Redcliffe to Pisani, November 4, 1853 (Siyasiyye: Ingiltere 1280).

139. Temperley, "Stratford de Redcliffe and the Origins of the Crimean War," pt. 2, p. 292.

140. Stratford de Redcliffe to Etienne Pisani, November 5, 1853, annexed to Stratford de Redcliffe to Clarendon, November 5, 1853, in Great Britain, *Sessional Papers,* 1854, "Correspondence . . . ," Part II, p. 251.

141. Stratford de Redcliffe to Clarendon, November 5, 1853, in ibid., p. 250.

142. AE: De la Cour to Drouyn de Lhuys, November 6, 1853, and November 10, 1853 (Turquie 316).

143. Temperley, "Stratford de Redcliffe and the Origins of the Crimean War," pt. 2, p. 292.

144. PRO: Stratford de Redcliffe to Dundas, November 11, 1853 (FO 78/940).

145. PRO: Stratford de Redcliffe to Clarendon, November 24, 1853 (FO 78/940).

146. Slade, *Turkey and the Crimean War,* p. 135.

147. Friedjung, *Der Krimkrieg,* pp. 8–9; Puryear, *Straits Question,* p. 326.

148. Friedjung, *Der Krimkrieg,* p. 9.

149. Nesselrode to Brunnov, November 1, 1853, in Nesselrode, 10:295; Nesselrode to Meyendorff, December 2, 1853, in ibid., 10:307.

150. Slade, *Turkey and the Crimean War,* pp. 139–41.

151. Stratford de Redcliffe to Clarendon, December 4, 1853, in Great Britain, *Sessional Papers,* 1854, "Correspondence . . . ," Part II, pp. 311–12.

152. Tarle, *Krymskaya Voyna,* 8:354.

153. Menshikov, quoted in Bogdanovich, 1:148.

154. Tarle, *Krymskaya Voyna,* 8:354.

155. Bogdanovich, 1:148.

156. Tarle, *Krymskaya Voyna,* 8:355.

157. Ibid., pp. 355–58.

158. Slade, *Turkey and the Crimean War,* p. 141.

159. Tarle, *Krymskaya Voyna,* 8:361.

160. Orders of Admiral Nakhimov, November 17, 1853, in Zaionchkovksy, 2:130; Karal, *Nizam-ı cedit,* p. 235.

161. Bartlett, *Great Britain and Sea Power,* p. 333; Clarendon to Seymour, December 27, 1853, in Great Britain, *Sessional Papers,* 1854, "Correspondence . . . ," Part II, p. 322. I am indebted to Samuel C. Post, Jr., for the observation that, since only eleven Turkish ships participated, the figure of four thousand Turkish dead suggests implausibly crowded conditions.

162. Guarracino to Stratford de Redcliffe, December 12, 1853, annexed to Stratford de Redcliffe to Clarendon, January 15, 1854, in Great Britain, *Sessional Papers,* 1854, "Correspondence . . . ," Part VII, p. 17. In addition to the sources already cited, substantially similar accounts of the battle may be found in Ahmet Lûtfi, "Tarih" (1270), pp. 87–88; *Takvim-i Vekâyi* #497 (26 Rebiyülevvel 1270/December 28, 1853); BA: Hariciye Iradesi 1270 #5151 lef [enclosure] 26; Bogdanovich, 1:147–59; Gorev, *Voyna 1853-1856,* pp. 105–58; PRO: Deposition of the Captain and Officers of the *Taif,* annexed to #380 (FO 78/941A).

163. Tarle, *Krymskaya Voyna,* 8:285–87.

Chapter VI

1. Slade, *Turkey and the Crimean War*, quoted in Temperley, *Crimea*, p. 372.
2. AE: Reshid Pasha to Baraguay d'Hilliers, December 3, 1853, annexed to Baraguay d'Hilliers to Drouyn de Lhuys, December 4, 1853 (Turquie 317).
3. AE: Baraguay d'Hilliers to Drouyn de Lhuys, December 4, 1853 (Turquie 317).
4. Bapst, *Origines,* pp. 464–65.
5. [Joseph Alexander,] comte de Hübner, *Neuf ans de souvenirs . . . , 1851–1859,* ed. Comte Alexandre de Hüber, 1:162.
6. Stratford de Redcliffe to Lady Stratford, December 24, 1853, quoted in Lane-Poole, *Stratford Canning,* 2:334; Stratford de Redcliffe to Clarendon, December 24, 1853, quoted in ibid., 2:335.
7. DB: [Baraguay d'Hilliers] to Reshid Pasha, December 3, 1853 (Siyasiyye: Ingiltere 1280); AE: Porte to Baraguay d'Hilliers and Stratford de Redcliffe, December 3, 1853, annexed to Baraguay d'Hilliers to Drouyn de Lhuys, December 4, 1853 (Turquie 317).
8. Temperley, *Crimea,* p. 372; Stratford de Redcliffe to Reshid Pasha, December 11, 1853, annexed to Stratford de Redcliffe to Clarendon, December 17, 1853, in Great Britain, *Sessional Papers,* 1854, "Correspondence . . . ," Part II, p. 342.
9. Unckel, *Österreich und der Krimkrieg,* p. 109. Text of the protocol appears in Jasmund, 1:206–9, and in Zaionchkovsky, 2:252–53.
10. AE: Baraguay d'Hilliers to Drouyn de Lhuys, December 4, 1853 (Turquie 317); Stratford de Redcliffe to Clarendon, December 5, 1853, in Jasmund, 1:211–12.
11. Stratford de Redcliffe to Clarendon, December 17, 1853, in ibid., pp. 215–16.
12. Collective note of the representatives of Austria, Prussia, France, and Great Britain to the Porte, December 15, 1853, in ibid., pp. 210–11.
13. Unckel, *Österreich und der Krimkrieg,* p. 113.
14. AE: Baraguay d'Hilliers to Drouyn de Lhuys, December 24, 1853 (Turquie 317).
15. PRO: Stratford de Redcliffe to Clarendon, December 19, 1853 (FO 78/941B).
16. AE: Lysimaque Tavernier to Baraguay d'Hilliers, November 30, 1853, annexed to #17 (Turquie 317).
17. Alder, "India and the Crimean War," p. 20.
18. AE: Baraguay d'Hilliers to Drouyn de Lhuys, December 8, 1853 (Turquie 317).
19. Kelly, *Britain and the Persian Gulf,* p. 455.
20. AE: Baraguay d'Hilliers to Drouyn de Lhuys, December 31, 1853 (Turquie 317); Ibragimbeili, *Kavkaz v Krymskoi voine,* p. 240.
21. Garry J. Alder, "The Key to India? Britain and the Herat Problem, 1830–1863-Part I," p. 197.
22. Alder, "India and the Crimean War," pp. 22, 27, 32.
23. Schmitt, "Diplomatic Preliminaries of the Crimean War," p. 65; PRO: Stratford de Redcliffe to Clarendon, December 5, 1853, #374 (FO 78/941A).
24. Baraguay d'Hilliers and Stratford de Redcliffe to Reshid Pasha, December 12, 1853, in Testa, vol. 4, pt. 2, p. 35.
25. AE: Hamelin to Baraguay d'Hilliers, December 13, 1853 (Turquie 317).
26. AE: Ducos to Hamelin, December 4, 1853 (Turquie 317).
27. AE: [Baraguay d'Hilliers] to Stratford de Redcliffe, December 21, 1853 (Turquie 317).
28. AE: Slade to Stratford de Redcliffe, December 15, 1853 (Turquie 317).

29. AE: [Baraguay d'Hilliers] to Stratford de Redcliffe, December 21, 1853 (Turquie 317).

30. Türkgeldi, 1:322–23.

31. AE: Baraguay d'Hilliers to Drouyn de Lhuys, December 24, 1853 (Turquie 317); HHSA: Bruck to Buol, December 19, 1853, #61 (PA XII/47).

32. Temperley, *Crimea,* p. 379.

33. İnal, 1:64.

34. PRO: Stratford de Redcliffe to Clarendon, December 23, 1853 (FO 78/941B).

35. Stratford de Redcliffe to Lady Stratford, Christmas Eve, 1853, quoted in Lane-Poole, *Stratford Canning,* 2:332–33; PRO: Stratford de Redcliffe to Reshid Pasha, December 21, 1853, annexed to Stratford de Redcliffe to Clarendon, December 23, 1853 (FO 78/941B).

36. PRO: Stratford de Redcliffe to Clarendon, December 23, 1853 (FO 78/941B).

37. Stratford de Redcliffe to Lady Stratford, Christmas Eve, 1853, quoted in Lane-Poole, *Stratford Canning,* 2:333.

38. PRO: Stratford de Redcliffe to Clarendon, December 23, 1853 (FO 78/941B).

39. İnal, 1:64.

40. PRO: Reshid Pasha to Stratford de Redcliffe, December 23, 1853, annexed to Stratford de Redcliffe to Clarendon, December 23, 1853 (FO 78/941B).

41. PRO: Stratford de Redcliffe to Clarendon, December 23, 1853 (FO 78/941B).

42. Stratford de Redcliffe to Clarendon, December 26, 1853, in Great Britain, *Sessional Papers,* 1854, "Correspondence . . . ," Part II, p. 347.

43. *Takvim-i Vekâyi* #499 (4 Cemaziyelevvel 1270/February 3, 1854).

44. Lynn M. Case, *French Opinion on War and Diplomacy during the Second Empire,* pp. 19–23; Simpson, *Louis Napoleon and the Recovery of France,* p. 238; [Jomini,] *Diplomatic Study,* 1:280.

45. See Napoleon III's revealing remarks to Seebach, recounted in Comte de Seebach to Nesselrode, February 7, 1854, in Nesselrode, 11:7.

46. Anderson, *Eastern Question,* p. 130.

47. Schroeder, *Crimean War,* p. 123.

48. Martin, *Triumph of Lord Palmerston,* pp. 150–53, 157–60.

49. Conacher, *The Aberdeen Coalition,* pp. 220–22.

50. Martin, *Triumph of Lord Palmerston,* p. 159.

51. Ibid., pp. 178–86; Simpson, *Louis Napoleon and the Recovery of France,* pp. 241–42.

52. Entry for January 21, 1854, in James Howard Harris, third earl of Malmesbury, *Memoirs of an Ex-Minister,* 1:422.

53. Anderson, *Eastern Question,* p. 130.

54. AE: Baraguay d'Hilliers to Drouyn de Lhuys, December 26, 1853 (Turquie 317).

55. PRO: Stratford de Redcliffe to Clarendon, December 23, 1853 (FO 78/941B).

56. Slade, *Turkey and the Crimean War,* pp. 160–61.

57. Collective note, Porte to French, British, Austrian, and Prussian representatives, December 31, 1853, in Jasmund, 1:227–28; Testa, vol. 4, pt. 2, pp. 47–49; and Great Britain, *Sessional Papers,* 1854, "Correspondence . . . ," Part II, pp. 362–63. For the further history of this démarche, see chapter VII.

58. Protocol of the meeting of the *Meclis-i umumî* . . . concerning the occurrence at Sinope and the proposals of the English and French ambassadors, in Türkgeldi, 1:321–28. For dating of this document, see ibid., p. 31.

59. Ibid.

60. Temperley, *Crimea*, p. 381.
61. AE: Baraguay d'Hilliers to Drouyn de Lhuys, December 31, 1853 (Turquie 317).
62. *Takvim-i Vekâyi* #499 (4 Cemaziyelevvel 1270/February 3, 1854).
63. AE: Baraguay d'Hilliers to Drouyn de Lhuys, December 31, 1853 (Turquie 317).
64. AE: Baraguay d'Hilliers to Drouyn de Lhuys, January 5, 1854 (Turquie 318B).
65. Schroeder, *Crimean War*, pp. 120–21.
66. Stratford de Redcliffe to E. Pisani, January 4, 1854 annexed to Stratford de Redcliffe to Clarendon, January 5, 1854, in Great Britain, *Sessional Papers*, 1854, "Correspondence . . . ," Part II, p. 377.

Chapter VII

1. Slade, *Turkey and the Crimean War*, p. 164.
2. AE: Baraguay d'Hilliers to Drouyn de Lhuys, January 25, 1854 (Turquie 318B).
3. Slade, *Turkey and the Crimean War*, p. 169.
4. Nesselrode to Meyendorff, January 20, 1853, in Nesselrode, 10:212.
5. [Jomini,] *Diplomatic Study*, 1:256.
6. Simpson, *Louis Napoleon and the Recovery of France*, pp. 247–48.
7. Anderson, *Eastern Question*, p. 131.
8. Guichen, *La Guerre de Crimée*, pp. 126–27.
9. HHSA: Bruck to Buol, February 6, 1854, #12 (PA XII/52).
10. Unckel, *Österreich und der Krimkrieg*, pp. 113–14; for text, see Jasmund, 1:230.
11. Seymour to Clarendon, January 30, 1854, in Great Britain, *Sessional Papers*, 1854, "Correspondence . . . ," Part VII, p. 27.
12. Unckel, *Österreich und der Krimkrieg*, p. 119.
13. For texts, see Jasmund, 1:269–72.
14. Unckel, *Österreich und der Krimkrieg*, pp. 120–21; Martin, *Triumph of Lord Palmerston*, p. 41.
15. For text see Zaionchkovsky, 2:184–86, and Testa, vol. 4, pt. 2, pp. 56–58.
16. Simpson, *Louis Napoleon and the Recovery of France*, p. 247.
17. [Jomini,] *Diplomatic Study*, 1:257; Tarle, *Krymskaya Voyna*, 8:414; for text of Nicholas's refusal, see Zaionchkovsky, 2:186–89, and Testa, vol. 4, pt. 2, pp. 73–76.
18. Simpson, *Louis Napoleon and the Recovery of France*, p. 244; see also Case, *French Opinion*, pp. 18–25. The contention that the French public opposed the war has been challenged by Roger Bellet in *Presse et journalisme sous le second Empire*, but Bellet's evidence related to the provinces and not to Paris, where opinion was most visible.
19. Kinglake, *Invasion of the Crimea*, 1:259.
20. Cowley to Clarendon, January 13, 1854, quoted in Sir Victor Wellesley and Robert Sencourt, *Conversations with Napoleon III*, p. 52.
21. Tarle, *Krymskaya Voyna*, 8:383, 388.
22. Orlov to [Nicholas I], January 23, 1854, in Zaionchkovsky, 2:262–63.
23. Tarle, *Krymskaya Voyna*, 8:392, 393, 396.
24. Orlov to Nesselrode, January 22/February 3, 1854, in Zaionchkovsky, 2:268.
25. Tarle, *Krymskaya Voyna*, 8:396–97.
26. Westmorland to Clarendon, February 4, 1854, in Great Britain, *Sessional Papers*, 1854, "Correspondence . . . ," Part VII, p. 19; Westmorland to Clarendon, February 23, 1854, in ibid., p. 58.
27. Unckel, *Österreich und der Krimkrieg*, pp. 117–18.
28. Tarle, *Krymskaya Voyna*, 8:404.

29. Nesselrode to Meyendorff, March 9, 1854, in Nesselrode, 11:25.

30. Tarle, *Krymskaya Voyna,* 8:430.

31. İnal, 1:67.

32. PRO: Stratford de Redcliffe to Clarendon, January 25, 1854 (FO 78/989); Stratford de Redcliffe to Clarendon, February 2, 1854 (FO 78/990).

33. *Takvim-i Vekâyi* #499 (4 Cemaziyelevvel 1270/February 3, 1854).

34. PRO: Stratford de Redcliffe to Clarendon, February 23, 1854 (FO 78/990).

35. İnal, 1:65–68. Mehmet Ali's banishment was of very short duration (*Türk Meşhurları Ansiklopedisi,* p. 245).

36. This had been amply demonstrated by the end of the Crimean War; see W. E. Mosse, "The Return of Reschid Pasha."

37. PRO: Stratford de Redcliffe to Clarendon, January 25, 1854 (FO 78/989).

38. Gooch, *Bonapartist Generals,* p. 66. Gooch notes that "none of the positions . . . labelled 'next to useless' were taken" (p. 84).

39. Cowley to Clarendon, February 12, 1854, in Great Britain, *Sessional Papers,* 1854, "Correspondence . . . ," Part VII, p. 37; Clarendon to Stratford de Redcliffe, February 16, 1854, in ibid., p. 41.

40. AE: Baraguay d'Hillers to Drouyn de Lhuys, March 5, 1854 (Turquie 318B).

41. Gooch, *Bonapartist Generals,* pp. 67, 74–75.

42. Ibid., pp. 67–69, 62–63.

43. *Takvim-i Vekâyi,* Supplement to #498; ibid., #499 (4 Cemaziyelevvel 1270/February 3, 1854); Gorchakov to Nicholas I, December 29, 1853, in Zaionchkovsky, 2:157–58.

44. Kovalevsky, *Der Krieg Russlands,* p. 93.

45. Stratford de Redcliffe to Clarendon, January 15, 1854, in Great Britain, *Sessional Papers,* 1854, "Correspondence . . . ," Part VII, p. 16.

46. AE: Baraguay d'Hilliers to Drouyn de Lhuys, January 15, 1854 (Turquie 318B).

47. PRO: Fonblanque to Stratford de Redcliffe, November 11, 1853 (FO 195/407).

48. HHSA: Bruck to Buol, December 29, 1853, #64 (PA XII/47).

49. AE: Baraguay d'Hilliers to Drouyn de Lhuys, January 15, 1854 (Turquie 318B).

50. PRO: Fonblanque to Stratford de Redcliffe, January 26, February 4, 1854 (FO 195/436); Sergey Aleksandrovich Nikitin, *Ocherki po istorii yuzhnykh Slavyan y russko-balkanskikh svyazey v 50–70e gody XIX v.,* p. 134. (Hereafter cited as Nikitin.)

51. PRO: Stratford de Redcliffe to Clarendon, February 14, 1854 (FO 78/990).

52. Schroeder, *Crimean War,* pp. 138–39.

53. Popov, *Rossiya i Serbiya,* 2:343–44; Nikitin, p. 134.

54. Nesselrode to Meyendorff, March 3, 1854, in Nesselrode, 11:19.

55. AE: Baraguay d'Hilliers to Drouyn de Lhuys, March 12, 1854 (Turquie 318B).

56. PRO: Enclosure with Longworth to Stratford de Redcliffe, March 9, 1854 (FO 195/392).

57. Unckel, *Österreich und der Krimkrieg,* pp. 81–82.

58. Nomikos, "International Position of Greece," p. 89.

59. DB: Neşet Bey to Reshid Pasha, 17 Safer 1270/November 19, 1853 (Siyasiyye: Rusya 610).

60. BA: A. Paicos to Neşet Bey, December 14/26, 1853 (two letters) (Hariciye Iradesi 1270 #5151 lef [enclosure] 14 and 13).

61. Kovalevsky, *Der Krieg Russlands,* pp. 112–13.

62. [Jomini,] *Diplomatic Study,* 1:538.

63. Nesselrode to Meyendorff, March 21, 1854, in Nesselrode, 11:42.

64. Nikitin, p. 139.

65. Nomikos, in her important dissertation based on Greek archival sources, suggests that the Russians were closer to the mark than the English, French, and Turks: the inhabitants of Epirus and Thessaly, in her view, failed to contribute significantly to the campaign; indeed, she maintains, the insurrection would have succeded if it had received local help ("International Position of Greece," p. 102). This judgment seems rather unfair. There were many instances in which insurrections that had a strong local base still failed in the end (Crete is a case in point); furthermore, given the possibility of reprisals, local elements could not have been expected to commit themselves too soon. In any case, whether or not local Greeks joined in (and the bias of Nomikos's Greek sources must not be overlooked), the anxiety felt by the British, French, and Turks was genuine.

66. PRO: Clarendon to Stratford de Redcliffe, December 17, 1853 ("Private") (FO 352/36).

67. Edouard Engelhardt, *La Turquie et le Tanzimat*, 1:77.

68. Slade, *Turkey and the Crimean War*, p. 188.

69. AE: Drouyn de Lhuys to Lavalette, December 8, 1852 (Turquie 310).

70. See DB: Petition to Stratford de Redcliffe from thirteen Greek inhabitants of Rhodosto, December 6, 1853 (Siyasiyye: Ingiltere W1254).

71. DB: Extract, Longworth to Stratford de Redcliffe, December 31, 1853 (Siyasiyye: Ingiltere W1254).

72. DB: Kanunnâme [imperial order] from the Porte to the vali of Yanina (Siyasiyye: Rusya 661).

73. DB: Kanunnâme [imperial order] from the Porte to the vali of Yanina (Siyasiyye: Rusya 661).

74. DB: "Proclamation à tous les Grecs et Philhellènes, croyant à Jésus Christ" (Siyasiyye: Rusya 661). Translation is from enclosure in Consul Saunders to Clarendon, February 7, 1854, in Great Britain, *Sessional Papers, 1854*, "Correspondence Respecting the Relations between Greece and Turkey [March 1853–May 1854]," p. 357.

75. Nomikos, "International Position of Greece," pp. 149–51.

76. PRO: Stratford de Redcliffe to Clarendon, February 14, 1854 (FO 78/990). Nomikos dates the invasion February 5 ("International Position of Greece," p. 152).

77. DB: Neşet Bey to Reshid Pasha, 8 Cemaziyelevvel 1270/February 7, 1854 (Siyasiyye: Rusya 661), and 17 Cemaziyelevvel 1270/February 15, 1854, with the report enclosed from frontier official Ismail Bey (Siyasiyye: Rusya 661).

78. PRO: Longworth to Stratford de Redcliffe, February 14, 1854 (FO 195/392).

79. Nomikos, pp. 121–22.

80. PRO: Roberts (Préveza) to resident (Santa Maura), February 4, 1854 (FO 195/456).

81. PRO: H. G. Ward to Captain Peel, February 13, 1854 (FO 195/456); Captain Peel to H. G. Ward, February 14, 1854 (FO 195/456).

82. Captain Peel to Vice-Admiral Dundas, February 7, 1854, enclosure #2 to #47, in Great Britain, *Sessional Papers, 1854*, "Correspondence . . . Greece and Turkey," p. 345.

83. Mr. Fraser (Secretary to the Lord High Commissioner) to Captain Peel, February 6, 1854, enclosure #3 to #47, in ibid., p. 345.

84. Clarendon to the Lords Commissioners of the Admiralty, February 17, 1854, in ibid., pp. 347–48.

85. PRO: Longworth to Stratford de Redcliffe, February 14, 1854, #5 (FO 195/392).

86. PRO: Longworth to Stratford de Redcliffe, February 14, 1854, [unnumbered] (FO 195/392).

87. PRO: "Intelligence from the Greek Frontier," February 16, 1854 (FO 195/435); DB: Neşet Bey to Reshid Pasha, 17 Cemaziyelevvel 1270/February 15, 1854 (Siyasiyye: Rusya 661).

88. PRO: Longworth to Stratford de Redcliffe, February 14, 1854, #5 (FO 195/392), and February 18, 1854 (FO 195/392).

89. PRO: H. G. Ward to Stratford de Redcliffe, February 20, 1854 (FO 195/456).

90. Nomikos, "International Position of Greece," pp. 153-54.

91. PRO: Joseph Phillips to Blunt, February 22, 1854 (FO 195/435).

92. PRO: Longworth to Stratford de Redcliffe, February 23, 1854 (FO 195/392).

93. PRO: H. G. Ward to the Duke of Newcastle, March 4, 1854 (FO 195/456).

94. Nomikos, "International Position of Greece," pp. 199-200. Nomikos says that actually King Otto's motive was discouragement at the revolution's lack of success, but British sources give a more alarmist picture of the progress of the revolt.

95. PRO: Blunt to Stratford de Redcliffe, March 2, 1854 (FO 195/435).

96. PRO: [?] to Blunt, March 9, 1854, annexed to Blunt to Stratford de Redcliffe, March 12, 1854 (FO 195/435).

97. PRO: Blunt to Stratford de Redcliffe, March 12, 1854, (FO 195/435).

98. PRO: H. G. Ward to Stratford de Redcliffe, March 12, 1854 (FO 195/456).

99. PRO: Reshid Pasha to Stratford de Redcliffe, 20 Cemaziyelevvel 1270/February 19, 1854 (FO 78/990).

100. PRO: Stratford de Redcliffe to Reshid Pasha, February 21, 1854 (FO 78/990); DB: Baraguay d'Hilliers to Reshid Pasha, February 20, 1854 (Siyasiyye: Ingiltere 1280).

101. PRO: Stratford de Redcliffe to Clarendon, February 26, 1854 (FO 78/990).

102. AE: Baraguay d'Hilliers to Drouyn de Lhuys, February 25, 1854 (Turquie 318B).

103. BA: Mehmet Neşet to Reshid Pasha, 26 Rebiyülâhır 1270/January 26, 1854 (Hariciye Iradesi 1270 #5151 lef [enclosure] 12); DB: Neşet to Reshid Pasha, February 7/19, 1854 (Siyasiyye: Rusya 661).

104. Nomikos, "International Position of Greece," pp. 89-101.

105. King Otto, quoted in Driault and Lhéritier, *Grèce,* 2:389-90, 392.

106. DB: Neşet Bey to Reshid Pasha, 27 Cemaziyelevvel 1270/February 25, 1854 (Siyasiyye: Rusya 661); DB: A. Paicos to Porte, February 23/March 7, 1854 (Siyasiyye: Rusya 661).

107. PRO: Stratford de Redcliffe to Clarendon, March 15, 1854 (FO 78/991).

108. Driault and Lhéritier, *Grèce,* 2:391.

109. Accounts of these tense days are to be found in DB: "Events of the First and Second Day"; "Third Day"; "The Fourth Day" (Siyasiyye: Rusya 661), and in PRO: Stratford de Redcliffe to Clarendon, March 13, 1854, and enclosures (FO 78/991).

110. PRO: Wyse to Stratford de Redcliffe, March 21, 1854, annexed to #130 (FO 78/991).

111. Cowley to Clarendon, February 10, 1854, in Great Britain, *Sessional Papers,* 1854, "Correspondence . . . ," Part VII, p. 37.

112. AE: Drouyn de Lhuys to Baraguay d'Hilliers, February 18, 1854 (Turquie 318B); Baraguay d'Hilliers to Drouyn de Lhuys, February 25, 1854 (Turquie 318B).

113. Cowley to Clarendon, February 20, 1854, in Great Britain, *Sessional Papers,* 1854, "Correspondence . . . ," Part VII, p. 52.

114. Guichen, *La Guerre de Crimée,* p. 122.

115. Clarendon to Wyse, February 16, 1854, in Great Britain, *Sessional Papers,* 1854, "Correspondence . . . ," Part VII, p. 42.

116. For a description of the occupation, see Driault and Lhéritier, *Grèce,* 2:395-417, and Nomikos, "International Position of Greece," pp. 272-89.

117. AE: Bourée to Drouyn de Lhuys, November 3, 1853 (Turquie 318B).

118. See AE: Bourée to Drouyn de Lhuys, August 5, 1853, August 24, 1853, #8, and August 26, 1853 (Turquie 318A). Bourée's attitude towards the Ottoman Empire was actually more positive than that of most of his colleagues at the Quai d'Orsay and even than that of the Emperor himself, a fact that ultimately caused him severe professional difficulties (Jean Boissel, "Un diplomate du XIXe siècle, défenseur de l'Empire ottoman: Prospère Bourée," pp. 120, 123.

119. AE: Baraguay d'Hilliers to Drouyn de Lhuys, April 20, 1854 (Turquie 318B).

120. Great Britain, *Hansard's Parliamentary Debates,* vol. 131, cols. 593–603.

121. The Ecclesiastical Titles Bill, as originally brought forward by Lord John Russell, was intended to prevent implementation of the Pope's plan to give territorial jurisdiction to prelates assigned to Great Britain. For an excellent discussion of this problem and the issues it raised in the public mind, see Ralls, "The Papal Aggression of 1850."

122. Berkes, *The Development of Secularism in Turkey,* p. 150.

123. *Hansard's Parliamentary Debates,* vol. 131, col. 611.

124. BA: *Newcastle Guardian,* December 17, 1853, annexed to Musurus Bey to Reshid Pasha, December 17, 1853 (Hariciye Iradesi 1270 #5151).

125. See, for instance, PRO: Longworth to Stratford de Redcliffe, July 26, December 1, 1853 ("Private") (FO 195/392); see also Gordon L. Iseminger, "The Old Turkish Hands: the British Levantine Consuls, 1856–1876," pp. 299–301.

126. Clarendon to Nesselrode, February 27, 1854, in Jasmund, 1:277–78.

127. Text printed in Zaionchkovsky, 2:222–24, in Jasmund, 1:283, and in Gabriel Efendi Noradounghian, *Recueil d'actes internationaux de l'empire ottoman,* 2:420–22.

128. Jasmund, 1:291–93.

129. Simpson, *Louis Napoleon and the Recovery of France,* p. 243.

Chapter VIII

1. BA: *Newcastle Guardian,* December 17, 1853, annexed to Musurus Bey to Reshid Pasha, December 17, 1853 (Hariciye Iradesi 1270 #5151).

2. Kinglake, *Invasion of the Crimea,* 1:210–11, 214.

3. Baumgart, *Friede,* pp. 256–57.

4. For a recent analysis based on extensive reading in Italian sources, see Baumgart, *Friede,* pp. 188–203.

5. See, for example, Ann Pottinger Saab, "Review of Winfried Baumgart, *Der Friede von Paris, 1856;* Paul W. Schroeder, *Austria, Great Britain, and the Crimean War.*"

6. Baumgart, *Friede,* pp. 15–19, 110–25.

7. Lynn M. Case's *Edouard Thouvenel et la diplomatie du second Empire* (Paris, 1976) appeared too late for use in this study, but Case's lifetime of experience in quest of Napoleon III makes it of obvious interest for the diplomacy of this period.

Bibliography

I. Unpublished Documents

Istanbul—Başvekâlet Arşivi (cited as BA).
Consulted: diplomatic correspondence and papers from the classification Hariciye Iradesi 1264 through Hariciye Iradesi 1270 (1848–54); diplomatic papers from the Yildiz Collection.
Istanbul—Dişişleri Bakanliği Hazine-i Evrak (cited as DB).
Consulted: diplomatic correspondence and papers from the Siyasiyye classification relating to the years 1848–54.
London—Public Record Office (cited as PRO).
Consulted: dispatches from the embassy at Constantinople, 1848–54; consular reports from Corfu, Monastir, Salonica, Varna, Belgrade, 1853–54; private letters from Clarendon to Stratford de Redcliffe, 1853, in Stratford de Redcliffe's private papers.
Paris—Archives des Affaires Etrangères, Ministère des Affaires Etrangères (cited as AE).
Consulted: correspondence to and from the embassy at Constantinople 1848–54; reports from Bourée's special mission, 1853.
Vienna—Haus- Hof- und Staatsarchiv (cited as HHSA).
Consulted: correspondence to and from the internunciate at Constantinople, August 15–September 15, 1849; 1853–54.

II. Published Documents

The Annual Register (1853 and 1854). Vols. 95 and 96. London, 1854 and 1855.
Aristarchi Bey. *Législation ottomane.* 7 vols. Constantinople, 1873–88.
Great Britain. *Hansard's Parliamentary Debates.* 3rd ser. Vols. 127–32. London, 1853–54.
Great Britain, House of Commons. "Communications Respecting Turkey Made to Her Majesty's Government by the Emperor of Russia" ("Eastern Papers," Part V). In *Sessional Papers,* 1854, vol. 71. London, 1854.
Great Britain, House of Commons. "Correspondence Respecting the

Relations between Greece and Turkey [March 1853–May 1854]. In *Sessional Papers,* 1854, vol. 72. London, 1854.

Great Britain, House of Commons. "Correspondence Respecting the Rights and Privileges of the Latin and Greek Churches in Turkey" ("Eastern Papers," Parts I–III; Part VII). In *Sessional Papers,* 1854, vol. 71. London, 1854.

Great Britain, House of Commons. "Instructions of the British and French Governments for the Joint Protection of British and French Subjects and Commerce" ("Eastern Papers," Part IV). In *Sessional Papers,* vol. 71. London, 1854.

Great Britain, House of Commons. "Memorandum by Count Nesselrode, June 1844" ("Eastern Papers," Part VI). In *Sessional Papers,* 1854, vol. 71. London, 1854.

Jasmund, J. von. *Aktenstücke zur orientalische Frage.* 3 vols. Berlin, 1855–59.

Martens, F. *Recueil des traités et conventions conclus par la Russie avec les puissances étrangères.* 15 vols. Saint Petersburg, 1874–1909.

Noradounghian, Gabriel Efendi. *Recueil d'actes internationaux de l'empire ottoman.* 4 vols. Paris, 1897–1903.

Poschinger, Heinrich von, ed. *Preussens auswärtige Politik, 1850 bis 1858.* 3 vols. Berlin, 1902.

Takvim-i Vekâyi (1264–70/1848–54).

Temperley, H. W. V., and Penson, Lilian M. *Foundations of British Foreign Policy from Pitt (1792) to Salisbury (1902).* Cambridge, 1938.

Testa, I. de [et al.]. *Recueil des traités de la Porte ottomane avec les puissances étrangères.* 11 vols. Paris, 1864–1911.

Türkgeldi, Ali Fuat. *Mesail-i Mühimme-i Siyasiyye.* Edited by Bekir Sıtkı Baykal. Ankara, 1957.

Zaionchkovsky, A. M. *Vostochnaya Voyna 1853–1856, Prilozheniya.* 2 vols. St. Petersburg, 1908.

III. Books and Articles

Abdurrahman Sheref. *Tarih Musahabeleri.* Istanbul, 1339/1920–21.

Abu Jaber, Kamel S. "The Millet System in the Nineteenth-Century Ottoman Empire." *The Muslim World* 57 (1967):212–23.

Ahmet Lûtfi. "Tarih" (1269–70/1853–54). Unpublished manuscript.

Albrecht-Carrié, René. *A Diplomatic History of Europe since the Congress of Vienna.* New York, 1958.

Alder, Garry J. "India and the Crimean War." *Journal of Imperial and Commonwealth History* 2 (1973):15–37.

————. "The Key to India? Britain and the Herat Problem, 1830–1863—Part I." *Middle Eastern Studies* 10 (1974):186–209.

Ali Fuat. "Rical-i Tanzimattan Sadık Rifat Paşa." *Türk Tarih Encumeni Mecmuası.* 1 (1929):1–11.

"Ali Paşa (Mehmed Emin-)." Pp. 293–307 in *Islam-Türk Ansiklopedisi,* vol. 1. Istanbul, 1941.

Allen, [William Edward Davis,] and Muratoff, Paul. *Caucasian Battlefields: A History of the Wars on the Turco-Caucasian Border, 1828–1921.* Cambridge, 1953.

Anderson, M. S. *The Eastern Question, 1774–1923.* New York, 1966.

Anderson, Olive. "Cabinet Government and the Crimean War." *English Historical Review* 79 (1964):548–51.

————. "Great Britain and the Beginnings of the Ottoman Public Debt." *Historical Journal* 7 (1964):47–63.

————. *A Liberal State at War.* London, 1967.

Argyll, George Douglas Campbell, eighth duke of. *Autobiography and Memoirs.* Edited by the Dowager Duchess of Argyll. 2 vols. London, 1906.

Arnakis, George G., [and Vucinich, Wayne S.]. *The Near East in Modern Times.* Vol. 1. Austin, Tex., 1969.

Ashley, Evelyn. *The Life of Henry John Temple, Viscount Palmerston: 1846–1865.* 2 vols. London, 1876.

Ausubel, Herman. *John Bright, Victorian Reformer.* New York, 1966.

Averbukh, [Revekka A.]. *Tsarskaya Interventsiya v bor'be s vengerskoy revolyutsey, 1848–1849.* Moscow, 1935.

Baczkowski, Wlodzimierz. "Russia and the Holy Land." *Eastern Quarterly* 2 (1949):42–49.

Baddeley, John F. *The Russian Conquest of the Caucasus.* London, 1908.

Bailey, [Frank Edgar]. *British Policy and the Turkish Reform Movement: A Study in Anglo-Turkish Relations, 1826–1853.* Cambridge, Mass., 1942.

Balfour, Lady Frances. *The Life of George, Fourth Earl of Aberdeen.* 2 vols. London, [1922].

Bamberg Felix. *Geschichhe der orientalischen Angelegenheit.* Berlin, 1892.

Bapst, Edmond. *Les Origines de la guerre de Crimée.* Paris, 1912.

Barker, A. J. *The Vainglorious War, 1854–56.* London, 1970.

Barnes, Donald G. *A History of the English Corn Laws from 1660–1846.* London, 1930.

Bartlett. C. J. *Great Britain and Sea Power, 1815–1853.* Oxford, 1963.

Bassett, A. Tilney, ed. *Gladstone to his Wife.* London, 1936.

Baumgart, Winfried. *Der Friede von Paris, 1856.* Munich, 1972.

————. "Der Krimkrieg in der angelsächsischen und russischen militärgeschichtlichen Literatur der sechziger Jahre." *Militärgeschichtliche Mitteilungen* 2 (1970):181-94.

————. "Probleme der Krimkriegsforschung: Eine Studie über die Literatur des letzten Jahrzehnts (1961-1970)." *Jahrbücher für Geschichte Osteuropas* 19 (1971):49-109, 243-64, 371-400.

Baykal, Bekir Sıtkı. "Die Frage der Heiligen Stätten im gelobten Lande und die Hohe Pforte." *Geschichte in Wissenschaft und Unterricht,* 10 (1959):407-16.

————. "Makamat-ı mübareke meselesi ve Babiâli," *Belleten* 23 (1959):241-66.

Bell, H. C. F. *Lord Palmerston.* 2 vols. London, 1936.

Bellet, Roger. *Presse et journalisme sous le Second Empire.* Paris, 1967.

Benedetti, Vincent. *Studies in Diplomacy.* New York, 1896.

Benedikt, Heinrich. *Die wirtschaftliche Entwicklung in der Franz-Joseph-Zeit,* Vienna, 1958.

Berkes, Niyazi. *The Development of Secularism in Turkey.* Montreal, 1964.

Bessé, Alfred de. *The Turkish Empire.* Translated, revised, and enlarged by Edward Joy Morris. Philadelphia, 1854.

Best, G. F. A. *Shaftesbury.* London, 1964.

Bestuzhev, I. V. *Krymskaya Voyna 1853-1856 gg.* Moscow, 1956.

————, and Sverev, B. I., eds. *Sovetskaya istoricheskaya entsiklopediya.* 12 vols. Moscow, 1961-69.

Beyens, [Napoléon Eugène,] baron. *Le Second Empire vu par un diplomate belge.* 2 vols. Paris, [1924-26].

Blaisdell, Donald C. *European Financial Control in the Ottoman Empire.* New York, 1929.

[Blunt, Mrs. John Elijah.] *The People of Turkey: Twenty Years' Residence among Bulgarians, Greeks, Albanians, Turks, and Armenians.* Edited by Stanley Lane-Poole. London, 1878.

Bogdanovich, [Modest Ivanovich]. *Vostochnaya Voyna 1853-1856 godov.* 2 vols. Saint Petersburg, 1876.

Boicu, L. "Les Principautés roumaines dans les projets de Karl von Bruck et Lorenz von Stein pour la constitution de la 'Mitteleuropa' à l'époque de la guerre de Crimée." *Revue roumaine d'histoire.* 6 (1967):233-56.

Boissel, Jean. "Un diplomate du XIXe siècle, défenseur de l'Empire ottoman: Prospère Bourée." *Revue d'histoire diplomatique* 87 (1973): 115-38.

Bolsover, G. H. "Aspects of Russian Foreign Policy, 1815-1914." In

Essays presented to Sir Lewis Namier, edited by Richard Pares and A. J. P. Taylor. London, 1956.

————. "David Urquhart and the Eastern Question, 1833–37." *Journal of Modern History* 8 (1936):444–67.

————. "Nicholas I and the Partition of Turkey." *Slavonic and East European Review* 27 (1948):115–45.

Borries, Kurt. *Preussen im Krimkrieg (1853–1856).* Stuttgart, 1930.

Bossy, Raoul. "Les Roumaines et l'idée fédéraliste au XIXᵉ siècle." *Revue d'histoire diplomatique* 81 (1967):168–75.

Bourgeois, Emile. *Manuel historique de politique étrangère.* 10th ed. 4 vols. Paris, 1920–28.

Bourne, Kenneth. *The Foreign Policy of Victorian England, 1830–1902.* Oxford, 1970.

Bower, Leonard, and Bolitho, Gordon. *Otho I, King of Greece: A Biography.* London, 1939.

Briggs, Asa. *Victorian People.* Chicago, 1955.

Bright, John. *Diaries.* Edited by R. A. J. Walling. New York, 1931.

————. *Speeches on Questions of Public Policy.* Edited by James E. Thorold Rogers. London, 1878.

Byrne, Leo Gerald. *The Great Ambassador.* Columbus, Ohio, 1964.

Cadot, Michel. *La Russie dans la vie intellectuelle française, 1839–1856.* Paris, 1967.

Campbell, John C. "1848 in the Roumanian Principalities." *Journal of Central European Affairs* 8 (1948):181–90.

————. "The Influence of Western Political Thought in the Rumanian Principalities, 1821–1848." *Journal of Central European Affairs* 4 (1944):262–73.

Case, Lynn M. *French Opinion on War and Diplomacy during the Second Empire.* Philadelphia, 1954.

Castille, Hippolyte. *Réchid-Pacha.* Paris, 1857.

Çavli, Emin Âli. *Kırım Harbi.* Istanbul, 1957.

Charmatz, Richard. *Minister Freiherr von Bruck, Der Vorkämpfer Mitteleuropas.* Leipzig, 1916.

Christmas, Walter. *King George of Greece.* New York, 1914.

Cobden, Richard. *Political Writings.* 2nd ed. 2 vols. New York, 1868.

————. *Speeches on Questions of Public Policy.* Edited by John Bright and James E. Thorold Rogers. 2 vols. London, 1870.

Collin, Bernardin. *Le Problème juridique des lieux-saints.* Cairo, [1956].

————. "Question et problème des lieux-saints." *Nouvelle Revue Théologique* 75 (1953):727–38.

Conacher, J. B. *The Aberdeen Coalition, 1852–1855.* London, 1968.

Connell, Brian, ed. *Regina v. Palmerston: The Correspondence between Queen Victoria and Her Foreign and Prime Minister, 1837–1865.* London, 1962.

Cook, Sir Edward. *Delane of the Times.* London, 1915.

Cunningham, Allan. "Stratford Canning and the *Tanzimat.*" Pp. 245–64 in William R. Polk and Richard L. Chambers, eds., *Beginnings of Modernization in the Middle East: The Nineteenth Century.* Chicago, 1968.

Curtiss, John S. "Nicholas I, Austria, and the Eastern Question." Paper presented at the American Historical Association meeting, December 1968.

————. *The Russian Army under Nicholas I, 1825–1855.* Durham, N.C., 1965.

————. "Russian Diplomacy in the Mid-Nineteenth Century." *South Atlantic Quarterly* 72 (1973):396–405.

Danilevsky, N. I. *Russland und Europa.* Translated from Russian by Karl Nötzel. Stuttgart, 1920. Reissued Osnabrück, 1965.

Dasent, Arthur Irwin. *John Thadeus Delane.* 2 vols. London, 1908.

Davison, Roderic H. *Reform in the Ottoman Empire, 1856–1876.* Princeton, 1963.

————. *Turkey.* Englewood Cliffs, N.J., 1968.

————. "Turkish Attitudes concerning Christian-Muslim Equality in the Nineteenth Century." *American Historical Review* 59 (1954): 844–64.

————. "Westernized Education in Ottoman Turkey." *Middle East Journal* 15 (1961):289–301.

Dawson, William H. *Richard Cobden and Foreign Policy.* New York, 1927.

Delaygue, Louis. *Essai sur les finances ottomanes.* Paris, 1911.

Derry, John W. *The Radical Tradition.* London, 1967.

Devereux, Robert. *The First Ottoman Constitutional Period.* Baltimore, 1963.

Dowty, Alan. *The Limits of American Isolation: The United States and the Crimean War.* New York, 1971.

Driault, Edouard. *La Question d'orient.* Paris, 1921.

————, and Lhéritier, Michel. *Histoire diplomatique de la Grèce de 1821 à nos jours.* 5 vols. Paris, 1925–26.

Du Velay, A. *Essai sur l'histoire financière de la Turquie.* Paris, 1903.

Eckhart, Franz. *Die deutsche Frage und der Krimkrieg.* Berlin, 1931.

Eichmann, F. *Die Reformen des osmanischen Reiches.* Berlin, 1858.

Emin Ahmed. *The Development of Modern Turkey as Measured by Its Press.* New York, 1914.

Engelhardt, Edouard. *La Turquie et le Tanzimat.* 2 vols. Paris, 1882–84.

Entner, Marvin L. *Russo-Persian Commercial Relations, 1828–1914.* Gainesville, Fla., 1965.

Fejtö, François. *The Opening of an Era: 1848.* New York, 1966.

Fernau, Friedrich Wilhelm. *Patriarchen am Goldenen Horn: Gegenwart und Tradition des orthodoxen Orients.* Opladen, 1967.

Finn, James. *Stirring Times.* 2 vols. London, 1878.

Florescu, Radu R. "British Reactions to the Russian Regime in the Danubian Principalities, 1828–1834." *Journal of Central European Affairs* 22 (1962):27–42.

———. "The Rumanian Principalities and the Origins of the Crimean War." *Slavonic and East European Review* 43 (1964):46–67.

———. "Stratford Canning, Palmerston, and the Wallachian Revolution of 1848." *Journal of Modern History* 35 (1963):227–44.

———. *The Struggle against Russia in the Roumanian Principalities, 1821–1854.* Munich, 1962.

Fortunatov, P. K. *Der Krieg 1877/78 und die Befreiung Bulgariens.* Translated by E. Jeran. Berlin, 1953.

Franz, Georg. "Der Krimkrieg, ein Wendepunkt des europäischen Schicksals." *Geschichte in Wissenschaft und Unterricht* 7 (1956): 448–63.

Friedjung, Heinrich. *Der Krimkrieg und die österreichische Politik.* Berlin, 1907.

Gibbs, Peter. *Crimean Blunder.* London, 1960.

Gille, Geneviève. "Au temps de la guerre de Crimée: correspondance inédite du Comte de Morny et de la Princesse de Lieven." *Revue: litterature, histoire, arts, et sciences (Revue des deux mondes)* (1966), pp. 328–45, 545–59.

Gillespie, Frances E. *Labor and Politics in England, 1850–1867.* Durham, N.C., 1927.

Gleason, John H. *The Genesis of Russophobia in Great Britain.* Cambridge, Mass., 1950.

Godechot, Jacques, and Pernot, Françoise. "L'Action des représentants de la France à Turin et l'intervention sarde dans la guerre de Crimée." *Rassegna storica del risorgimento* 45 (1958): 39–56.

Gooch, Brison D. "A Century of Historiography on the Origins of the Crimean War." *American Historical Review* 62 (1956):33–58.

———. "The Crimean War in Selected Documents and Secondary Works since 1940." *Victorian Studies* 1 (1958):271–79.

———. *The New Bonapartist Generals in the Crimean War.* The Hague, 1959.

———. *The Reign of Napoleon III.* Chicago, 1969.

Gooch, G. P., ed. *The Later Correspondence of Lord John Russell, 1840–1878.* 2 vols. London, 1925.

Gopčević, Spiridion. *Russland und Serbien von 1804–1915.* Munich, 1916.

Gordon, Sir Arthur. *The Earl of Aberdeen.* New York, 1893.

Gorev, L. *Voyna 1853–1856 gg. i oborona Sevastopolya.* Moscow, 1955.

Goriainov, Serge. *Le Bosphore et les Dardanelles.* Paris, 1910.

Gövsa, İbrahim Alâettin. *Türk Meşhurları Ansiklopedisi.* n.p., n.d.

Greer, Donald M. *L'Angleterre, la France, et la révolution de 1848.* Paris, 1925.

Guedalla, Philip, ed. *Gladstone and Palmerston, Being the Correspondence of Lord Palmerston with Mr. Gladstone, 1851–1865.* New York, 1928.

Guériot, Paul. *Napoléon III.* 2 vols. Paris, 1933–34.

Guichen, [Eugène,] vicomte de. *La Guerre de Crimée (1854–1856) et l'attitude des puissances européennes.* Paris, 1936.

Habberton, William. *Anglo-Russian Relations concerning Afghanistan, 1837–1907.* Urbana, Ill., 1937.

Hajek, Alois. *Bulgarien unter der Türkenherrschaft.* Berlin, 1925.

Hall, Major John. *England and the Orleans Monarchy.* London, 1912.

Hallberg, Charles W. *Franz Joseph and Napoleon III, 1852–1864.* New York, 1955.

Handelsman, Marcel. *Czartoryski, Nicolas Ier, et la question du Proche Orient.* Paris, 1934.

_____. "Les Eléments d'une politique étrangère de la Pologne (1831–1856)." *L'Académie des sciences morales et publiques: Revue des travaux et comptes-rendus* 90 (1930):107–38.

_____. "La Guerre de Crimée, la question polonaise, et les origines du problème bulgare." *Revue Historique* 169 (1932):271–315.

Hardinge, Sir Arthur. *The Life of Henry Howard Molyneux Herbert, Fourth Earl of Carnarvon, 1831–1890.* 3 vols. London, 1925.

Hayreddin. *1270 Kırım Muharebesinin Tarih Siyasiyye.* n.p., 1326/1908.

Hayreddin. *Vesaik-i Tarihiye ve Siyasiyye.* n.p., 1326/1908.

Heindl, Waltraud. *Graf Buol-Schauenstein in St. Petersburg und London (1848–1852).* Vienna, 1970.

Heller, Isidore, ed. *Memoiren des Baron Bruck aus der Zeit des Krimkriegs.* Vienna, 1877.

Henderson, Gavin Burns. *Crimean War Diplomacy.* Glasgow, 1947.

_____. "The Diplomatic Revolution of 1854." *American Historical Review* 43 (1937):22–50.

————. "The Foreign Policy of Lord Palmerston." *History* 22 (1938): 335–44.

Herkless, J. L. "Stratford, the Cabinet, and the Outbreak of the Crimean War." *Historical Journal* 18 (1975):497–523.

Heurtley, W. A., Darby, H. C., Crawley, C. W., and Woodhouse, C. M. *A Short History of Greece.* Cambridge, 1965.

Heyd, Uriel, ed. *Studies in Islamic History and Civilization.* Jerusalem, 1961.

Hibbert, Christopher. *The Destruction of Lord Raglan.* London, 1963.

Hodder, Edwin. *The Life and Work of the Seventh Earl of Shaftesbury.* 3 vols. London, 1886.

Hoetzsch, Otto, ed. *Peter von Meyendorff, ein russischer Diplomat an den Höfen von Berlin und Wien: Politischer und privater Briefwechsel, 1826–1863.* Berlin, 1923.

Homsy, Basile. *Les Capitulations et la protection des chrétiens au Proche-Orient aux XVIᵉ, XVIIᵉ, et XVIIIᵉ siècles.* [Harissa, Lebanon, 1956.]

Hopwood, Derek. *The Russian Presence in Syria and Palestine, 1843–1914.* Oxford, 1969.

Horváth, Eugene. "Kossuth and Palmerston, 1848–1849." *Slavonic Review* 9 (1931):612–31.

————. *Origins of the Crimean War.* Budapest, 1937.

————. "Russia and the Hungarian Revolution." *Slavonic Review* 12 (1934):628–45.

Hösch, E. "Neuere Literatur (1940–1960) über den Krimkrieg." *Jahrbücher für Geschichte Osteuropas* 9 (1961):399–434.

Hoskins, Halford L. *British Routes to India.* New York, 1966.

Hourani, Albert. "Ottoman Reform and the Politics of Notables." Pp. 41–68 in William R. Polk and Richard L. Chambers, eds., *Beginnings of Modernization in the Middle East: The Nineteenth Century.* Chicago, 1968.

Howard, H. E. "Brunnow's Reports on Aberdeen, 1853." *Cambridge Historical Journal* 4 (1932–34):312–21.

————. "Lord Cowley on Napoleon III in 1853." *English Historical Review* 49 (1934):502–5.

Hübner, [Joseph Alexandre,] comte de. *Une année de ma vie, 1848–1849.* Paris, 1891.

————. *Neuf ans de souvenirs d'un ambassadeur d'Autriche à Paris sous le second empire, 1851–1859.* Edited by Comte Alexandre de Hübner. 2 vols. Paris, 1904.

Hurewitz, J. C. "The Beginnings of Military Modernization in the

Middle East: A Comparative Analysis." *Middle East Journal* 22 (1968):144–58.

_____. *Middle East Politics: The Military Dimension.* New York, 1969.

_____. "Ottoman Diplomacy and the European State System." *Middle East Journal* 15 (1961):141–52.

_____. "Russia and the Turkish Straits. A Revaluation of the Origins of the Problem." *World Politics* 14 (1961–62):605–32.

Ibragimbeili, Khadzhi Murat. *Kavkaz v Krymskoi voine 1853–1856 gg. i mezhdunarodniye otnosheniya.* Moscow, 1971.

İnal, İbnülemin Mahmud Kemal. *Osmanlı Devrinde Son Sadriâzamlar.* 14 vols. Istanbul, 1940–53.

İnalcik, Halil. "Tanzimat ve Fransa." *Tarih Vesikaları* 2 (1942):128–39.

Iseminger, Gordon L. "The Old Turkish Hands: the British Levantine Consuls, 1856–1876." *Middle East Journal* 22 (1968):297–316.

Issawi, Charles. "The Tabriz-Trabzon Trade, 1830–1900: Rise and Decline of a Route." *International Journal of Middle East Studies* 1 (1970):18–27.

_____, ed. *The Economic History of the Middle East, 1800–1914.* Chicago, 1966.

Itzkowitz, Norman, and Shinder, Joel. "The Office of Şeyh ül-islam and the Tanzimat." *Middle Eastern Studies* 8 (1972):93–101.

Jánossy, Dénes. "Die ungarische Emigration und der Krieg im Orient." *Archivum Europae Centre-Orientalis* 5 (1939):113–275.

Jelavich, Barbara. *Russia and the Greek Revolution of 1843.* Munich, 1966.

_____. *Russland 1852–1871: Aus den Berichten der bayerischen Gesandtschaft in St. Petersburg.* Wiesbaden, 1963.

Jelavich, Charles, and Jelavich, Barbara. *The Balkans.* Englewood Cliffs, N.J., 1965.

_____. "The Danubian Principalities and Bulgaria under Russian Protectorship." *Jahrbücher für Geschichte Osteuropas* 9 (1961):349–66.

Jenks, Leland H. *The Migration of British Capital to 1875.* New York, 1938.

Jerrold, Blanchard. *The Life of Napoleon III.* 4 vols. London, 1874–82.

[Jomini, Aleksandr, baron.] *Diplomatic Study on the Crimean War (1852 to 1856).* 2 vols. London, 1882.

Jorga, [Nicolae]. *Geschichte des Osmanischen Reiches.* 5 vols. Gotha, 1908–13.

Kaehler, Siegfried A. "Realpolitik zur Zeit des Krimkriegs—Eine Säkularbetrachtung." *Historische Zeitschrift* 174 (1952):417–78.

Karal, Enver Ziya. *Nizam-ı cedit ve Tanzimat devirleri, 1789–1856.* In *Osmanlı Tarihi*, vol. 5, pt. 2. Ankara, 1954.

————. *Islâhat Fermani devri, 1856–1861.* In *Osmanlı Tarihi*, vol. 6. Ankara, 1961.

Karpat, Kemal. *An Inquiry into the Social Foundations of Nationalism in the Ottoman State.* Princeton, 1973.

Kaynar, Reşat. *Mustafa Reşit Paşa ve Tanzimat.* Ankara, 1954.

Kelly, J. B. *Britain and the Persian Gulf, 1795–1880.* Oxford, 1968.

Kerner, Robert J. "Russia's New Policy in the Near East after the Peace of Adrianople." *Cambridge Historical Journal* 5 (1935–37) 280–90.

Kinglake, Alexander W. *The Invasion of the Crimea.* 6 vols. New York, 1863–88.

Kırım Muharebesi Tarihi. 2 vols. Unpublished manuscript: Staatsbibliothek, Marburg.

Klapka, George. *The War in the East.* Translated from French by A. Mednyánszky. London, 1855.

Kovalevsky, Eg[or Petrovich]. *Der Krieg Russlands mit der Türkei.* Translated from Russian by Christian von Sarauw. Leipzig, 1869.

Kubie, Nora Benjamin. *Road to Ninevah.* Garden City, N.Y., 1964.

Kukiel, Marian. *Czartoryski and European Unity, 1770–1861.* Princeton, 1955.

Kurat, Akdes Nimet. *Türkiye ve Rusya... (1798–1919).* Ankara, 1970.

La Gorce, Pierre de. *Histoire du second Empire.* 7 vols. Paris, 1894–1905.

————. *Histoire de la seconde République française.* 2 vols. Paris, 1898.

Lamartine, Alphonse de. *Souvenirs, impressions, pensées, et paysages, pendant un voyage en orient, 1832–1833.* In *Oeuvres complètes*, vols. 7 and 8. Paris, 1845.

Lane-Poole, Stanley. *The Life of the Right Honourable Stratford Canning.* 2 vols. London, 1888.

Langer, William L. *Political and Social Upheaval, 1832–1852.* New York, 1969.

Laughton, John Knox. *Memoirs of the Life and Correspondence of Henry Reeve.* 2 vols. 2nd ed. London, 1898.

Layard, Sir A. Henry. *Autobiography and Letters.* Edited by William N. Bruce. 2 vols. New York, 1903.

————. *A Popular Account of Discoveries at Nineveh.* New York, 1854.

Lee, Dwight E. *Great Britain and the Cyprus Convention Policy of 1878.* Cambridge, Mass., 1934.

Lefèvre, André. "L'Angleterre et l'avènement du second Empire (février-décembre 1852)." *Revue d'histoire diplomatique* 83 (1969): 142–56.

Lesueur, Emile. *Le Prince de La Tour d'Auvergne.* Paris, 1930.

Lewis, Bernard. *The Emergence of Modern Turkey.* London, 1961.

————. "Some English Travellers in the East." *Middle Eastern Studies* 4 (1968):296–315.

Lockhart, Laurence. "The 'Political Testament' of Peter the Great." *Slavonic Review* 14 (1936):438–41.

Lohmann, Otto. "Der Konflikt der Türkei mit Oesterreich und Russland wegen der ungarische Flüchtlinge von 1849." *Zeitschrift für Internationales Recht* 22 (1912):228–50.

Malcolm-Smith, E. F. *The Life of Stratford Canning.* London, 1933.

Malmesbury, James Howard Harris, third earl of. *Memoirs of an ex-Minister.* 3rd ed. 2 vols. London, 1884.

Mange, Alyce Edythe. *The Near Eastern Policy of the Emperor Napoleon III.* Urbana, Ill., 1940.

Ma'oz, Moshe. *Ottoman Reform in Syria and Palestine, 1840–61.* Oxford, 1968.

Mardin, Şerif. *The Genesis of Young Ottoman Thought.* Princeton, 1962.

Marinescu, Beatrice. "Economic Relations between the Romanian Principalities and Great Britain (1848–1859)." *Revue roumaine d'histoire* 8 (1969):271–81.

Marlin, Roger. *L'Opinion franc-comtoise devant la guerre de Crimée.* Paris, 1957.

Marriott, J. A. R. *The Eastern Question.* 4th ed. Oxford, 1947.

Martin, Kingsley. *The Triumph of Lord Palmerston.* Rev. ed. London, 1963.

Marx, Karl. *The Eastern Question.* Edited by Eleanor Marx Aveling and Edward Aveling. London, 1897.

————. *The Story of the Life of Lord Palmerston.* Edited by Eleanor Marx Aveling. London, 1899.

Matter, Paul. "Cavour et la guerre de Crimée." *Revue Historique* 145 (1924):161–202.

Maxwell, Sir Herbert. *The Life and Letters of George William Frederick, Fourth Earl of Clarendon.* 2 vols. London, 1913.

Midhat, Ali Haydar. *The Life of Midhat Pasha.* London, 1903.

Monnier, Luc, ed. *Souvenirs d'Alexis de Tocqueville.* 6th ed. Paris, 1942.

Morawitz, Charles. *Les Finances de la Turquie.* Paris, 1902.

Morley, John. *The Life of Richard Cobden.* 2 vols. London, 1908.

Mosely, Philip E. *Russian Diplomacy and the Opening of the Eastern Question in 1838 and 1839.* Cambridge, Mass., 1934.

Mosse, W. E. *The European Powers and the German Question, 1848–71.* Cambridge, 1958.

――――. "The Return of Reschid Pasha." *English Historical Review* 68 (1953):546–73.

Nechkina, M. V. *Russia in the Nineteenth Century, Part I.* In *The History of Russia,* vol. 2, translated by Sir Bernard Pares and Oliver J. Frederiksen. Ann Arbor, Mich., 1953.

Nesselrode, Karl Robert, comte de. *Lettres et papiers du chancelier comte de Nesselrode, 1760–1856.* Edited by Comte A. de Nesselrode. 11 vols. Paris, [1904–1912?].

Nicolson, Harold. *The Congress of Vienna.* New York, 1946.

Nikitin, Sergey Aleksandrovich. *Ocherki po istoriy yuzhnykh Slavyan y russko-balkanshikh svyazey v 50–70e gody XIX v.* Moscow, 1970.

Nomikos, Eugenia Voyiatzis. "The International Position of Greece during the Crimean War." Ph.D. dissertation, Stanford University, 1962.

Normanby, [Constantine Henry Phipps,] first marquis of. *A Year of Revolution.* 2 vols. London, 1857.

Ollivier, Emile. *L'Empire libéral.* 18 vols. Paris, 1895–[1918].

――――. *Journal, 1846–1869.* Edited by Theodore Zeldin and Anne Troisier de Diaz. 2 vols. Paris, 1961.

Onou, Alexander. "The Memoirs of Count N. Ignatyev." *Slavonic and East European Review* 10 (1931–32):386–407, 627–40; 11 (1932–33): 108–25.

Palm, Franklin Charles. *England and Napoleon III.* Durham, N.C., 1948.

Papadopoullos, Theodore H. *Studies and Documents Relating to the History of the Greek Church and People under Turkish Domination.* Brussels, 1952.

Parry, E. Jones, ed. *The Correspondence of Lord Aberdeen and Princess Lieven, 1832–1854.* Royal Historical Society, Third Series, vols. 60 and 62. London, 1938–39.

Persigny, [Jean Gilbert Victor Fialin,] duc de. *Mémoires.* Edited by H. de Laire, comte d'Espagny. Paris, 1896.

Phillimore, Sir Augustus. *The Life of Admiral of the Fleet Sir William Parker.* 3 vols. London, 1876–80.

Pinson, Mark. "Ottoman Bulgaria in the First Tanzimat Period—The Revolts in Nish (1841) and Vidin (1850)." *Middle Eastern Studies* 11 (1975):103–46.

Pintner, Walter McKenzie. *Russian Economic Policy under Nicholas I.* Ithaca, N.Y., [1967].

Platt, D. C. M. *The Cinderella Service: British Consuls since 1825.* [Hamden, Conn.], 1971.

_____. *Finance, Trade, and Politics in British Foreign Policy, 1815–1914.* Oxford, 1968.

_____. "The Role of the British Consular Service in Overseas Trade, 1825–1914." *Economic History Review* 15 (1962–63):494–512.

Ponsonby, [John Ponsonby,] first viscount. *Private Letters on the Eastern Question.* Brighton, 1854.

Popov, Nil A. *Rossiya i Serbiya.* 2 vols. Moscow, 1869.

Popova, A. A. "Politika Turtsiy i natsional'no-osvoboditel'naya bor'ba bolgarskogo naroda v 60-kh godakh XIX veka." *Voprosy istoriy* (1953), pp. 49–64.

Potiemkine, Vladimir. *Histoire de la diplomatie.* Translated by Xenia Pamphilova and Michel Eristov. 3 vols. Paris, [1946–47].

Poujoulat, M. *La France et la Russie à Constantinople: La question des lieux saints.* Paris, 1853.

Prevelakis, Eleutherios. *British Policy towards the Change of Dynasty in Greece, 1862–1863.* Athens, 1953.

Purves, J. G., and West, D. A., eds. *War and Society in the Nineteenth Century Russian Empire.* Toronto, 1972.

Puryear, Vernon John. *England, Russia, and the Straits Question, 1844–56.* Berkeley, Calif., 1931.

_____. *France and the Levant.* Berkeley, Calif., 1941.

_____. *International Economics and Diplomacy in the Near East.* Stanford, Calif., [1935].

_____. "New Light on the Origins of the Crimean War." *Journal of Modern History* 3 (1931):219–34.

Quazza, Guido. "La politica orientale sarda nei dispacci del Tecco (1850–1856)." *Rassegna storica del Risorgimento* 48 (1961):663–80.

Rall, Hans. "Griechenland zwischen Russland und dem übrigen Europa: Die 'Grosse Idee' der Griechen zwischen 1847 und 1859." *Saeculum: Jahrbuch für Universalgeschichte* 18 (1967):164–80.

Ralls, Walter. "The Papal Aggression of 1850: A Study in Victorian Anti-Catholicism." *Church History* 43 (1974):242–56.

Rambaud, Alfred. *Histoire de la Russie.* Paris, 1878.

Randon, [Jacques,] comte. *Mémoires du maréchal Randon.* 2 vols. Paris, 1875–77.

Read, Donald. *Cobden and Bright: A Victorian Political Partnership.* London, 1967.

Reid, T. Wemyss. *The Life, Letters, and Friendships of Richard Monckton Milnes, First Lord Houghton.* 2 vols. New York, 1891.

Ridley, Jasper. *Lord Palmerston.* New York, 1971.

Rifat Pasha, Mehmet Sadık, "Rusya Muharebesi Tarihi." In *Anzâr-i Rif'as Pasha.* Constantinople, 1275/1859.

Robertson, Priscilla. *Revolutions of 1848: A Social History.* New York, 1960.

Robinson, Gertrude. *David Urquhart.* Oxford, 1920.

Robinson, Ronald, and Gallagher, John. *Africa and the Victorians.* New York, 1961.

Robson, Robert, ed. *Ideas and Institutions of Victorian Britain: Essays in Honour of George Kitson Clark.* New York, 1967.

Rodkey, Frederick Stanley. "Ottoman Concern about Western Economic Penetration in the Levant, 1849–1856." *Journal of Modern History* 30 (1958):348–53.

——. *The Turco-Egyptian Question in the Relations of England, France, and Russia, 1832–1841.* Urbana, Ill., [1924–25].

Rothenberg, Gunther E. "The Croatian Military Border and the Rise of Yugoslav Nationalism." *Slavonic and East European Review* 43 (1964):34–45.

——. *The Military Border in Croatia, 1740–1881.* Chicago, 1966.

——. "The Struggle over the Dissolution of the Croatian Military Border, 1850–1871." *Slavic Review* 23 (1964):63–78.

Saab, Ann Pottinger. "Review of Winfried Baumgart, *Der Friede von Paris, 1956;* Paul W. Schroeder, *Austria, Great Britain, and the Crimean War.*" *Central European History* 8 (1975):51–68.

Sage, Leland Livingston. "Lord Stratford de Redcliffe and the Origins of the Crimean War." Ph.D. dissertation, University of Illinois, 1932.

Salibi, Kamal S. "The 1860 Upheaval in Damascus as seen by al-Sayyid Muhammad Abu'l-Su'ud al-Hasibi, Notable and *Naquib al-Ashraf* of the City." Pp. 185–202 in William R. Polk and Richard L. Chambers, eds., *Beginnings of Modernization in the Middle East: The Nineteenth Century.* Chicago, 1968.

Salih Munir Pasha. *La Politique orientale de la Russie.* Lausanne, 1918.

Salomon, Richard. "Die Anerkennung Napoleons III." *Zeitschrift für osteuropäische Geschichte* 2 (1912):312–66.

Şapolyo, Enver Behnan. *Mustafa Reşit Paşa ve Tanzimat Devri Tarihi.* Istanbul, 1945.

Schiemann, Theodor. *Geschichte Russlands unter Kaiser Nikolaus I.* 4 vols. Berlin, 1904–19.

Schmitt, B. E. "Diplomatic Preliminaries of the Crimean War." *American Historical Review* 25 (1919):36–67.

Schöningh, Franz. "Karl Ludwig Bruck und die Idee Mitteleuropas." *Goerres-Gesellschaft zur Pflege der Wissenschaft im katholischen Deutschland: Historisches Jahrbuch* 56 (1936):1–14.

Schroeder, Paul W. "Austria and the Danubian Principalities, 1853–1856." *Central European History* 2 (1969):216–36.

———. *Austria, Great Britain, and the Crimean War.* Ithaca, N.Y., 1972.

———. "Bruck versus Buol: The Dispute over Austrian Eastern Policy, 1853–1855." *Journal of Modern History* 40 (1968):193–217.

Seaman, L. C. B. *From Vienna to Versailles.* New York, 1963.

Senior, Nassau William. *Conversations with M. Thiers, M. Guizot, and other Distinguished Persons during the Second Empire.* 2 vols. London, 1878.

———. *Journals kept in France and Italy from 1848 to 1852.* Edited by M. C. M. Simpson. 2 vols. London, 1871.

Seton-Watson, Hugh. *The Russian Empire, 1801–1917.* Oxford, 1967.

Seton-Watson, R. W. *A History of the Roumanians.* Cambridge, 1934.

———. *The Southern Slav Question and the Hapsburg Monarchy.* London, 1911.

Shaw, Stanford J. "The Central Legislative Councils in the Nineteenth Century Ottoman Reform Movement before 1876." *International Journal of Middle East Studies* 1 (1970):51–84.

———. "The Ottoman View of the Balkans." Pp. 56–80 in Charles and Barbara Jelavich, eds., *The Balkans in Transition.* Berkeley, 1963.

Shopov, A. *Les Réformes et la protection des chrétiens en Turquie, 1673–1904.* Paris, 1904.

Shukla, Ramlakhan. *Britain, India, and the Turkish Empire, 1853–1882.* New Delhi, 1973.

Simpson, F. A. *Louis Napoleon and the Recovery of France, 1848–1856.* New York, 1923.

Slade, Sir Adolphus. *Records of Travels in Turkey, Greece, etc. . . . , in the Years 1829, 1830, and 1831.* 2nd ed. 2 vols. London, 1833.

———. *Turkey and the Crimean War.* London, 1867.

Southgate, Donald. *"The Most English Minister...,"* *The Policies and Politics of Palmerston.* New York, 1966.

Spencer, Edmund. *Travels in European Turkey.* 2nd ed. 2 vols. London, 1853.

Sproxton, Charles. *Palmerston and the Hungarian Revolution.* Cambridge, 1919.

Stan, Apostol. "L'Organisation de la lutte de libération des peuples balkaniques dans les principautés roumaines pendant la phase danubienne de la guerre de Crimée (1853–1854)." *Revue roumaine d'histoire* 11 (1972):833–41.

Standish, J. F. "The Persian War of 1856–1857." *Middle Eastern Studies* 3 (1966):18–45.

Stavrianos, L. S. *Balkan Federation.* Hamden, Conn., 1964.

———. *The Balkans since 1453.* New York, 1958.

Stavrou, Theofanis George. "Russian Interest in the Levant, 1843–1848." *Middle East Journal* 17 (1963):91–103.

Stephan, John J. "The Crimean War in the Far East." *Modern Asian Studies* 3 (1969):257–77.

Stoianovich, Traian. "The Conquering Balkan Orthodox Merchant." *Journal of Economic History* 20 (1960):234–313.

———. "The Pattern of Serbian Intellectual Evolution, 1830–1880." *Comparative Studies in Society and History* 1 (1959):242–72.

Sumner, B. H. "Ignatyev at Constantinople, 1864–76." *Slavonic Review* 11 (1933):341–53, 556–71.

Szenczi, N. J. "Great Britain and the War of Hungarian Independence." *Slavonic Review* 17 (1939):556–70.

Tarle, Evgeniy Viktorovich. *Krymskaya Voyna.* In *Sochineniya,* vols 8 and 9. Moscow, 1959.

Tatischev, S. S. "Diplomaticheskiy Razryv Rossiy s Turtsiei 1853 g." *Istoricheskiy Vestnik* 47 (1892):153–76.

Taylor, A. J. P. "John Bright and the Crimean War." *Bulletin of the John Rylands Library* 36 (1954):501–22.

———. *The Struggle for Mastery in Europe, 1848–1918.* Oxford, 1954.

———. *The Trouble Makers: Dissent over Foreign Policy, 1792–1939.* Bloomington, Ind., 1958.

Temperley, H. W. V. "The Alleged Violations of the Straits Convention by Stratford de Redcliffe between June and September, 1853." *English Historical Review* 49 (1934):657–72.

———. "British Policy towards Parliamentary Rule and Constitutionalism in Turkey, 1830–1914." *Cambridge Historical Journal* 4 (1933):156–91.

———. "British Secret Diplomacy during the Palmerstonian Period." In *Festskrift til Halvdan Koht.* Oslo, 1933.

———. *England and the Near East.* London, [1936]. Reissued Hamden, Conn., 1964.

———. *History of Serbia.* London, 1917. Reissued New York, 1969.

———. "Stratford de Redcliffe and the Origins of the Crimean War," pts. 1 and 2. *English Historical Review* 48 (1933):601–21; 49 (1934): 265–98.

———. "The Treaty of Paris of 1856 and its Execution." *Journal of Modern History* 4 (1932):387–414, 523–43.

Thomas, Daniel H. "The Reaction of the Great Powers to Louis Napoleon's Rise to Power in 1851." *Historical Journal* 13 (1970): 237–50.

Thouvenel, L[ouis]. *Nicolas Ier et Napoléon III.* Paris, 1891.

Tibawi, A. L. *British Interests in Palestine, 1800–1901.* London, 1961.

[Tocqueville, Alexis de.] *Correspondence and Conversations of Alexis de Tocqueville with Nassau William Senior.* Edited by M. C. M. Simpson. 2 vols. London, 1872.

Trevelyan, George Macaulay. *The Life of John Bright.* New York, 1913.

"The Turkish Loan: Its Negotiation and Repudiation." *Bankers' Magazine (London)* 13 (1853):252–60.

Tyrrell, Henry. *The History of the War with Russia.* 3 vols. London, [1855–58].

Ubicini, [Jean Henry Abdolonyme]. *Lettres sur la Turquie.* 2 vols. Paris, 1853–54.

Unckel, Bernhard. *Österreich und der Krimkrieg.* Lübeck, 1969.

Urquhart, David. *Progress of Russia in the West, North, and South.* 3rd ed. London, 1853.

———. *Recent Events in the East.* London, 1854.

Vacaresco, Hélène. "La Mystique nationale roumaine aux environs de 1848." *Revue d'histoire diplomatique* 43 (1929):8–19.

Valsecchi, Franco. "Europa 1859." In *Atti del XXXVIII Congresso di storia del Risorgimento italiano (28 maggio–1 giugno 1959).* Rome, 1960.

———. *Il Risorgimento e l'Europa: L'alleanza di Crimea.* Verona, 1948.

Victoria, Queen of Great Britain. *The Letters of Queen Victoria.* Edited by Arthur C. Benson and Viscount Esher. 3 vols. New York, 1907.

Vinogradov, V. N. *Rossiya y ob'edineniye rumynskikh knyazhestv.* Moscow, 1961.

Vitzthum von Eckstaedt, Charles Frederick. *St. Petersburg and London in the Years 1852-1864.* Edited by Henry Reeve; translated by Edward Fairfax Taylor. 2 vols. London, 1887.

Walpole, Spencer. *The Life of Lord John Russell.* 2 vols. 2nd ed. London, 1889.

Waterfield, Gordon. *Layard of Nineveh.* London, 1963.

Webster, Sir Charles. *The Foreign Policy of Palmerston, 1830-1841.* 2 vols. London, 1951.

Wellesley, Colonel F. A. *Secrets of the Second Empire.* New York, 1929.

Wellesley, Sir Victor, and Sencourt, Robert. *Conversations with Napoleon III.* London, 1934.

Wertheimer, Eduard von. "Die Kossuth-Emigration in der Türkei." *Ural-altäische Jahrbücher* 8 (1928):377-82.

Wieczynski, Joseph L. "The Myth of Kuchuk-Kainardja in American Histories of Russia." *Middle Eastern Studies* 4 (1968):376-79.

Wilson, Philip Whitwell, ed. *The Greville Diary.* 2 vols. New York, 1927.

Woodham Smith, Mrs. Cecil. *The Reason Why.* London, 1953.

Wyse, Sir Thomas. *Impressions of Greece.* London, 1871.

Index